MARKET EVOLUTION
IN DEVELOPING COUNTRIES:
THE UNFOLDING
OF THE INDIAN MARKET
Subhash C. Jain, PhD

ADVANCE REVIEW

"Professor Jain's book makes a significant contribution to our understanding of the developing world and its future significance to U.S. business. . . . [a] significant contribution to the literature on marketing in developing countries with focus on India."

C. P. Rao, PhD, CPM
University Professor and Wal-Mart Lecturer
in Strategic Marketing
Department of Marketing
University of Arkansas

Market Evolution in Developing Countries
The Unfolding of the Indian Market

INTERNATIONAL BUSINESS PRESS
Erdener Kaynak, PhD
Executive Editor

New, Recent, and Forthcoming Titles:

International Business Handbook edited by V. H. (Manek)
  Kirpalani

Sociopolitical Aspects of International Marketing
  edited by Erdener Kaynak

How to Manage for International Competitiveness
  edited by Abbas J. Ali

International Business Expansion into Less-Developed Countries:
  The International Finance Corporation and Its Operations
  by James C. Baker

Product-Country Images: Impact and Role in International
  Marketing edited by Nicolas Papadopoulos and Louise A. Heslop

The Global Business: Four Key Marketing Strategies
  edited by Erdener Kaynak

Multinational Strategic Alliances edited by Refik Culpan

Market Evolution in Developing Countries: The Unfolding
  of the Indian Market by Subhash C. Jain

A Guide to Successful Business Relations with the Chinese: Opening
  the Great Wall's Gate by Huang Quanyu, Richard Andrulis,
  and Chen Tong

Industrial Products: A Guide to the International Marketing Economics
  Model by Hans Jansson

Euromarketing: Effective Strategies for International Trade and Export
  edited by Erdener Kaynak and Pervez N. Ghauri

Globalization of Consumer Markets: Structures and Strategies edited by
  Salah S. Hassan and Erdener Kaynak

Market Evolution in Developing Countries

The Unfolding of the Indian Market

Subhash C. Jain, PhD

International Business Press
An Imprint of The Haworth Press, Inc.
New York • London • Norwood (Australia)

Published by

International Business Press, an imprint of The Haworth Press, Inc., 10 Alice Street, Binghamton,
NY 13904-1580

Library of Congress Cataloging-in-Publication Data

Jain, Subhash C., 1942-
    Market evolution in developing countries : the unfolding of the Indian market / Subhash C.
Jain.
        p.   cm.
    Includes bibliographical references and index.
    ISBN 1-56024-360-0 (alk. paper)
    1. Market surveys–India. 2. United States–Foreign economic relations–India. 3. India–For-
eign economic relations–United States. I. Title.
HC435.2.J33   1993
382′.0954073–dc20
                                                                                              92-22619
                                                                                                   CIP

CONTENTS

List Of Exhibits

ABOUT THE AUTHOR

Subhash C. Jain, PhD, is Professor of Marketing and Director of the Institute for the Study of International Markets at the University of Connecticut School of Business Administration. He offers seminars for the International Trade Center (UNCTAD/GATT) in Geneva and serves as a visiting faculty member at the Graduate School of Business Administration, Zurich in their executive MBA program. Dr. Jain also has presented seminars in the United States and abroad on a variety of marketing topics, including market segmentation, marketing strategy, export strategy, and global marketing strategy formulation. He frequently has served as a consultant to such organizations as Xerox Corporation, Mead Corporation, General Motors, NCR, Control Data, Pitney Bowes, and Corning Glass and has advised government agencies in Malaysia, Chile, India, Pakistan, St. Lucia, Kenya, and Indonesia on their trade problems. The author of more than one hundred publications, including several books, he is an active member of the American Marketing Association, the Academy of Marketing Science, the Academy of International Business, and several other professional organizations.

Preface

The growing power of the Third World countries is the corporate challenge of the next century. These countries are much too important in economic and human terms to be ignored. Over three-fourths of the world's population resides in these countries. Geographically, more than two-thirds of the earth's land area belongs to Third World nations, and they account for a significant share of the earth's resources in agriculture and minerals.

Traditionally, Third World countries, despite their importance in terms of population and natural resources, did not count much as far as multinational business activity was concerned. However, in the 1980s, many Third World countries achieved steady growth, becoming significant players in the global arena. As their economies grew, their demand for goods and services increased simultaneously. By and large, workers in Third World countries receive low wages relative to their counterparts in developed countries. This provides them a comparative advantage in producing labor-intensive products. The global sourcing strategies of many multinational enterprises, along with the increased emphasis on export-led development policies that a number of these countries pursue, make them a vital link in the world commerce as exporters of manufactured goods and services. Such linkages promise continued prosperity for the people in these countries.

The increased wealth, accompanied by the new awareness that the diffusion of television brings, results in the emergence of a huge demand for different kinds of consumer goods. This demand, in turn, leads to increases in manufacturing capacity, creating demand for producer and capital goods.

Today we live in a world with interdependent economies. Third World nations may play a more or less important role in global business activity, depending on their economic, political, cultural, and historical perspectives, but as a group they are an essential part of the global economy.

From the viewpoint of marketers, an important concern is how the "new" prosperity in Third World countries relates to consumer markets. Of course, the overall demand will increase and the markets will continue to evolve. But how will the market evolution shape up? Will the evolution process go through stages? How can these stages be characterized? What underlying conditions may affect smoother evolution of the market? What strategies will be appropriate for multinational enterprises to tame these markets? What might Third World countries do to attract these enterprises to their markets? This book seeks to answer these questions.

A model of market evolution in Third World countries is developed, identifying stages through which the evolution progresses. Characteristics of each stage are identified and the enabling conditions that initially trigger the evolution and influence the progression from stage to stage are examined. Application of the model is tested with reference to India, where a large and growing market is shaping up. Forty-four years ago, in the middle of a night in August when the world was asleep, the knock of freedom struck on the door of this ancient land. That knock may have set the clock ticking toward the eventual dissolution of the largest empire ever known. But it also started the countdown toward the transformation of the prized jewel in the British crown into the foremost industrial nation in the Third World.

In the days of the "Raj," India was a land of startling economic contrasts: Croesus-rich maharajahs and their often impoverished subjects, landed gentry and landless laborers. Myriad contrasts still persist, but a quiet transformation has taken place. The extent of this change, involving one-sixth of humanity, cannot be fully reflected in statistics or economic indices, but it can be sensed in the brightly visible symbols of progress in diverse fields. One of the most striking examples is the green revolution that has transformed Northern India into the nation's granary. Another is the proliferation of new industrial townships across the land embodying the vibrant spark of entrepreneurial activity. Other, less visible, symbols—nuclear power plants, offshore oil rights, and satellite tracking stations—also speak of the country's capability in harnessing newer and more esoteric technologies. They speak of a coming of age, a rite of passage.

The transformation is most evident in the marketplace. The Indian economy has traditionally been one of shortages, with production capacity rigidly controlled. However, in recent years, with the relaxation of controls, production capacity has rocketed and new products are entering the marketplace at a furious pace. In industry after industry, from computers to automobiles, from cooking ranges to VCRs, the white heat of competition is being felt, spurring product innovations and improvements on an unprecedented scale.

The 200 million citizens who constitute India's new middle-class market could ultimately emerge as the largest single market in the world. It makes an interesting study in market evolution in Third World countries. Such questions as the following become pertinent: Through what stages has this market evolved? How could each stage be characterized? What conditions influenced progression from one stage to another? Answers to these questions are sought using the market evolution model mentioned above.

Hitherto deprived of many consumer durables, this market is already attracting a host of international brand leaders. Their ranks include consumer electronics giants Toshiba and Sony, appliance makers Whirlpool and Hoover, and automobile companies such as Daimler-Benz, Honda, and Suzuki. Collaborations between Indian firms have changed, or are changing, the face of Indian industry. They are introducing contemporary standards, designs, and state-of-the-art technology into a previously somnolent market.

Interestingly, American firms have not taken as keen an interest in capitalizing on emerging opportunities in India as have their counterparts in Europe and Japan. Why have U.S. companies been slow in responding to opportunities in India? What concerns prevent them from expanding into India? What strategies might they pursue to seek entry into India? The book probes these questions in depth. The answers are relevant for American firms seeking opportunities, not only in India, but elsewhere in the Third World. A basic theme that emerges here is that the history, geography, politics, and culture of Third World countries require new and innovative approaches on the part of multinational enterprises to successfully conduct business there. These countries are going to be the booming markets in the twenty-first century. Companies capable of looking beyond the immediate future will harvest bumper crops if they, in a timely fashion, sow the seeds ahead of their competitors.

India has come a long way and yet it has miles to go. It must not detract from the path of liberalization it adopted in the mid-1980s. What strategies India might adopt and what policy initiatives the government must incorporate to make the journey toward economic prosperity for its growing population are difficult but important questions. The book makes an attempt to answer these questions, making recommendations for formulating and implementing a unified strategy to globalize the economy. An underlying message is delivered which seeks to alleviate constraints on the growth of industry. Most Third World countries suffer from excessive controls on business. Yet no nation can economically progress until entrepreneurship is inspired, private initiative is supported, and competition is encouraged. The strategic recommendations for India to liberalize the economy thus carry an important lesson for other Third World countries.

Writing a book such as this, as I reluctantly discovered, is a monumental task. It would not have been possible without much patience and perseverance on the part of all the people who responded to questions, assisted in the research, and remained at my side during the preparation of the manuscript. I owe these people my greatest appreciation and special thanks. They belong to organizations in the U.S. (Indian Investment Center, World Bank, Business International Corporation, Embassy of India, and Overseas Development Council), India (National Council of Applied Economic Research, Planning Commission, Indian Institute of Foreign Trade, Federation of Indian Chambers of Commerce and Industry, Indo-American Chamber of Commerce, Indian Institute of Management at Ahmedabad and at Calcutta, International Management Institute–India, Center for Monitoring Indian Economy, Institute of Economic Growth, and Delhi School of Economics), and elsewhere (GATT, Asian Development Bank, International Trade Center–UNCTAD/GATT, Pakistan's Export Promotion Bureau, Malaysia's Productivity Center, Indonesia's Institute for Management Education and Development, International Business Management Institute–Beijing, and Mexico's Banco Nacional de Comercio Exterior, S.N.C.).

The scope of this book is wide. Indeed, I could hardly claim expertise in all of the areas it covers; the ideas are based on a variety of experiences of different individuals. I would like to thank all the company executives, diplomats, lawyers, and managers who willingly granted their time and openly shared their views. I am grateful to numerous scholars in many academic disciplines in the U.S. and India who readily gave their permission to use themes contained in their nonpublished and published works. While it is not feasible to recognize them all here, I would like to thank Sushil Vachani, Boston University; Nikhilesh Dholakia, University of Rhode Island; Rajiv Khanna, LeBoeuf, Lamb, Leiby & MacRea; Abhinandan Jain, Indian Institute of Management, Ahmedabad; Ashok Pratap Arora, Indian Institute of Management, Calcutta; Sharad Sarin, Xavier Labour Research Institute (XLRI); Nagesh Kumar, Research and Information System for the Non-aligned and Other Developing Countries; Siddhartha Roy, Hindustan Lever Limited; D. R. Pendse, Tata Services, Limited; Prem Pandhi, International Management Institute–India; Claude Cellich, International Trade Center (UNCTAD/ GATT); Alan R. Andreason and John Clair Thompson, The University of Connecticut; Albert Stahli and Cornel J. Wietlisbach, Graduate School of Business Administration, Zurich; V. Rangaraj, Indo-American Chamber of Commerce; Eric Outwater, U.S. Department of Commerce; John O'Connor, Connecticut Small Business Development Center; Peter J. Pattinson, Intertech; Richard P. Weber, Weber, Neville & Shaver; Ronald J. Patten, DePaul University; Hasmukh Shah, *Indo-American Business Times*; David Freeman, Loctite Corporation; and Robert Werner, Timex Corporation. I am grateful to Mahendra Gujarathi, Bentley College, and Suresh Nair, The University of Connecticut, for carefully going over several chapters and making useful suggestions. Their insightful comments on chapters dealing with India were particularly helpful in tightening the manuscript. I am indebted to Pathfinders, India and Indo-American Chamber of Commerce for their permission to let me use their material liberally.

My gratitude also extends to Erdener Kaynak (Senior Editor, International Business Press), Pennsylvania State University at Middletown for his valuable comments on the manuscript. Without his personal interest in the project and perennial encouragement, this book would not have been completed.

The talented staff at The Haworth Press deserves praise for their role in shaping the book, especially Eric L. Roland, Assistant Editor, for networking the people who got the project underway, Lisa McGowan, Production Editor, and Patricia Malone, Assistant Editor, for managing the manuscript to completion.

I am indebted to Marie Palmer and her clerical assistants, Joan Bowley and Sue Levesque at The University of Connecticut, for their administrative support in the completion of this project; Huong Ly for typing portions of the manuscript, Janice Bittner of Fenton River Office Services for readying the final manuscript, and my doctoral student, Kiranjit Ahluwalia, and graduate assistant, Teresa Grusauskas, for library research. I also want to thank Dipa Roy in The University of Connecticut Library for her help in researching reference material. Financial support for this project was provided by the GE Foundation and the University of Connecticut Research Foundation, and I gratefully acknowledge their help. My colleagues and students at The University of Connecticut and those at the Oekreal Graduate School of Business Administration, Zurich, provided valuable feedback on initial ideas and read early drafts of the manuscript.

Finally, I owe my greatest debt to my wife and our children who cheerfully put up with many inconveniences so that the writing could go on.

Subhash C. Jain
Storrs, Connecticut

Chapter 1

Markets in Developing Countries

The slowing of economic growth in the industrialized countries in the past decade raises an important question about the viability of Third World countries as markets for the United States, and as competitors for American business. Third World countries present a strange enigma that American businesses find difficult to comprehend. On the one hand, there is mass hunger and poverty in the Third World; on the other hand, these countries exhibit growing economic strength. Thus, how the Third World countries should be viewed in the realm of global business remains a paradox.

The reality of life in developing countries cannot be denied in a world where finance, communication, and technology are increasingly international, and nations are increasingly interdependent. The trend toward economic globalism is so rapid and so pronounced that the choice remaining to Americans is not whether to accept it, but how to do business in the midst of the unique circumstances that Third World countries present.

These are the countries for which a business needs to develop careful goals and strategies. Besides being emerging markets for capital goods and likely efficient suppliers for many U.S. companies, they will seize an international economic role far exceeding their combined GNP.

The Third World economies will continue to forge ahead despite considerable political uncertainty in some regions. In some ways, one wonders if anyone should invest a dime in any Third World country. Brazil is burdened with external debt. India continues to roadblock foreign enterprises. Egypt's survival is dependent on U.S. foreign aid. The Philippines are politically unstable. Still, these countries, in their own ways, are going all out to attain economic growth. Seeking market niches, for many products they will cut into newly-industrialized countries' (NICs') turf.

This book is a treatise on Third World markets with a focus on India. Specifically, it has a three-fold purpose. First, the perspectives of markets in developing countries as an economic opportunity for American business are examined. Second, the market evolution process in these countries is described. Third, strategic moves that American business may make to capitalize on opportunities in these markets are outlined.

Essentially, the book develops two scenarios: a general scenario of Third World markets at large and a specific scenario of market opportunity in India. It presents a theme that, despite poverty and hunger, Third World markets are growing fast, and in twenty years or so, these markets will offer the most business opportunity. However, firms aspiring to be a part of this growth must establish their presence in these markets today; otherwise, the opportunity will be lost forever. European and Japanese companies are more willing to take a long-term view of these markets and, hence, make a humble entry in order to be there. American businesses need to do some thinking about giving up their traditional attitude toward investment in Third World countries in order not to be outcompeted in these huge markets which are expected to be growing at an accelerating rate in the 1990s and beyond.

DEFINING DEVELOPING COUNTRIES

The division of the world into developed and developing countries is a post-World War II phenomenon. After the war, as the colonial system began to dissolve, it became apparent that three-fourths of humanity lived in misery and squalor while the remaining one-fourth was blessed with plenty. A convenient way of dividing countries into two groups was to label the poor ones as underdeveloped and the others as developed. As the years went by, the word underdeveloped gave way to developing since it was claimed that these countries, at least most of them, were making a persistent effort to come out of impoverishment and, therefore, given time, they would become developed.

Developing countries are also called by another name, Third World. This term was coined by a French scholar in 1952 referring to the less developed countries of Asia, Africa, Oceania, and Latin

America.[1] Third World is now employed more or less synonymously with a number of other terms used to identify low- and middle-income nations as different from the industrial economies and the industrial nonmarket (communist) countries. These terms include underdeveloped, less developed, developing, and nonindustrialized–terms that have spawned a number of subgroups including middle-income countries (MICs) and newly-industrialized countries (NICs).

Much has changed in the 1980s. Today a number of so-called Third World countries are so advanced that they should no longer be considered as developing. These are the newly-industrialized countries (NICs), ranking at the top among developing countries in terms of economic development and industrialization. In many ways, these nations are more similar to Japan than to the poor countries of Africa, Latin America, and Asia.

Which countries are NICs is a matter of debate. There is a common agreement about the inclusion of four East Asian countries in the group–South Korea, Taiwan, Hong Kong, and Singapore–also known as the "Four Tigers" or the "Four Dragons." Some scholars consider Brazil, India, Mexico, Argentina, Malaysia, Thailand, Chile, Iran, Iraq, Panama, Venezuela, and Syria as emerging economies that should also be labeled as NICs, or at least second-tier or peripheral NICs.[2]

For the purpose of this book different countries are classified in the following five categories: First World, Second World, Third World, Fourth World, and Fifth World.

First World

This includes the advanced industrial nations of Europe, North America, and Asia that accept a more-or-less capitalistic, market-oriented economy. The core of the First World consists of members of the Organization for Economic Cooperation and Development (OECD); that is, the industrialized West and Japan. New Zealand and Australia also qualify; Greece and Spain are borderline cases.

Second World

This group includes high-income oil exporters and newly industrialized countries. In the last fifteen years they have achieved significant economic progress, either through investing their oil revenues (for example, Saudi Arabia) or by competing aggressively in the international markets (South Korea).

Third World

This group is made up of countries that need time and technology, rather than massive foreign aid, to build modern, developed economies. These include nations whose development may be guaranteed by other key resources and nations that are developed enough to attract foreign investment and borrow on commercial terms. Examples of the former group are Zambia (copper) and Morocco (phosphate). Mexico, Brazil, and India fall into the latter group.

Fourth World

This group includes the 1.5 billion people of the world's hitherto centrally planned Communist-run nations.

Fifth World

The 200 million inhabitants of the Fifth World live in hard-core poverty. Many Fifth World countries have few presently known resources. Usually a large part of the population is engaged in subsistence farming or nomadic herding, and some are isolated from the outside world. Life expectancy is below fifty years, and nutritional intake is significantly less than the minimum considered necessary for health. Notable examples are Mali, Chad, Ethiopia, Somalia, Rwanda, and Bangladesh.

Exhibit 1-1 identifies countries in each category.

The distinguishing characteristics of countries in each category are summarized in Exhibit 1-2. Mainly, the countries in each group differ in terms of per capita income, rate of population growth, quality of life, sectorial distribution of gross domestic product, and life expectancy at birth. These factors together lead to economic differences among nations. The First World countries can be favorably positioned on one extreme on these factors while the Fifth World represents the other extreme. The Second World, in terms of wealth, is closer to First World, while on social aspects it is similar to Third World. As a matter of fact, in the social arena some Second World countries may represent a perspective of Fourth and Fifth Worlds. The Third World stands in the middle, with a section of the population living like people in the First World. The Fourth World ranks behind Third World on most measures simply because politics stood in the way of economic initiative. With recent changes in the communist world, most of the Fourth World countries would move to the Second or Third World category.

Economic development is characterized by such factors as comparatively small allocation of labor force to agriculture; energy available in large amounts at low cost per unit; high level of gross national product and income; high levels of per capita consumption; relatively low rates of population growth; complex modern facilities for transportation, communication, and exchange; a substantial amount of capital for investment; urbanization based on production as well as exchange; diversified manufacturing that accounts for an important share of the labor force; numerous tertiary occupations; specialization of both physical and mental labor; surpluses of both goods and services; and a highly developed technology that includes ample media and methods for experiment.[3] These factors can be utilized to examine economic standing of nations. Needless to say, a large variety of information is needed to categorize *countries* on an economic development scale. For many characteristics, hard data are not available and judgment becomes the determining factor.

The focus of this book is on developing nations referred to as Third World countries. While the "Four Tigers" have received a lot of attention, other emerging countries have not been considered adequately from the viewpoint of U.S. business, particularly as significant markets for American goods and services.

PROFILING DEVELOPING COUNTRIES

As mentioned above, there is a lack of agreement as to what countries should be categorized as Third World countries. It is because the distinction between developed and developing countries is based on a variety of factors, all of which cannot be objectively measured. To simplify the matter, however, we will identify a few

EXHIBIT 1-1. Economic Grouping of Countries

First World (Industrial Market Economies)	Second World (High-Income Oil Exporters and Newly Industrialized Countries)	Third World (Emerging Countries)		Fourth World (East Eurpoean Nonmarket Economies)	Fifth World (Least Developed Countries)
Australia	Hong Kong	Algeria	Jordan	Albania	Afghanistan
Austria	Kuwait	Angola	Kenya	Bulgaria	Bangladesh
Belgium	Libya	Argentina	Korea, Rep.	Czechoslovakia (former)	Benin
Canada	Malaysia	Bolivia	Lebanon	Hungary	Bhutan
Denmark	Oman	Brazil	Liberia	Poland	Botswana
Finland	Saudi Arabia	Burma	Mexico	Romania	Burkina Faso
France	Singapore	Cameroon	Mongolia	USSR (former)	Burundi
Germany	South Korea	Chile	Morocco		Cape Verde
Ireland	Taiwan	China	Nicaragua		Central African Rep.
Italy	United Arab Emirates	Colombia	Nigeria		Chad
Japan		Congo, People's Rep.	Pakistan		Comoros
Luxembourg		Costa Rica	Papua New Guinea		Democratic Yemen
Netherlands		Cuba	Paraguay		Djibouti
New Zealand		Cyprus	Peru		Equatorial Guinea
Norway		Dominican Republic	Philippines		Ethiopia
Spain		Ecuador	Portugal		Gambia
Sweden		Egypt, Arab Rep.	Senegal		Guinea
United Kingdom		El Salvador	South Africa		Guinea-Bissau
United States		Ghana	Sri Lanka		
			Syrian Arab Rep.		

Greece	Thailand	Haita
Guatemala	Tunisia	Kiribati
Honduras	Turkey	Lao People's Dem. Rep.
India	Uruguay	Lesotho
Indonesia	Venezuela	Malawi
Iran, Islamic Rep.	Vietnam	Maldives
Iraq	Yemen Arab Rep.	Mali
Israel	Yemen, PDR	Mauritius
Ivory Coast	Yugoslavia (former)	Mozambique
Jamaica	Zambia	Madagascar
	Zimbabwe	Myanmar
		Nepal
		Niger
		Rwanda
		Samoa
		Sao Tome and Principe
		Sierra Leone
		Somalia
		Sudan
		Togo
		Tuvalu
		Uganda
		United Rep. of Tanzania
		Vanuatu
		Yemen
		Zaire

EXHIBIT 1-2. Distinguishing Characteristics of Countries in Each Category

Characteristic	First World	Second World
Per capita income	very high	high
Rate of population growth	low	low to medium
Quality of life	very high	low to medium
Sectorial distribution of gross domestic product	services most important	dependence on a few industries
Life expectancy	very high	medium
Rate of inflation	low	low to medium
Currency convertibility	convertible	convertible
Energy consumption	very high	high
Infrastructure	highly adequate	mostly adequate
Per capita consumption	very high	high
Urbanization	high	low to medium

factors that may be used to establish economic differences among countries.

The following three factors may be used, either individually or together, to characterize a country as developing: (a) per capita gross national product, (b) percentage of labor force engaged in primary activities, and (c) per capita consumption of inanimate energy.

The World Bank uses GNP per capita as the main criterion, classifying countries into six groups.[4]

Grouping	*GNP per capita*
• Low-income countries	$425 or less
• Middle-income countries	Between $426 and $1600
• Upper-middle-income countries	Between $1600 and $7500
• Higher income oil exporters	$5000 or more
• Industrial market economies	$5000 or more
• Communist countries	Not reported

The above classification is a convenient way of grouping countries, although not without problems. For example, Hong Kong and Singapore, with GNP per capita of about $7,000, are listed as upper-

Third World	Fourth World	Fifth World
medium to low	medium	very low
high	medium	very high
medium	low to medium	low
increasing importance of industry	mainly industry	mainly agriculture
medium	medium to high	low
medium to high	indeterminable	high
most inconvertible	inconvertible	inconvertible
medium to low	medium	very low
tolerable	inadequate	highly inadequate
medium	low to medium	low
medium	medium	low

middle-income countries while Spain and Ireland, with less than $6,000 GNP per capita, are considered industrial market economies.

Generally speaking, agriculture in developing countries accounts for a large proportion of economic activity and employment. For example, according to World Bank data, several low-income countries depend on agriculture for about half of their domestic product, with an average of 32 percent for low-income countries and 15 percent for middle-income economies.[5] On the other hand, among the industrial market economies, agriculture accounts for less than 10 percent of gross domestic product, and the average is only 3 percent (only 2 percent for the U.S. and West Germany). Similar patterns are evident in the labor force. On the average, 70 percent of the labor force in low-income countries is engaged in agriculture, 40 percent in middle-income countries, and as low as 7 percent in industrial market economies.[6]

Energy consumption is another factor that distinguishes between developed and developing countries. It indicates the extent to which human and animal power have been replaced by inanimate energy. In 1986, per capita energy consumption in low-income countries averaged 314 kilowatts, while it was 883 kilowatts for middle-income countries and over 2000 kilowatts among industrial market economies.[7]

MARKET INTERDEPENDENCIES

One of the most significant developments in recent decades is the internationalization of markets for goods and services. Although trade has been conducted across national boundaries for centuries, it is only since World War II that business operations have escalated to a global scale. Today practically all aspects of a business–financing, manufacturing, commerce and technology–are global.

According to Morgan Stanley & Company, on the average, in 1987 over $420 billion moved through the world's financial exchanges every day. This is more than one-third of the U.S. Federal budget.[8] At the end of 1990, according to a U.S. Department of Commerce report, U.S. direct investment abroad stood at $410.0 billion, up from $229.7 billion in 1985. Foreigners hold $1.3 trillion in liquid assets in this country, a fourth of that in U.S. federal debt. Overseas production by U.S. corporations amounted to $800 billion a year. A Ford car assembled in England and West Germany has components produced in ten other countries on three continents–truly a product of a global factory.[9]

In 1990, U.S. exports and imports of goods and services amounted to almost one-fourth of the gross national product, more than twice as much as twenty years ago. U.S. manufacturers export over 20 percent of their output. As far as agriculture is concerned, the produce of over two cropland acres out of five is exported. Technology probably has gone farthest in becoming global. Fifty pounds of fiberglass transmit as many phone messages as a ton of copper. Synthetics are fast replacing steel. Microelectronics and satellites support global communication networks enabling a manager to control factories on the other side of the globe. Research in ceramics, superconductors, and biotechnology flows readily across borders, creating the so-called Third Industrial Revolution. In summary, the powerful force of technology is driving the world toward a converging commonality.[10]

The global market has emerged. Millions worldwide want all the things they have heard about, seen, or experienced via new communication technologies. To capitalize on this trend, American companies must learn to operate globally, as if the world were one large market, ignoring superficial regional and national differences. Global markets offer unlimited opportunities. Corporations geared to this new reality can benefit from enormous economies of scale in production, distribution, marketing, and management. By translating these benefits into reduced world prices, they can dislodge competitors who still operate with the perspectives of the 1960s and 1970s. In future years, only companies capable of changing their mentality and becoming global will achieve long-term success.[11] At the macro-level, the overwhelming message of market globalization is that living standards of countries that seek to resist the tide will decline relative to others, and perhaps even in absolute terms. The benefits of global markets are simply too great to forego, especially when neighbors and competitors take advantage of them.

ATTRACTIVE MARKETS

Earlier we classified countries into six groups. In the Third World category–the principal focus of this book–there are 60 countries. Of these, many countries may be dropped because of political uncertainty in the foreseeable future (for example, Burma). Further, markets that are too small in terms of population (for example, Paraguay) may be eliminated because of the limited demand potential. The surviving countries can then be assessed for strategic attractiveness using the following criteria:

a. *Economic potential*–GNP growth
b. *Wealth*–per capita market size of the country as a whole and specific segments
c. *Infrastructure*–institutional framework and physical environment
d. *Technology orientation*–ability to absorb technology in the economy
e. *Resource availability*–access to vital resources (qualified labor force, raw materials, capital)

Applying the above parameters (based on macroeconomic data and historical events), the following Third World countries qualify as the most attractive markets with substantial long-term economic potential:

- China
- India
- Kenya
- Pakistan
- Indonesia
- Argentina
- Brazil
- Peru
- Philippines
- Colombia
- South Africa
- Thailand
- Malaysia
- Venezuela
- Nigeria
- Mexico
- Egypt
- Morocco
- Algeria
- Sri Lanka

The above 20 countries are distinct from other Third World countries in the nature and degree of their structural strength to enhance national development, and in their capacity to adapt to the international economic environment. Although there are vast differences among these countries, the common factor that characterizes them is their strength of economic, institutional and, ultimately, human capacities–a strength which is compounded in many cases by geophysical advantages.

A plethora of social and economic factors makes these countries exceptionally complex and difficult marketplaces. They exhibit bewildering variety, dramatic contrast, and constant change.

Variety

The Third World 20 countries vary on several dimensions. They are small and large, rich and poor, rural and urban. Politically, they are communist (China), monarchist (Thailand), and democratic (everywhere else, more or less).

Economically, they practice everything from China's timid capitalism to India's semi-socialism to the free market economy of Sri Lanka. Their populations are mainly Catholic (Argentina), mainly Buddhist (Thailand), mainly Hindu (India), and mainly Protestant (South Africa). They speak a polyglot of languages from the most simplistic (Spanish) to the most complex (Mandarin).

Contrast

Per capita incomes in the Third World 20 countries are a study in contrasts ranging from about $300 per year in China to over $3,000 annually in Venezuela. These extremes in income are mirrored by equally stark differences in lifestyles. While affluence and high-tech sophistication typify Argentina, in the remote jungles of Irian Jaya, Indonesia, loincloths are still the fashion and shrunken heads acceptable decor.

Change

Each of the Third World 20 countries is now engaged in a unique and dramatic process of evolution. Mexico, for example, is adapting to a new, more competitive world in which its traditional union dominance and bountiful welfare programs play a greatly reduced role. In India, change means coming to grips with a newly affluent middle class, massive rural poverty, and high unemployment among the educated people.

For marketers, so much variety, contrast, and change make for a passel of hassles. Yet in coming years, as rising incomes continue to bolster the spending power of these newborn consumer populations, the opportunities for savvy marketers will be unparalleled. Exhibit 1-3 supplies basic macro information on the Third World 20s. Exhibits 1-4 and 1-5 depict indicators of their market size.

As markets, these countries exhibit common perspectives, but they pursue different strategies to seek economic growth. Following Dholakia's classification,[12] these nations may be grouped into three categories: (a) miracle exports, (b) noncapitalist countries, and (c) regional powers. The miracle exporters (for example, Thailand and Philippines) seek growth through export-led strategies, emulating such countries as South Korea and Taiwan. Noncapitalist countries (for example, China and Burma) rely mainly on their own resources to pursue growth without depending on the world capitalist system. Regional powers (for example, India and Brazil), taking advantage of their large industrial base and market size, rely on a mixture of export-led growth and self-reliance, depending what suits them best

EXHIBIT 1-3. Macro Information on 20 Third World Countries

Countries	Total Population 1988 (Millions)	Total Gross Domestic Product 1988 ($ Billions)	Per Capita Gross Domestic Product 1988 ($)	Average Hourly Wage 1988 ($)	Life Expectancy at Birth 1986 (Years)
1. Algeria	23.84	54.1	2,269	--	62
2. Argentina	32.0	84.8	2,655	0.79	70
3. Brazil	144.4	351.0	2,430	1.95	65
4. China	1,096.10	332.8	304	0.19	69
5. Colombia	30.2	38.9	1,286	--	65
6. Egypt	51.90	74.4	1,434	--	61
7. India	796.60	269.7	339	0.48	57
8. Indonesia	175.59	82.7	471	--	57
9. Kenya	23.88	8.6	360	0.78	57
10. Malaysia	16.96	37.5	2,210	1.45	56
11. Mexico	82.7	183.8	2,222	1.13	68
12. Morocco	23.91	22.0	920	--	60
13. Nigeria	104.96	33.4	318	0.85	51
14. Pakistan	105.41	40.1	381	--	52
15. Peru	21.3	34.2	1,607	0.37	60
16. Philippines	58.72	39.1	667	0.35	63
17. Sri Lanka	16.59	7.0	421	0.21	70
18. South Africa	33.75	88.7	2,628	2.71	61
19. Thailand	54.54	57.9	1,062	--	64
20. Venezuela	18.80	60.0	3,199	2.94	70

Source: From different government and United Nations publications.

Average Annual Rate of Inflation 1980-1986 (Percentage)	Area (Thousands of Square Meters)	Physical Quality of Life Index Early 1970s	Local Currency	Exchange Rate Per U.S. Dollar January, 1991
6.1	2,382	41	Dinar	9.66
326.2	2,767	85	Austral	7,301.00
157.1	8,512	68	Cruzeiro	201.28
3.8	9,561	69	Renmimbi	5.23
22.6	1,139	71	Peso	563.11
12.4	1,001	41	Pound	2.25
7.8	3,288	43	Rupee	18.44
8.9	1,919	48	Rupiah	1,885.01
9.9	583	39	Shilling	22.47
1.5	330	66	Ringgit	2.63
63.7	1,973	73	Peso	2,945.00
7.7	447	41	Dirham	8.08
10.5	924	25	Naira	7.87
7.5	804	38	Rupee	22.02
100.1	1,285	62	New Sol	0.49
18.2	300	71	Peso	27.20
13.5	66	82	Rupee	40.46
13.6	1,221	53	Rand	2.54
3.0	514	68	Baht	25.15
8.7	912	79	Bolivar	54.52

EXHIBIT 1-4. Indicators of Market Size for 20 Third World Countries (Consumer Markets)

Countries	Private Consumption Expenditure		Percentage Share of Total Household Consumption (Range of years, 1980-85)					
	Total 1988 ($ Bil.)	Average Annual Real Increase 1986-90 (%)	Food		Clothing and Footwear	Gross Rents, Fuel and Power		Medi-cal Care
			Total	Cereals and Tubers		Total	Fuel and Power	
1. Algeria	26.8	--	--	--	--	--	--	--
2. Argentina	--	−1.9	35	4	6	9	2	4
3. Brazil	19.9	2.8	35	9	10	11	2	6
4. China	--	5.6	—	--	--	--	—	--
5. Colombia	20.1	3.3	29	--	6	13	2	7
6. Egypt	59.1	1.8	36	7	4	5	1	14
7. India	158.8	6.6	52	--	10	8	5	3
8. Indonesia	48.0	3.7	48	21	7	13	7	2
9. Kenya	5.2	2.3	42	18	8	13	3	0
10. Malaysia	19.5	6.6	45	22	7	11	3	7
11. Mexico	116.5	0.8	35	--	10	8	--	5
12. Morocco	15.1	5.2	48	14	10	14	3	3
13. Nigeria	--	1.9	52	18	7	10	2	3
14. Pakistan	27.3	4.9	54	17	9	15	6	3
15. Peru	1.2	−2.0	35	8	7	15	3	4
16. Philippines	28.6	4.6	47	--	6	11	--	4
17. Sri Lanka	5.4	2.3	48	21	5	6	2	3
18. South Africa	50.1	2.7	--	--	--	--	--	--
19. Thailand	35.5	6.6	34	--	11	6	3	6
20. Venezuela	13.0	0.1	38	--	4	8	--	8

Source: From different government and United Nations publications.

| Educa-tion | Transport and Communica-tion | | Other Consumption | | Passenger Cars | | Tele-phones | Televisions | |
	To-tal	Motor Cars	To-tal	Other Con-sumer Dura-bles	Total 1988 (Thou)	Cumula-tive Increase 1983-88 (%)	Total 1988 (Thou)	Total 1989 (Thou)	Cu-mula-tive Increase 1984-89 (%)
--	--	--	--	--	725	27.0	944	1,600	11.1
6	13	0	26	6	4,060	14.7	2,745	7,165	21.1
5	8	1	27	8	9,527	2.7	9,085	36,000	56.5
--	--	--	--	--	995	895.0	9,426	126,000	1,172.7
5	13	--	27	--	632	−22.9	2,032	5,500	205.4
11	3	1	26	2	425	−2.5	1,453	3,500	−9.3
4	11	--	12	--	1,506	52.7	4,482	20,000	852.4
4	4	0	22	5	965	31.3	931	2,000	−33.4
2	9	1	26	6	128	0.8	356	200	163.2
6	12	2	12	8	1,172	15.6	1,646	2,350	125.5
5	12	--	25	--	5,403	15.7	3,775	9,500	25.8
6	5	0	13	5	565	25.6	371	1,210	--
4	4	1	20	6	773	4.6	283	5,600	1,117.4
3	1	0	15	5	434	20.2	748	1,600	59.2
6	10	0	24	7	391	3.7	626	1,600	82.9
8	3	--	21	--	353	−1.9	1,010	6,750	575.0
3	11	1	24	6	148	12.1	184	750	1370.6
--	--	--	--	--	3,079	12.9	4,914	2,650	26.2
6	13	--	24	--	507	11.2	116	4,500	50.0
7	10	--	25	--	1,601	7.1	1,749	2,760	37.9

EXHIBIT 1-5. Indicators of Market Size for 20 Third World Countries (Industrial Markets)

Countries	Trucks and Buses		Steel	
	Total 1988 (Thousands)	Cumulative Increase 1983-88 (Percentage)	Total 1988 (KMT)	Cumulative Increase 1983-88 (Percentage)
1. Algeria	480	48.1	2,828	9.3
2. Argentina	1,482	9.0	2,956	1.5
3. Brazil	2,410	20.4	11,720	36.6
4. China	3,128	84.0	70,348	35.7
5. Colombia	587	193.5	1,280	35.2
6. Egypt	247	18.2	4,462	76.2
7. India	1,377	40.4	16,349	33.6
8. Indonesia	1,040	17.0	1,393	−51.1
9. Kenya	143	17.2	212	11.6
10. Malaysia	351	39.3	2,022	−17.4
11. Mexico	2,383	24.4	6,998	11.1
12. Morocco	227	13.5	590	−7.2
13. Nigeria	606	2.4	429	−78.3
14. Pakistan	288	31.5	1,885	31.5
15. Peru	221	11.1	701	106.2
16. Philippines	506	−2.1	1,436	−11.9
17. Sri Lanka	133	23.1	--	--
18. South Africa	1,355	17.4	5,991	12.1
19. Thailand	819	37.4	3,176	2.7
20. Venezuela	558	−34.9	3,126	85.2

Source: From different government and United Nations publications.

Cement		Electricity		Energy Consumption	
Total 1988 (KMT)	Cumulative Increase 1983-88 (Percentage)	Total 1988 (Billion KWH)	Cumulative Increase 1983-88 (Percentage)	Per Capita 1987 (kg oil equivalent)	Cumulative Increase 1982-87 (Percentage)
7,541	101.5	13.32	46.2	1,008	153.3
6,302	8.3	48.67	24.6	1,338	14.3
25,332	21.3	214.12	32.2	75,916	15,650.2
204,144	69.9	593.52	68.9	524	29.4
6,312	33.5	35.37	38.1	572	0.2
8,762	141.0	32.50	44.0	472	15.7
43,152	45.9	221.12	58.1	192	24.7
12,096	40.7	34.81	137.7	192	5.5
1,248	−5.5	2.84	27.4	72	1.4
4,800	38.4	21.48	57.4	956	14.5
21,996	13.7	101.88	23.7	1,188	−4.0
3,864	4.2	5.92	0.2	235	2.6
3,084	2.4	9.90	13.6	116	−32.2
7,032	73.5	35.22	78.9	1,751	5.1
2,520	28.0	16.20	25.1	8,919	2.4
4,092	−12.6	24.59	30.2	185	−13.1
5,012	30.0	2.80	32.4	87	−4.4
6,000	−27.8	156.74	27.6	1,971	0.8
11,520	35.5	32.64	65.0	345	41.4
6,204	40.1	54.70	36.9	2,113	−7.1

in a particular case. While some countries neatly fall into one of these categories, others follow a mixed perspective that varies from one time period to another and from industry to industry.

MARKET CHARACTERISTICS

Unlike markets in the West, Third World markets are still evolving. While each market, dictated by its social, economic, cultural, historical, and geographical factors, assumes its unique attributes, there are traits common to most markets.[13]

(a) *Regional disparities.* Often markets are geographically dispersed in terms of their size and potential. Overall, urban markets appear to be more advanced than the rural markets in comparison with markets in the developed world. Further, some regions may be ahead of others which may be explained by varying educational levels, industrial growth, or such similar factors.

(b) *Income inequalities.* In Third World countries wealth is so extremely maldistributed that a small segment of the population controls a disproportionately high amount of monetary resources. The income inequalities limit the size of the market, prohibiting developing mass markets.

(c) *Lack of services.* The marketing systems of Third World countries suffer from inadequate services of all kinds—from poor information to poor before and after sales support, including financing. Let the buyer beware is the common philosophy that typifies marketing transactions in these markets.

(d) *Inefficiency.* Productivity of marketing institutions in Third World countries, compared to those in the industrialized countries, is very low. This characteristic leads to not only low level of customer satisfaction but a great waste of human and capital resources. A comparable retail store, for example, may employ twice as many people as in the U.S. and yet provide less than one-fourth the service.

(e) *Monopolistic dominance.* Limited amount of information and lack of services lead customers to depend on recognized brands. Thus, brand dominance, leading to monopolistic competition, is more prevalent in the Third World countries than in the advanced nations.[14] Foreign brands or local brands with foreign collaboration achieve monopolistic control in the market.

CONCLUSION

Third World countries represent a large proportion of world population. Notwithstanding the large differences in history and culture that separate these countries, the size of their populations and the vastness of their lands have stimulated similar responses to the changing international environment of the modern era. Today, these countries share a common predicament: How can these nations with ambitious foreign policies but with underdeveloped, technology-poor economies make headway in a relentlessly demanding, rapidly changing, and ever more intrusive global economy? From the viewpoint of American business, the Third World countries represent potentially lucrative markets as they sort out their problems, adopt growth strategies, and raise their living levels from the present low levels of consumption.

Chapter 2

U.S. Business with Developing Countries

Over 75 percent of U.S. direct investments has traditionally been in developed countries. Similarly, developed countries account for a significantly greater share of U.S. foreign trade. Slowly, Third World countries are becoming important, both for investment and trade, especially countries that are politically stable. Interestingly, while for cultural, political, and economic reasons, the more viable opportunities for U.S. corporations are found in Western Europe, Canada, and, to a lesser extent, Japan, many Third World countries provide a better return on U.S. direct investments.

An individual developing country may not provide adequate potential for U.S. corporations, but developing countries as a group constitute a major market. In 1990, over one-third of our trade was with LDCs. In future years, the flow of U.S. trade with Third World countries should increase. An Organization of Economic Cooperation and Development (OECD) study shows that in 1970 the OECD countries with just 20 percent of the world's people had 83 percent of the world's trade in manufactures, while the developing countries, with 70 percent of the world's people, had 11 percent of the trade. In the year 2000, however, it is estimated that the OECD countries with 15 percent of the population will have 63 percent of the world's trade in manufactures, while the developing countries, with 78 percent of the population, will account for 28 percent of the trade.[1]

U.S. TRADE WITH THIRD WORLD COUNTRIES

Since the 1970s, manufacturing activity in the Third World has grown faster than in developed countries. This increase in output

23

has led to a simultaneous increase in their manufactured exports. In 1985, Third World countries had over 18 percent of world production compared with 14.5 percent in 1970. Their share of manufactured exports rose from 7.3 percent to 17.4 percent since 1970.[2]

Putting it differently, in 1965 no developing country could count itself among the top 30 exporters of manufactured goods. By 1985 a number of the Third World 20 countries–for example, Brazil and China–were in the top 20, with export sales close to Denmark and Finland.[3]

Manufacturing activity in Third World countries is gradually becoming sophisticated, diversifying from traditional labor-intensive products (e.g., textiles) or those based on natural resources (e.g., crude petrochemicals, cork, and paper) to chemicals and engineering products.

In those Third World countries that now challenge the developed world, production and trade have evolved far beyond the old pattern through which industrial countries exported manufactures to the developing countries in exchange for primary commodities. Today, the reverse is often true: A developing country may export manufactures and import primary commodities. Brazil, for example, exports automobiles to the United States and imports U.S. grain and other farm products.

Third World Countries as Customers

In the 1980s, Third World countries provided a market for about one-third of all U.S. exports. In 1990, U.S. exports to Third World 20 countries alone came to $128.08 billion, 32.5 percent of total exports of $393.9 billion. Exports to Third World 20 countries in 1990 showed an increase of 7 percent over 1989. In the same period, the increase to developed countries came to 4.5 percent.

U.S. exports to developing countries can be grouped in three major categories: machinery and transport equipment, agricultural products, and chemicals. The role of manufactured products is gradually increasing in importance over basic products. This shift reflects the change in the world economy. Exhibit 2-1 shows the import perspectives of Third World 20 countries.

U.S. exports to the Third World follow closely the economic growth trends recorded in these countries. For example, U.S. exports declined sharply in the early and middle 1980s as the purchasing power in these countries was reduced by debt-service problems, declining commodity prices, and the global recession. U.S. exports to industrial country markets also declined in those years, but the impact on Third World markets was substantially greater. Between 1981 and 1983, U.S. exports to developed countries fell by 9 percent, but exports to developing countries declined by almost 19 percent. Exports to developed countries also recovered more rapidly, with the result that, in 1987, the developing countries accounted for only 32 percent of U.S. total exports, compared with 37 percent at the beginning of the decade. By 1987, however, the Third World market was recovering more rapidly. Sales to those countries in 1987 showed a gain of $11 billion or 16 percent over the preceding year. This compares with increases of only 9 percent in sales to developed countries.[4]

Third World Countries as Suppliers

In 1990, 22 percent of U.S. imports came from developing countries. Exhibit 2-2 summarizes information on Third World exports. Two-thirds of these imports were manufactured goods, the category most frequently viewed as a competitive threat to the U.S. economy. In the last two decades, Third World manufacturing has grown more rapidly than that of developed countries, in both production and exports. This has led to a shift in the kind of products that these countries import and export. It is argued that U.S. imports from these countries are much less a threat to American jobs than the imports from industrialized countries, particularly Japan and NICs. In fact, studies show that trade with the Third World has resulted in net job gains for developed countries.[5] Yet Third World trade practices have often been the target of U.S. complaints.

In 1990, the excess of Third World exports over imports generated a U.S. negative trade balance of $25.5 billion or 25 percent of the overall U.S. trade deficit. However, $18 billion of that deficit was accounted for by petroleum imports, and $5 billion by coffee, rubber, and other tropical farm products not produced commercially in the U.S. The U.S. also looks to the Third World for important quantities of strategic materials: imports meet more than 50 percent of U.S. needs for twenty important minerals. The U.S. imports 99

EXHIBIT 2-1. Import Perspectives of 20 Third World Countries

Countries	Total Imports		Imports from US		Imports from EC		Imports from Japan		Major Imports
	1988 C.I.F. ($ Million)	Average Annual Increase 1983-88 (%)	1988 C.I.F. ($ Million)	Average Annual Increase 1983-88 (%)	1988 C.I.F. ($ Million)	Average Annual Increase 1983-88 (%)	1988 C.I.F. ($ Million)	Average Annual Increase 1983-88 (%)	
1. Algeria	8,036	-4.2	495	-3.8	4,739	-3.1	274	-8.8	Machinery 37%; food products 21%; packaged consumer goods 17%
2. Argentina	6,194	7.7	1,161	4.8	1,700	8.8	328	4.2	Machinery 28%; steel 22%; chemicals 15%; mineral fuels 8%
3. Brazil	16,048	-0.7	3,347	5.5	3,464	13.1	1,058	13.5	Petroleum 51%; machinery 19%; chemicals 10%; minerals 6%
4. China	55,352	23.1	6,633	11.0	8,176	23.1	11,062	21.5	—
5. Colombia	5,030	0.8	1,848	1.6	1,030	4.9	545	1.8	Machinery and equipment 38%; chemicals 14%; agricultural products 13%; ores and metals 10%
6. Egypt	13,651	6.1	2,574	13.1	4,758	-0.3	530	2.9	Cereals 14%; transport equipment 11%; chemicals 8%; electrical machinery 7%
7. India	24,310	9.1	2,748	12.5	7,284	13.8	2,291	9.9	Petroleum and petroleum products 39%; non-electrical machinery 9%; steel 19%; fertilizer 5%; chemicals 3%
8. Indonesia	13,489	-2.4	1,734	0.9	2,598	2.1	3,427	-1.1	Machinery 37%; minerals and lubricants 21%; basic manufactures 16%; chemicals 10%; food products 7%
9. Kenya	2,214	10.1	101	7.9	1,045	8.0	252	14.2	Crude petroleum 34%; transport equipment 27%; non-electrical machinery 8%; electrical machinery 5%; glass and glassware 5%

Country									Imports — major commodities
10. Malaysia	22,585	11.9	3,803	12.0	3,137	12.1	5,438	12.0	Telecommunications equipment 15%; computer software and services 11%; oil and gas production equipment 9%; computer hardware and peripherals 1%
11. Mexico	28,841	29.4	20,644	35.8	2,795	18.2	1,772	43.2	Agricultural products 21%; industrial machinery 18%; chemicals 11%; transportation equipment 9%; food products 7%
12. Morocco	4,612	5.2	322	7.7	1,822	-0.7	73	13.1	Crude petroleum 26%; machinery and equipment 21%; food products 14%; steel 5%
13. Nigeria	5,278	-9.2	392	-12.5	2,747	-2.2	339	-4.4	Machinery and equipment 46%; manufactured goods 26%; chemicals 12%; food products 10%
14. Pakistan	6,589	4.7	856	13.4	1,709	8.2	972	5.4	Machinery 17%; transport equipment 8%; edible oils 6%; steel 4%; fertilizers 3%
15. Peru	2,531	7.2	630	2.7	533	9.9	99	-6.6	Machinery and equipment 33%; food products 16%; packaged consumer goods 9%
16. Philippines	8,662	4.1	1,823	0.8	1,049	7.1	1,503	6.0	Crude petroleum 25%; non-electrical machinery 11%; chemicals 10%; steel 4%; motor vehicles 4%
17. Sri Lanka	2,211	4.4	153	9.9	383	5.3	305	-0.6	Petroleum 52%; machinery 28%; food and beverages 9%; textiles 6%
18. South Africa	18,737	5.6	1,691	-2.1	7,893	13.6	2,047	9.1	—
19. Thailand	16,292	11.3	2,733	22.9	3,154	21.1	1,901	-3.7	Fuels 30%; machinery 10%; steel 8%; electrical machinery 7%; organic chemicals and fertilizers 6%
20. Venezuela	11,624	12.8	4,611	12.2	3,095	10.2	555	11.7	Non-electrical machinery 12%; motor vehicles 12%; chemicals 11%; electrical machinery 10%; steel 8%

EXHIBIT 2-2. Export Perspectives of 20 Third World Countries

Countries	Total Exports		Major Export Destinations	Major Exports
	1988 F.O.B. ($ Mill.)	Average Annual Increase 1983-88 (%)		
1. Algeria	8,216	6.5	France 23%; Germany 22%; U.S. 11%; Italy 10%; Eastern Europe 7%	Petroleum 73%
2. Argentina	9,307	5.6	Italy 22%; former U.S.S.R. 18%; Netherlands 6%; Brazil 5%; U.S. 3%	Grains and cereals 24%; meat and meat products 22%; wool 10%; animal feed 8%
3. Brazil	33,785	10.4	U.S. 12%; Spain 8%; U.K. 6%; Japan 6%; Germany 4%	Coffee 10%; soybeans 10%; raw sugar 6%; iron ore 6%
4. China	47,663	16.8	—	—
5. Colombia	4,890	10.9	U.S. 72%; Japan 8%; Brazil 4%; U.K. 2%	Coffee 63%; fuel oils 23%
6. Egypt	4,285	9.5	Italy 23%; Israel 15%; France 7%; Romania 6%; Netherlands 6%	Petroleum and petroleum products 67%; textile fibers 14%
7. India	15,324	9.9	former U.S.S.R. 20%; U.S. 12%; Japan 9%; U.K. 6%; Germany 6%	Engineering goods 12%; textile goods 10%; leather goods 5%; iron ore 5%; chemicals 5%
8. Indonesia	19,376	-0.6	Japan 50%; U.S. 16%; Singapore 14%	Petroleum and petroleum products 70%; natural gas 13%; rubbers 3%; wood 3%; tin 2%
9. Kenya	1,353	4.9	U.K. 13%; Germany 12%; Uganda 10%; U.S. 6%; Netherlands 5%	Coffee 27%; petroleum products 26%; tea 14%; cement 4%; sisal 2%

			Trading partners	Commodities
10. Malaysia	25,049	9.7	Japan 33%; U.S. 28%; West Germany 14%; U.K. 13%	Rubber and other natural resources 40%; agricultural products 23%; electrical machinery and electronic devices 22%
11. Mexico	29,373	9.3	U.S. 54%; Spain 9%; Japan 7%; France 5%; U.K. 5%	Crude petroleum 67%; petroleum products 4%; transportation and communication equipment 4%; chemicals 3%
12. Morocco	3,374	9.5	France 24%; Germany 8%; Spain 7%; Italy 7%; India 6%	Metals and minerals 34%; food products 25%; chemicals 17%; textiles 9%
13. Nigeria	8,872	-2.8	U.S. 47%; Netherlands 12%; France 10%; Germany 7%; U.K. 3%	Petroleum 99%
14. Pakistan	4,509	9.0	Saudi Arabia 9%; Iran 9%; Japan 8%; Dubai 7%; U.S. 6%	Rice 11%; cotton fabrics 11%; cotton yarn 10%; carpets 6%; petroleum products 3%
15. Peru	2,689	1.5	U.S. 33%; Japan 9%; Germany 6%; Italy 5%	Petroleum 18%; copper 15%; silver 13%; zinc 11%; lead 10%
16. Philippines	7,034	8.2	U.S. 31%; Japan 22%; Netherlands 6%; West Germany 5%; Hong Kong 4%	Clothing 11%; sugar 10%; coconut oil 10%; copper centrates 8%; fruits and vegetables 8%
17. Sri Lanka	1,463	8.1	U.S. 15%; U.K. 7%; West Germany 6%; Japan 6%; India 3%	Tea 30%; rubber 11%; coconut products 5%; precious and semiprecious stones 4%
18. South Africa	25,847	8.8	—	—
19. Thailand	15,992	21.1	Japan 14%; Singapore 8%; Malaysia 6%; Hong Kong 5%	Rice 8%; rubber 6%; corn 6%; tin 5%; shrimp 2%
20. Venezuela	10,365	-3.8	U.S. 37%; Netherlands Antilles 22%; Canada 10%; U.K. 3%	Petroleum and petroleum products 93%

percent of its manganese, 96 percent of its bauxite/alumina, and 95 percent of its cobalt.[6] For example, cobalt, on which the aircraft industry is crucially dependent for manufacturing jet engine blades, comes from Zambia and Zaire.[7]

Many companies find Third World countries as viable places for offshore manufacturing.[8] For example, Nike set up production facilities in the People's Republic of China in search of cheaper labor. IBM made a major investment in Mexico to manufacture microcomputers, mainly for export to the U.S. AT&T set up operations in Thailand to manufacture phones for the U.S. market. It is interesting to note that this new facility would enable AT&T to shift its existing production of cord phones from Singapore to Thailand, leaving the former to concentrate on more sophisticated cordless phones. This underlines the importance of Third World countries as emerging production centers for labor-intensive jobs.

U.S. INVESTMENTS IN THE THIRD WORLD

The United States is the largest source of private direct investment in the world. At the end of 1990, the U.S. direct investment overseas reached $410 billion, up from $314 billion in 1987. About 80 percent of this investment is in industrialized countries. The remaining 20 percent is invested in Third World countries, including NICs. Among the Third World countries, only a few are the major beneficiaries of U.S. direct investments: Argentina ($5.8 billion), Brazil ($18.84 billion), Mexico ($14.5 billion), Indonesia ($8.4 billion), China ($4.6 billion), Colombia ($3.6 billion), Thailand ($3.2 billion), Venezuela ($3.3 billion), South Africa ($2.5 billion), and India ($350.5 million).[9]

Historically in the Third World countries, direct investments were made first in extractive operations in natural resources and public utility areas, such as minerals and petroleum. In recent years, a major proportion of direct investments has shifted to the processing of raw materials and the production of consumer goods. Currently, about one-third of U.S. direct investments in Third World countries is represented by manufacturing, 30 percent in petroleum, 10 percent in finance, and the remainder in other areas.[10]

Of the 500 largest U.S. companies, 55 percent had assets in Third

World countries in 1985.[11] The annual outflow of profits of foreign direct investment in developing countries rose by 22 percent a year between 1985 and 1989, reaching $30 billion in 1989,[12] compared with only 3 percent a year between 1980 and 1984. Again, during 1985-1989, the return on U.S. foreign direct investment in Third World countries averaged 18.3 percent, compared to 11.3 percent on direct investment in industrialized countries.[13]

The tempo of foreign direct investment in Third World countries is expected to continue in the 1990s. It is a matter of fact that, with the trend toward privatization of industry in Third World nations and their realization of the significance of foreign direct investment in their economic development efforts, more and more multinational corporations (MNCs) may find these countries as potentially good markets to enter. MNCs today are more willing to meet these nations halfway to make it convenient for the investment to flow despite the regulations that governments impose on such investments.

Foreign direct investment enables MNCs to enter new markets and/or seek access to natural resources and raw materials. Third World countries prefer direct investment by MNCs over developmental loans/aid because it is usually accompanied by technology and access to global marketing networks. Furthermore, direct investment means MNCs bear the risk if the project fails.

Conceptual explanation of an MNC's interest in making direct investments in Third World countries is provided by the international product life cycle model. The product life cycle model states that products go through the following four stages:[14]

- Phase I: U.S. export strength builds.
- Phase II: Foreign production starts.
- Phase III: Foreign production becomes competitive in export markets.
- Phase IV: Import competition begins in domestic U.S. markets.

During Phase I, the product is manufactured in the United States for a high income market and afterward introduced into foreign markets through exports. At that point, the U.S. usually holds a monopoly position as the only country able to supply the product. It continues to be manufactured only in the United States since business acumen suggests locating operations close to markets where the demand exists. Overseas customers, however, import the U.S. product in response to their own market demands and, thus, create a program of export for the U.S. product.

During Phase II, as the product becomes popular, entrepreneurs in other advanced countries, perhaps in Western Europe, venture into producing the same product. The technology involved is, by then, fairly routine and easily transferred from the United States. Subsequently, the overseas manufactured product begins to outsell the U.S. export in selected markets because the overseas product benefits from lower labor costs and savings in transportation. The stage where overseas manufacturers are able to compete effectively against U.S. exports has been reached.

In the third phase, the foreign producers begin to compete against the U.S. exports in Third World countries. This further adds to the declining market for the U.S. exports. Between Phases II and III the U.S. firms begin to consider making direct investments abroad to sustain or regain their original market position.

The fourth phase occurs when the foreign firms have lower costs so that, despite ocean freight and U.S. customs costs, they are able to compete effectively against the domestically produced U.S. products. These four phases complete the product life cycle and describe how American firms that once commanded a monopoly position in a product find themselves being pushed out of their home market.

The product life cycle theory of world trade holds that advanced countries, like the United States, play the innovative role in product development. Later on, other relatively advanced countries, like Japan or Western European countries, take over the market position held by the innovative country. The second-stage countries would go through the same cycle as did the innovative country and, in turn, would lose their markets to the next group of countries, say Third World countries. In other words, a product initially produced in the United States could eventually be produced only in newly-industrialized countries (NICs) and, subsequently, in less-developed countries (LDCs), with the result that the United States, Western Europe, Japan, and NICs would meet their needs for that product through import from LDCs.

The product life cycle model has been helpful in explaining the history of a number of products, particularly textiles, shoes, bicycles, radios, televisions, industrial fasteners, and standardized components for different uses. These products, available in the United States, Western Europe, and Japan, are being imported from Korea, Taiwan, Hong Kong, Brazil, Indonesia, India, and other Third World countries.

MNCs IN THE THIRD WORLD

The institution behind the upsurge of overseas direct investment has been the multinational corporation (MNC). MNCs have distinct advantages which can be put to the service of the Third World. Their ability to tap financial, physical, and human resources around the world and to combine them in economically feasible and commercially profitable activities, their capacity to develop new technology and skills, and their productive and managerial ability to translate resources into specific outputs have proven to be outstanding. They are credited for making, through direct investment, important contributions to Third World countries in two critical and related areas: the transfer of technology and the transformation of many countries from exporters of primary commodities into exporters of manufactures. Indeed, this direct contribution to structural change in developing countries appears to be far more important than the transfer of financial resources associated with foreign direct investment.

Despite these contributions, questions have been raised in Third World countries (as well as in industrialized countries) on the economic, political, and social significance of MNCs' overseas activities. The power concentrated in their hands and their actual or potential use of it, their ability to shape demand patterns and values and to influence the lives of people and policies of governments, as well as their impact on the international division of labor, have raised concerns about their role in world affairs. This concern is probably heightened by the fact that there is no systematic process of monitoring their activities and discussing them in an appropriate forum.[15]

The criticism of MNCs is not limited to host countries. For example, domestic labor unions in the United States have decried the MNCs for transferring jobs overseas and for entering into shady deals through bribery and politicking.

There are as many arguments that favor MNCs as those that

oppose them. Multinational corporations, on the whole, have made significant positive contributions to economic and social progress throughout the world. Through their technological and managerial capabilities, MNCs have helped to develop the material and productive resources of many nations and have worked to meet the world's growing needs for goods and services. Their investments have stimulated the diversification of local national economies. Their capital input has helped host governments to fulfill nationally defined economic development goals. They have provided jobs and helped to raise living standards in many areas. The important contribution that MNCs make to world welfare needs to be understood in the context of the objectives that they pursue. While their operations are often global, their interests are corporate. Their size and spread imply increased productive efficiency and reduction of risks, both of which have positive effects from the point of view of the allocation of resources.

As far as the U.S. is concerned, the overseas investment is necessary to maintain competitiveness and to protect markets abroad. MNCs contend that their overseas activities enable them to expand manufacturing and create jobs at home. This argument has been supported by consultants and academics. According to Peter Drucker, U.S. exports are increasingly dependent on U.S. foreign direct investment since three-fourths of the resulting output is sold in foreign markets. Drucker mentions:[16]

> It is simply not possible to maintain substantial market share in an important area unless one has physical presence as a producer. . . . By now, about one-fifth of the total capital invested in U.S. manufacturing firms is in facilities outside the U.S. In addition, a similar portion of the output of U.S. manufacturing industries is being produced offshore. Three-quarters of the output is for sale abroad and one-quarter is for export back to the U.S., to be sold or incorporated into goods for the American market. Major American commercial banks and major brokerage firms have a similar proportion of their assets invested abroad and derive an even larger proportion of their total business through their foreign branches.

A number of studies have addressed the question as to whether U.S. employment and manufacturing output have been reduced or increased by overseas investment, whether exports have been lost or enhanced, and whether the industrial base has been weakened or strengthened. Analysts have examined the motivation for overseas projects, the domestic performance of the companies involved, and the question of cost competitiveness. For example, Moran points out:[17]

> The results of all these approaches point in the same direction: A large part of U.S. investment overseas acts as a magnet, actually drawing exports of parts, components, and other sub-products and services out of the United States to those overseas plants. Of the rest, a large fraction goes to preserving a position in an existing market that would be lost if the operations were kept at home.

Financially, also, the direct investments in Third World countries have been rewarding for the U.S.' MNCs. The rate of return on operations in developing countries is often much higher than in industrial countries. In 1981, for example, U.S. firms earned about 20 percent on their investments in developing countries, and their returns averaged 15 percent in the following year, even though these were recession years around the world. A study of returns on U.S. investments in fourteen developing countries covering more than a decade found that the rate of returns on investments in ten of the developing countries was greater than in the U.S.–more than 10 percent greater in several cases.[18] Another study found that U.S. firms' joint ventures in India enjoyed an average increase of 20 percent per year in their after tax-profits.[19]

In addition, diversifying operations into countries outside the United States or other industrial countries can reduce the aggregate risks for U.S. firms. Since business cycles in individual developing countries are not perfectly correlated with U.S. cycles, U.S. companies can partially alleviate the impact of cyclical downturns at home.

THIRD WORLD COUNTRIES AS U.S. COMPETITORS

Competition from low-income countries is sometimes viewed as a threat to the American standard of living. Large populations working for pennies, under substandard conditions, are seen as undermining the American labor force and jeopardizing higher wage levels hard won over generations by U.S. industrial workers and farmers.

Actually, Third World competition is not primarily from low income countries but rather from half a dozen NICs. United States' critics of Third World competition often overstate the importance of the labor component in imported products and understate wage levels in the offending countries. The composition of Third World industrial exports has changed, with traditional labor-intensive products such as shoes and textiles giving way to higher technology products such as chemicals and electrical equipment.

It is true that in the 1980s the U.S. received a growing share of Third World exports, primarily because the U.S. was expanding as a market and other developed countries were not. Even so, most of the U.S. job losses linked to trade with Third World countries have been due to a loss of exports, not to an inordinate surge in imports.

Recognizing the fact that two-way trade generates economic activity on both sides, U.S. trade with the Third World has generated large employment gains in U.S. high-value-added sectors while reducing employment in low-value-added sectors such as apparel, leather, wood, food, and paper products. As a matter of fact, the work of University of Texas economist Marshall indicates that trade between developed and developing countries has resulted in net job gains to developed countries. In these studies, the United States tended to fare less well than other developed countries, apparently because the U.S. has suffered greater export declines in its Third World trade. As has been said: "The evidence clearly shows that North-South trade in fact results in job gains. Therefore, policymakers need to develop strategies for increasing North-South trade while at the same time ameliorating the localized dislocations, thus maximizing the overall gain for the United States and developing countries."[20]

It is pointed out that U.S.-Third World trade figures are sometimes distorted by the international character of manufacturing today. In many cases, "foreign competition" may actually be competition from American-owned and operated companies doing business in other countries. In 1985, for example, U.S. companies in Japan manufactured and sold $80 billion worth of products in that country, but very little of this value showed up as American exports. By the same token, autos made in Japanese-owned factories in this country are not counted as U.S. imports.

The United States has taken action on several fronts to improve the competitive situation with developing countries as well as with other trading partners. It has brought pressure, bilaterally and in the General Agreement on Tariffs and Trade (GATT), to change trade practices that this country considers unfair. U.S. negotiators have sought to end human rights violations in many developing countries. They have used bilateral pressure to halt the counterfeiting of U.S. products and the piracy of U.S. brands and designs, and have sought to strengthen GATT rules covering violations of intellectual property rights.

In addition, the Omnibus Trade and Competitiveness Act of 1988 provides a variety of trade-remedy tools for use in opening foreign markets for the U.S. For example, in May 1989, the United States issued unfair trader designations under the Super 301 provision of the Act to India and Brazil (also to Japan). India was named for restricting foreign investment and for not permitting foreign-based insurance companies to do business there. Brazil was cited for its import licensing practices. The Act requires the Administration to negotiate the removal of the barriers within 12-18 months. If talks are not successful, tariffs of up to 100% can be levied on selected imports from an offending country.

The force behind Third World competition is the multinational corporations belonging to these countries. The Birla Group of India, United Laboratories from the Philippines, and Autlan of Mexico are among the several hundred multinationals from the Third World whose overseas subsidiaries have increased from dozens around 1960 to a few thousand today. They are successfully competing for a share of world markets. These multinationals have gone abroad following the international product life cycle concept. They began by seeking export markets. When tariffs, quotas, or other barriers threatened overseas markets, these companies started assembling abroad. Their initial move, and greatest impact so far, has been in neighboring developing countries.

The strength of Third World MNCs comes from their special experience with manufacturing for small home markets. Using low technology and local raw material, running job-shop kinds of plants, and making effective use of semiskilled labor, they are able to custom design products best suited to host countries. For example, a Philippines paper company has managed projects in countries ranging from Indonesia to Nigeria. Its managers have drawn on their ability to make paper from inexpensive, locally available materials. In addition, they run a very efficient job-shop operation with printing, folding, and cutting machinery selected or built in-house to make very short runs of a wide range of cigarette, candy, and other packages. These are skills that the Western multinationals have usually forgotten.

While small-scale manufacturing remains their unique strength, these companies also are moving in other areas that are particularly suited to local conditions. For example, a Thai company uses rice stalks for paper and plantain products for glue. A Brazilian company has developed sunfast dyes and household appliances that resist high humidity and can survive the fluctuating voltages common in the developing world.[21]

The rapid growth of Third World multinationals provides both a threat and an opportunity to the multinationals from the advanced countries. The Third World MNCs can be tough competitors in seeking contract work in building plants that do not require high technology, such as steel plants and chemical complexes. But these MNCs also offer profitable opportunities to Western companies for joint operations. Lacking in marketing skills, for example, they may share their special know-how with traditional multinationals in exchange for brand names and skills in promoting new lines. Further, as Third World MNCs become visible and viable economic entities, their governments may well become more sympathetic to the needs of MNCs from the developed world.

CAPITALIZING ON OPPORTUNITIES IN THIRD WORLD COUNTRIES

Most developing countries are achieving higher and higher growth rates every year. For example, during the decade of the 1980s, Brazil, Malaysia, and Thailand were among the five fastest-growing economies. For U.S. marketers such growth promises unprecedented opportunities. H. J. Heinz Company's expansion into developing countries illustrates how a firm can take advantage of opportunities in Third World markets.[22]

On the theory that everyone needs to eat, Heinz looked for business opportunities around the globe. The company has been active abroad since 1905. In fiscal 1985, more than one-third of Heinz's sales came from foreign affiliates in the United Kingdom, Australia, New Zealand, and a few other nations, mostly in Europe. In the early 1980s, the company realized that it served only 15 percent of the world's population. It had not tapped the remaining 85 percent, which represents a huge potential. The company felt that improved living standards in the Third World would increase demand for Western-style foods such as ketchup.

Therefore, the company developed a plan to expand its operations in developing countries from less than $100 million in 1982 to $2.5 billion in 2000. In 1983 Heinz became the first foreign investor in Zimbabwe, acquiring 51 percent of Olivine Industries Inc., a maker of cooking oils and margarines. Since then the company has formed joint ventures in the Ivory Coast, Cameroon, and Thailand. The company has a long list of countries it wants to enter–China, India, Nigeria, and Egypt–by carefully adapting its U.S. products to local tastes. In its entry decision, the company duly considers if the overseas investment and aid to Third World farmers could provide its processing operations with raw materials in the future. A company spokesman says: "Our strategy isn't just for today or next year, but for years from now. If we can grow enough in Zimbabwe, and make it cost-competitive, we might export raw materials to Heinz operations in Europe."

The company has different strategies for different regions of the world. It acquired local companies in Africa, while in Asia it would prefer joint ventures with successful local companies that understand local tastes and have access to distribution networks.

As a company executive said: "We must be flexible and patient in seeking access to Third World markets. We have to convince them that we can offer something unique–new production techniques or the chance to manufacture a wide variety of foods. We have to negotiate with patience and many tea ceremonies. We introduced our brands to a vast awaiting audience and we now stand at the threshold of these new markets."

FUTURE PROSPECTS

A variety of reasons point toward growing market opportunities for American business in Third World countries in the 1990s and beyond. The expanding populations, the potential for a rise in living standards based on present low levels of consumption, and the likelihood of renewed economic growth following a period of slow growth in the 1980s indicate that Third World countries are potential growth markets for American business.

The predicted Third World economic collapse, as some economists foresaw, did not occur and now many of these countries are poised for rapid economic growth. There is evidence that "privatization" is becoming more acceptable in many Third World nations, which further enhances the chances of swift economic growth.

Population Growth

Three of every four of this world's consumers live in developing countries. By the end of this century, four out of five consumers will live in those countries. At the same time, population growth in developed countries is decreasing. For example, between 1988-2000, the Third World countries will have grown by more than a fourth, while developed countries' growth will total less than 6 percent.

After World War II, Western Europe and Japan were the focus of U.S. marketing efforts. But with virtually static population growth, future prospects in these countries are bleak. Japan's population will grow by less than 6 percent in the 1990s and will show growth near zero in the first two decades of the twenty-first century. Western Europe's population will actually decline during the 1990s, and will be totally flat in the next three decades. To put it more succinctly, the Third World population increase alone between 1988-2000 (a twelve-year period) will exceed the total combined populations in the year 2000 of Japan, all of Europe, the former Soviet Union, the United States, and Canada.

The enormous size of the Third World market, assuming purchasing power, presents an unsurpassable opportunity for U.S. companies.

Growing Needs

At the minimum, Third World countries represent a tremendous market for life's essentials: food, clothing, and shelter. At best, they present a large opportunity as producers and consumers in the global economy. People without purchasing power do not constitute a market and that is why the large populations in Third World countries did not mean much for marketers in the past. But in the 1990s these countries are expected to achieve fast economic growth resulting in increased purchasing power which, in turn, will create new markets and propel Third World nations into the mainstream of the world economy. What the newly industrializing countries have already proven is going to be repeated in Third World countries, one after the other.

Typically, Third World countries are characterized by low consumption levels, poor health and human services, and inadequate education. In 1985, average daily calorie intake per capita in Third World countries measured only two-thirds the level of advanced countries. Such data demonstrate the market potential in Third World countries as they move toward the global economic mainstream. As a President's task force points out: "Attention to the developing world will mean bigger and better markets, a large manpower pool, and increasing operational flexibility for those businesses engaged in the international arena."[23]

Economic Growth

Prospects for Third World economic growth in the 1990s depend on how well and how fast these countries adopt proven growth strategies. The World Bank believes that growth will depend on the success of measures to improve the international outlook, domestic policy reform, new money, and creative debt financing. The Bank's "high case" scenario calls for prompt and convincing steps to reduce payments imbalance and renewed efforts at structural reform to expand private investment, eliminate bottlenecks in labor markets, and reduce protection and agricultural subsidies. Under that scenario, the World Bank predicts it should be possible to achieve real annual growth rates between 5-6 percent in developing countries.[24]

The U.S. Department of Agriculture, which closely follows developments in the Third World, predicts that in the 1990s these countries will register substantially faster growth rates than developed countries.[25] Third World expansion will be led by East Asian countries (for example, Thailand and Indonesia) but other countries (particularly Brazil, India, and Mexico) should also record growth rates substantially better than in the latter half of the 1980s.

Privatization

A large number of Third World countries, on gaining independence from their colonial rulers, established different kinds of state-owned enterprises to seek economic growth. Recent worldwide developments have abundantly proved that state-controlled enterprises are less efficient and a drain on resources. Country after country is realizing the futility of the government establishing and running business enterprises. For example, in July 1985, at a meeting of the Organization of African Unity in Addis Ababa, Ethiopia, the assembled heads of state publicly conceded that "the primacy accorded to the state has hindered rather than furthered economic development."

While information about privatization, i.e., conversion of government-owned services and industries to the private sector, in Third World countries is sketchy, recent developments have focused on asset sales. Other forms of privatization include award of foreign management contracts, leasing, and liquidation of enterprises.

Third World countries that have made significant progress in privatizing their enterprises include Chile, Malaysia, Niger, Brazil, Mexico, Philippines, India, and Sri Lanka. Among them, the achievements of the first three are most extensive. As has been noted:

> In the mid-1970s a large number of enterprises taken over by the Allende–Popular Unity–Government were denationalized. More recently, in 1983 the government intervened to prevent bank failures. Two of these banks, Concepción and Internacional, were capitalized and sold to the private sector in 1986. A third, Colocadora, was merged with Banco de Santiago. All shares in Banco de Santiago and Banco de Chile were sold to

over 57,000 shareholds. By end-1986, CORFO, the Chilean Development Corporation and its affiliates, sold over 50 percent of the shares of the following enterprises: CHILMETRO (urban transport-metro), CHILQUINTA (electricity distribution), SOQUIMICH (nitrates), and CAP (iron ore). Shares in CTC (domestic telecommunications), ENTEL (international telecommunications), CHILGENER (electricity generation), IANSA (sugar), and LAB Chile (airline) were also sold, although private sector holdings in these companies remain below 50 percent of the total. Shares in the power company, CHILECTRA, have been on sale since 1985.

Malaysia

Since 1985, the Malaysian Government has sold 49 percent of its holding in Malaysian Airline System Berhad, a 17-percent holding in the Malaysian International Shipping corporation, and half of its holding in the Port Kelong container terminal. There have also been a number of smaller sales. The Telecommunications Department is being prepared for sale over the next two to three years. In addition, the Malayan Railway, the National Electricity Board, and the Postal Department are listed among candidates for future sale.

Niger

A number of enterprises were privatized in recent years. These include SONIDEP (petroleum distribution), SONITEXTIL (textiles), SOTRAMIL (millet processing), RINI (rice milling), SNCP (hides and skins), LEYMA (insurance), NITRA (freight forwarding), and INN (government printing office). Some sales have been made to Nigerian interests.[26]

This growing consensus among the developing countries on privatization coincides precisely with the principal thrust of U.S. government policy since the Reagan era that the private sector is the engine of long-run economic development in the Third World. As more and more Third World countries come to realize the signifi-

cance of privatization and take steps to implement it, economic
growth should be positively affected.

PROBLEMS IN CONDUCTING BUSINESS
WITH THIRD WORLD NATIONS

Market opportunities in developing countries are emerging. Yet it
is not easy to do business in these nations. Many obstacles block
entry, make it difficult to run business smoothly, and repatriate
profits. These obstacles include protectionism, international policies
of some Third World countries, the continuing debt problem, and
the problems related to services and intellectual property rights.

Protectionism

For four decades GATT rules and procedures have guided international trade liberalization efforts. But as we enter the 1990s, the
GATT system appears to be breaking down. Protectionist forces
have been gaining momentum, particularly in the United States. In
Europe, where half of all economic activity relates to trade, America's protectionist sentiments have created uneasiness. The Third
World countries do not know what to do, since the Western nations
constitute a big market for their limited exportable products. Individual efforts of different nations to meet the protectionist threat
have not succeeded.

Developing countries argue for maintaining import restrictions at
their own borders while seeking greater access for their products in
other countries. The industrialized countries complain of the self-
serving trade policies employed by the newly industrialized countries.

Developed countries often use nontariff barriers as well as tariffs
to limit imports. Some, like the European Community and other
developed countries, have used export subsidies to gain unfair advantage in the export market. According to the World Bank, many
developing countries have retained or increased their own import
barriers and these remain considerably higher than those of industrial countries. At the same time the Bank believes that past GATT

negotiations have done little to liberalize trade in commodities important to the Third World countries, and these countries have been hurt by a sharp increase in the use of nontariff barriers in Europe and North America.

The recent GATT negotiations, the Uruguay Round, was expected to prevent countries, both developed and developing, from following the protectionist path. The Uruguay Round was generally acknowledged to be a make-or-break affair for GATT. The intention was to strengthen GATT rules in its traditional areas, especially in agriculture where the rules have been ambiguous, improve its enforcement powers, and extend its scope of neglected areas such as services. The negotiations were difficult, and concluded without any agreement. Sensitive economic and political interests were involved, and each of the 90 participants wanted to balance concessions with gains. As an example, the graduation issue was sensitive from the viewpoint of industrialized countries. Part IV of the GATT, added in 1965, declares that developing countries are entitled to "differential and more favorable" treatment and, in particular, that concessions should be given to poor nations without reciprocal action in return. During the Uruguay Round negotiations, the West wanted richer developing countries, such as South Korea, to shoulder more of the obligations of GATT membership.

Demands for reciprocity also surfaced as a major issue in the Uruguay Round. There was a growing feeling that developing countries would benefit from abandoning their reliance on "charity," which has weakened their bargaining power, in favor of a more active mainstream role in negotiations, offering concessions in return for greater benefits. Developing countries historically have played a minor role in negotiations under the GATT. They have looked instead to the United Nations Conference on Trade and Development (UNCTAD) to express their demands for more stability in commodity markets and improved access to developed country markets, often including preferential treatment.

Third World countries see GATT's acceptance of trade restrictions by developed countries on textiles and apparel, and on agricultural products such as sugar, as proof of bias against developing countries. Consequently, most Third World countries have not actively participated in previous rounds, even though this has inhibited their ability to secure tariff reductions for their exports and to influence codes of conduct for nontariff barriers to their benefit.[27]

Third World countries, however, were more prominent in the Uruguay Round than in any previous round, but not as a unified group. Attempts to forge such a unity collided with the obstacles of disparate interests. Export-oriented Thailand had little in common with autocratic Brazil or poverty-stricken Lesotho.

Third World National Policies

Domestic trade and development policies pursued by Third World countries have a direct bearing on their economic performance. These policies help to determine how vulnerable they will be to external factors. Prudent macroeconomic policies and outward looking trade strategies give developing countries greater resilience and flexibility. On the other hand, when direct controls replace market mechanisms, economies work less efficiently. Past experience has shown that for countries that rely on stringent government control and enact policies which discourage business rather than attract it, the economic consequences are negative.

Debt Problem

The cost and availability of international finance is another major determinant of the economic performance of developing countries. The debt crisis has had a profound impact. One of the most urgent tasks facing the international community is to find ways of reducing the drag exerted by the continuing debt overhang on economic growth in the developing world.

The debt crisis grew out of the rise and fall of oil prices, increasing interest rates, and a global recession that reduced demand for Third World products. With the quadrupling of oil prices, Western banks began recycling billions of "petrodollars" as loans to Third World countries. These countries borrowed to build up export-oriented industries, mistakenly believing that markets would be assured by continued growth in the industrialized countries. As trade deficits climbed and interest rates rose, debtor nations incurred further debt in order to meet repayment obligations. The crisis began when oil prices collapsed in the early 1980s and Mexico, Nigeria, and Venezuela–all oil producers–announced that they could not continue debt repayments. Brazil and Peru followed and the crisis soon enveloped at least 15 countries. As lending was reduced by the exposed Western banks, debtor countries were further hurt by a severe flight of capital to foreign banks. The result was austerity as debtor nations reduced imports in an effort to ease their financial troubles.

A combination of measures by developed countries and Third World debtor nations averted the total economic collapse that was widely feared early in the decade and, by 1989, the credit worthiness of the highly indebted countries had improved somewhat. Nevertheless, external debt continues to increase.

There can be no simple, single solution to the debt problem: a comprehensive framework is needed. Its main objectives should be, first, to enable debtor countries to allocate more resources to investment and consumption and, second, to strengthen their credit worthiness, thus eventually permitting a resumption of voluntary commercial lending. Debtors and creditors alike stand to gain from such an approach. As credit worthiness is restored, the secondary-market discounts on outstanding debt–which exceed 50 percent for many of the highly indebted countries–would drop. Moreover, the debtors' improving growth prospects would enable them to import more from the industrial countries. That would assist in the global correction of external imbalances.

A framework to reduce the burden of debt must have two elements. First, the debtors need to grow faster and export more. Second, the cost of debt service must fall. With the right policies in both industrial and developing countries, these elements can go hand in hand.

Numerous proposals have been offered to permit developing countries to resume economic growth, restore credit worthiness, and recover their ability to attract "spontaneous" lending by commercial banks. These include case-by-case debt reschedulings, comprehensive restructurings, interest capitalization schemes, and innovative solutions including what are known as debt equity swaps, a variation of foreign direct investment, which can generate inflows of new capital but with greater risk for the investor as compared with loans.

Services and Intellectual Property Rights

A major issue between the United States and developing countries is trade and investment in services–i.e., banking, law, insurance, telecommunications, engineering, data processing, and other knowledge-intensive fields. The United States was instrumental in getting this issue on the agenda of the Uruguay Round of the General Agreement on Tariffs and Trade because services offer trade opportunities for American firms.

Most developing countries opposed any treatment of services within GATT, contending that services are an investment issue and that trade rules could not be applied. They also argued that new GATT rules liberalizing trade in services would favor industrial countries with strong service industries and inhibit the growth of such industries in the Third World. A group of developing countries, led by India and Brazil, fought vigorously but unsuccessfully to keep services out of the Uruguay Round.

Closely related to trade in services is the issue of intellectual property rights, also a subject of major U.S. interest in the Uruguay Round. High technology especially suffers from violations of patent, copyright, and trademark law. The U.S. believes it has suffered disproportionately from the lack of rigorous and uniform international standards for intellectual property rights. Developing countries–not the only violators–nevertheless view weak intellectual property right laws as a vehicle for technology transfer.

On the positive side, it is believed there is an emerging trend in many developing countries toward reliance on the private sector which should improve the business climate and, hence, growth prospects. As far as trade restrictions are concerned, they would probably be lessened through bilateral negotiations and future GATT negotiations.

CONCLUSION

As consumers, suppliers, and competitors, Third World countries are of major and growing importance to the Western world. They no longer can simply be viewed as a burden to developed countries and a permanent supplicant for U.S. aid.

As we move toward and into the twenty-first century, Third World nations will become even more important in the global economy. Improvements in the well-being of their masses, however, depend on their ability to pursue proven growth policies and implement programs efficiently. In this endeavor, MNCs can play a significant role. The capacity of their managers to operate the productive apparatus in an efficient, effective, and equitable manner in these countries would go a long way in boosting economic growth and prosperity.

Chapter 3

Market Evolution Process

It is an intriguing question, from the viewpoint of multinational marketers, if Third World countries, where three-fourths of the world's population resides, will ever emerge as mass markets. From a short-term perspective, Third World markets in the absence of high purchasing power cannot exist. Appropriately, therefore, these markets do not interest the multinational enterprises (MNEs). They find the risk in these markets, in proportion to returns, high. In addition, the operating requirements in these markets are at variance from the policies that MNEs normally pursue. Whereas standardization of products and marketing programs, formalized decision-making, and rigid control have tended to be hallmarks of large enterprises, Third World countries want flexible approaches, personalized attention, and, above all, a significant "piece of action."

Academic scholars and concerned observers, however, are confident that, in the long run, Third World countries will develop into viable markets. They argue that their economies are changing rapidly, and most are experiencing some degree of industrialization, urbanization, rising productivity, higher personal incomes, and technological progress. Third World countries are aware of their economic plight and are not content with status quo; indeed, they seek economic growth, increased standards of living, and an opportunity for the good life.[1]

Accepting the view that Third World markets will eventually grow, it appears reasonable to expect that this growth will be a gradual progressing through a set of stages. These stages constitute both a theory of market evolution and a theory about the economic history of the developing world as a whole.

This chapter begins with an impressionistic definition of the five stages of market evolution. The following section examines the characteristics of each stage from the viewpoint of marketing management. The final section considers more analytically, and from contemporary experience, the conditions that affect the movement from one stage to the next.

STAGES OF MARKET EVOLUTION

Market evolution is characterized by five stages identified as elite market, affluent market, rural market, urban market, and mass market. It is submitted that these stages are an arbitrary and limited way of looking at the marketing transformation in the Third World.[2] These are designed to highlight the general sequence of modernization and the uniqueness of each nation's progression based on its socio-economic-political circumstances. They grapple with a quite substantial range of issues. Under what impulses does the evolution process begin? What forces impact the movement from stage to stage? In which directions does the uniqueness of each society express itself at each stage? What significant cultural and political factors that help shape the market may be discerned at each stage?

Elite Market

The elite market mainly consists of landlords, families with inherited wealth, and a limited number of professionals–successful doctors and lawyers, big business owners, political leaders, and high-ranking military officers. Together they constitute less than one percent of consumers. More or less, they are spread throughout the country. Their influence is local/regional, but they have a firm grasp on income above subsistence levels of consumption in their domain.

The economy is strictly land-based with agriculture accounting for the livelihood of over 90 percent of the population. The situation is static since members of the elite class have a vested interest in maintaining the status quo. Agricultural output triggers the market activity. The farmers get to keep the minimum product at the subsistence level while the surplus is sold for supporting the urban population. The cash proceeds accrue to landlords who willingly share their good fortune with political/military leaders in an alliance. Industrial entities are few and far between and are generally agriculture-based, for example, the cotton textile industry, the rubber industry, and the jute industry. Alternatively, the industry is dependent on extractive materials, such as oil, minerals, and stones. Science and technology play a meager role either in agriculture or industry. Whatever few improvements are made in agriculture, they are based on the farmers' self-initiative. Usually industrial units are foreign owned and constitute the main source of foreign exchange. Agricultural commodities and/or extractive materials may also be exported depending on market availability.[3]

Industrial activity in consumer goods is limited. As a matter of fact, some nations may not manufacture any packaged goods. The elite class, therefore, depends on imports to satisfy their needs. Imported goods are always in short supply and high in price. Most shopping is done in nearby towns with an occasional visit to the large metropolis. Life is a drag for the masses, while the elite consider it to be their right to buy and consume products and services that enrich living.

Affluent Market

The affluent market emerges as a result of political awareness. At the initiative of political leadership, steps are taken to prepare the country for economic take off, which may include, for example, formulating a plan for economic progress and growth. Resources are sought from multilateral organizations (for example, The World Bank) and in the form of foreign aid from industrialized countries to improve infrastructure, exploit natural resources, and establish basic industries. Often, these activities are organized in the public sector, with government retaining full control. The country progresses from being a static society to a developing nation.[4]

The initiation of developmental activity results in the emergence of a professional class engaged in managing different aspects of development, and a class of small business owners that runs ancillary enterprises to serve the needs of large public sector units.

A psychological change begins to be socially accepted during this stage. Men come to be valued in the society, not for their connection with clan or class, but for their individual ability to perform certain specific, increasingly specialized functions.[5]

During the affluent stage, the market is enlarged to include professionals and small business owners. While the discretionary resources of these customers are limited, they add a new dimension to the market by buying and consuming a variety of consumer goods, hitherto little in demand. In addition, they have a greater awareness of and desire for new things and a materialistic life.

The affluent market comprises about two percent of the population. An important aspect of this market is the fact that most professionals and small business owners are urban dwellers, are more educated than customers in the elite class, and are more willing to take risks (for example, willing to try out new products).

Assuming the developmental activities continue to grow, a simultaneous need for more professionals is created which, in turn, gives rise to growth in professional education. The aspiring professionals enter the market as customers early on in life as knowledge about different products is diffused on college campuses.

The motivating factor during the affluent market stage is instant gratification, and modern life for the individual–portraying achievement and success. In the elite market stage, however, the motive was to distinguish oneself as belonging to a class. In other words, the emphasis shifts from class belongingness to individual achievement.

Rural Market

The growth in manufacturing during the affluent market stage coincides with higher productivity in agriculture. It is because, while creating infrastructure and establishing basic industries, investments are made to improve agricultural practices to grow enough food for the increasing population, a common problem of economic life in developing countries.

As agricultural productivity increases, a country's ability to support an urban industrial population rises. Rural communities provide a market for industrial and consumer goods, and supply food and agricultural raw materials needed in industry. As less labor is needed in agriculture, new workers entering the labor force increasingly look for employment in manufacturing, and industrial and urban services.[6]

Demand grows throughout the economy, stimulating domestic

production and also trade. Surpluses provide commodities for export and help to pay for the imports increasingly demanded by a growing and prosperous population.

Economic growth is, thus, accompanied by increased use of mechanical and electrical power, and a shift away from dependence on agriculture. Health, education, and social services improve, and the country becomes a cash customer for the world's products, especially industrial goods. Typically, such a country will even increase imports of agricultural products at the same time its own agriculture is becoming more productive.

A psychological revolution of expectations takes place. People begin to accept that man need not regard his physical environment as virtually a factor given by nature and providence, but as an ordered world which, if rationally understood, can be manipulated in ways which yield productive change and progress. The spurt in agrarian prosperity enables the rural consumers to reach higher levels of income. Traditionally, such incremental income in rural areas, say as a result of good rains or some other natural cause, would have been spent on buying land and/or gold. But the development effort that led to this increase in income links rural prosperity to developments in urban areas. Thus, the spurt in agrarian prosperity induces behavior changes regarding consumption choices.[7]

The rural prosperity, however, is not shared by everybody alike. Traditionally, land has been owned by a small percentage of families while the majority worked as landless labor. As the developmental steps are initiated, efforts are made to reduce the land holdings of the landlords. Such land reforms succeed in some areas and not in others. But certainly a much larger proportion of village dwellers begin to own land; at the same time, a substantial percentage continues to live as landless farm workers.

Again, as a part of the development effort, steps are taken to improve agricultural productivity through mechanization, use of better quality inputs including fertilizers, and improvements in farm management in general. The productivity gains, however, are not widely distributed. In many cases, landholding is too small to permit optimum use of productivity enhancement programs. At the same time, farmers in some areas are more dynamic and take advantage of new farm improvement programs while, in others, tradition-bound farming prevails. The net result is that the rural market is uneven geographically and is limited to a rural "middle class" which may constitute about 5 to 10 percent of the people in rural areas. Interestingly, however, an improvement model is established and, other things being equal, one may expect that, slowly but definitely, this process will continue to bring more and more farmers within its fold.

The emphasis of the rural market is on buying goods that make life worth living. Compared with class prestige propounded by the elite market, or self-achievement pursued by the affluent market, the rural market stresses decent life, something beyond sheer survival but without indulgence. Two distinct characteristics of the rural market deserve mention. First, an increasing proportion of incremental income is spent on buying consumer durables, different from the previous state of buying more land and gold. Second, the purchasing pattern shifts from buying locally-made (mostly within the village) goods to buying those made in urban centers.

Urban Market

The boost in the agricultural sector enhances economic activity in urban areas. New industries begin to appear to serve the growing needs of rural markets. This development, in turn, raises urban incomes, concurrently increasing consumer demands in urban areas.

With the infrastructure in place, and if the political climate is conducive to attracting foreign investment and technology, the rising demand encourages the establishment of new industries, hitherto unknown. Convenience and the good life become the common cry which must be met through new kinds of products and services, either manufactured at home or imported. Indeed, a middle-class revolution takes place with a substantial percentage of the urban class going through a change resulting in an insatiable demand for material things.

As the urban middle-class market takes shape, seeds are sown for the development of a mass market. How fast that happens will depend on the number and condition of landless rural inhabitants and unskilled urban dwellers. In other words, before a dynamic situation is created (i.e., government measures create and improve infrastructure and trigger agricultural improvements, an increase in rural productivity results in the emergence of a rural market, and the rural market leads to the urban middle-class market which becomes the foundation of a mass market), a way must be found to bring landless farmers and unskilled urbanites into the mainstream of life. At what rate urban markets may lead to the emergence of mass market would depend on how well and at what rate the hitherto ignored segments of the population become a part of the change process. Specifically, if their number is large and if they continue to be ignored, they could become a threat to the prosperous middle class both in rural and urban markets.[8]

Overall, the urban middle class constitutes about 5 to 8 percent of the population. The urban middle class is motivated by material acquisitions and keeping up with their neighbors. More and more material things become the ultimate goal in life, even if it means incurring debt beyond limit. In other ways, the urban middle class in Third World countries is similar in the psychology of living to its counterpart in the West.

Mass Market

Passage to the mass market stage requires:[9] (1) rising prosperity of the urban middle class, and (2) opportunity for the rural and urban poor to become a part of the market. These requirements can be met only with these conditions: (a) There is a shift to a predominance for industry, communications, trade, and services from agriculture. As agricultural productivity continues to increase, the human labor required to till the land declines. Thus, surplus farm labor is shifted to the industrial sector for gainful employment.[10] (b) Population yields a decline in the birth rate. This way, economic gains are not nullified, either partially or fully, by growth in population to support. (c) There is an attitudinal change in the society toward fundamental and applied science and technology as essential for progress, toward the initiation of change in productive techniques, toward the taking of risk, and toward the conditions and methods of work. The change implied here is simply not a psychological change in orientation, but an effective change translated into working institutions and procedures. (d) Political and social economic performance encourages mass production and mass consumption.

The essence of the mass market stage involves a rise in the rate of investment to a level which regularly, substantially, and perceptibly outstrips population growth. The mass market encompasses the majority of the population (over 60 percent) except the hard core urban poor who are left out due to an improper surrounding environment and the lack of education, and the village poor who, forced by tradition, must continue the past ways.

STAGES OF MARKET EVOLUTION VIS-À-VIS ROSTOW'S STAGES OF ECONOMIC GROWTH

The use of the word "stages" to characterize any economic aspects of Third World countries has been suspect ever since Rostow used it in his *stages of economic growth*.[11] It is desirable, therefore, to clarify the market stages implied here from Rostow's. Rostow stated that nations could be categorized into five stages according to the economics of their industrial production functions. Countries in the *traditional stage* were characterized by "limited production functions, based on pre-Newtonian science and technology, and on pre-Newtonian attitudes towards the physical world." This stage was followed by three stages in the growth process: the pre-conditions for take-off, the take-off itself, and the drive to maturity. The final stage was "the age of mass consumption." Rostow qualitatively described these stages and examined factors tending to move a society from one stage to the next. Rostow's stages have been criticized for their arbitrariness and for their justification based on historical facts.[12]

To an extent, the stages of market evolution discussed here are subject to similar criticism. The stages are not clearly distinguishable from one another in practice; they do not display empirically testable characteristics and the dynamic characteristics tending to cause movement from one stage to the next are not identifiable. But the conceptual basis of these stages is strong.

The market evolution framework, the subject matter of this book, is much more limited in scope than Rostow's. It makes no pretense of setting specific time intervals for the progression from one stage to another. The framework is based on a set of variables that have been identified as important in moving a society from one kind of market to the next, to finally emerge as a mass market.

The framework is not intended to suggest any sort of dynamic or analytic connection causing movement from one stage to another. It has no sense of historical determinism or inevitability. Rather, it is policy-oriented in that it suggests that government leaders can learn from the experiences of other countries in more or less similar circumstances.

FORCES BEHIND MARKET EVOLUTION

Traditionally, markets in Third World countries have been static. Most people lived at the subsistence level. Agriculture was the mainstay. In the absence of agricultural modernization programs, economic fortunes depended on Mother Nature. In the post-World War II period, however, a number of broad forces have led to growing markets in Third World countries. Some of these forces are continuations of well-established trends, while others have emerged more recently.

Awareness of the Need to Achieve Economic Prosperity

Following World War II, a keen sense of awareness of the need to achieve economic prosperity grew among Third World nations. After the war, a number of countries were wresting political freedom from colonial rulers, particularly from Britain. It did not take long for these countries to realize that political freedom alone was not sufficient. Economic prosperity was not only necessary for existence but mandatory for long-term survival as a nation. For example, leadership in India, immediately after gaining independence in 1947 from the British rulers, faced the problem of how to eradicate mass poverty. The achievement of this goal required a radical reform of the land system, including abolition of landlordism. Agricultural indebtedness had to be liquidated and provision made for cheap credit for the rural population. Agriculture had to be put on a scientific basis with a view to increasing productivity.[13] In addition, a comprehensive scheme of industrial development was indispensable. A new industrial structure had to be built in place of the old one which had collapsed as a result of mass production abroad and alien rule at home. In brief, there was unanimity among Third World nations that political freedom would not last long unless explicit short- and long-term measures were taken to improve the economy and put it on a growth path.[14]

Availability of Opportunities for Economic Development

In the post-World War II period, the willingness of the Third World countries to improve their economic lot was matched by global realization of the need to develop economic reconstruction programs. A variety of multilateral agreements were made at the international level that helped Third World nations to spearhead their developmental efforts.[15] The International Monetary Fund was established to promote international monetary cooperation, to facilitate the expansion of trade, and, in turn, to contribute to increased employment and improved economic conditions. Multilateral development banks were founded to assist the growth of Third World countries through the provision of loans and technical assistance. These included the World Bank family, which consists of the International Bank for Reconstruction and Development (IBRD), its concessional window, the International Development Association (IDA), and the International Finance Corporation (IFC); the Inter-American Development Bank; the Asian Development Bank; and the African Development Bank.

Successive rounds of multilateral agreements under the auspices of GATT, and bilateral agreements have lowered tariff levels markedly since World War II. At the same time, regional economic pacts such as the European Community (EC) were formed to facilitate trade and other relations among countries. Aid programs were designed whereby rich countries provided loans and grants to Third World nations in their economic buildup.

Technology as a Strategic Resource

One of the hallmarks of the 1960s and 1970s has been the growth of existing technologies and the development of new ones. While the United States and the countries of Western Europe (and later on, Japan) continued to be the principals of technology, the worldwide diffusion of technology has been increasing. Nearly all Third World nations hoped to industrialize and to achieve economic growth by adopting the new technologies of production and distribution.[16] Joint ventures and licensing agreements between Western firms and Third World enterprises became a common vehicle to seek access to product-specific production technologies. In addition, new communications and information technology have helped in bringing countries together. Indeed, technology makes it a realizable, feasible goal for Third World nations to economically develop themselves on a par with the West.

Transfer of Managerial Know-How

The 1960s and 1970s were not only the years of technological innovation and diffusion, but they were also those of the diffusion of management know-how. The United States had been the pioneer in the development of administrative and financial controls, and overall management structures essential to the effective operation of modern enterprises.

The management know-how, however, did not remain the monopoly of the United States for long. U.S. business education rapidly spread worldwide, and U.S. management techniques were popularly discussed in corporate boardrooms everywhere.[17]

U.S. universities have trained thousands of students from Third World countries through professional education in business. Additionally, many U.S. business schools have aided in the establishment of similar institutions in developing nations. For example, the Harvard Business School has helped India in creating an institution for offering advanced education in business. U.S. educated students, whether actually instructed in the United States or their homeland, generate and support modern management ideas that have served U.S. business well. Third World firms can adapt proven quality, inventory, and other control systems, as well as the overall management structures worked out in developed countries, and thus compete effectively.

Globalization of Consumer Tastes

An interesting phenomenon in recent years has been the development of a common worldwide preference for a variety of consumer goods. More and more products and brands are available everywhere, manifesting similar buyer needs in different countries. People in Third World markets are eager to improve their economic conditions and their living standards, and they are aware of the products bought by customers in the developed world. Given a choice, they would prefer similar products.[18]

Political leaders in Third World countries are aware of this homogenization of demand. Some countries have made a positive response to the emerging consumer need and are, therefore, in accord with the people. Governments that avoid people's demand for products and brands do it at their own peril.

MARKET EVOLUTION AND MARKETING DECISIONS

The market evolution model presented in the previous section provides a framework for facilitating movement from a less developed, scattered market to a mass market. There are five identifiable stages of market evolution in Third World countries. Each succeeding stage is marked by an increase in market width and breadth. The level of marketing function roughly parallels the stages of market evolution.

Exhibit 3-1 illustrates perspectives of marketing in each stage. Presented here is a static situation representing an idealized evolutionary process. Technological change, the sociocultural context, economic policy, and the political situation can cause significant deviations in the evolutionary process and marketing specifics in each stage.

Market

Market evolves from being a negligible percentage in the first stage to almost two-thirds of the population in the final stage. Geographically, the market is initially scattered throughout the country. Then, the major market activity shifts to large cities where political initiatives help in the development of the affluent market. Next, the rural market flourishes, followed by the urban market. Finally, the market thrives all over. The evolution pattern shows that agricultural development in the initial stages is a prerequisite to the emergence of mass market.[19] Further, the rural market develops before the urban market takes shape.

The movement from one stage to the other cannot be timed since it is affected by the environmental constraints, on the one hand, and management of the economy, on the other. For example, corrupt political leadership could hinder movement beyond the affluent stage. Longer time periods may be required to achieve agricultural development in countries where large portions of land are arid.

Product

The durable goods required during the first three stages are mainly black and white televisions, radios, sewing machines, electric fans, bicycles, scooters, and electric irons. Automobiles, furnishings, furniture, air conditioners, washers, dryers, VCRs, stereo systems, lawn mowers, kitchen appliances, and the like are not demanded until the fourth stage. Until the mass market emerges, most customers are happy with standard products as long as they are functionally satisfactory.

In the first three stages, as far as nondurables are concerned, toiletries (including pharmaceuticals) and clothing (including ready-made garments) are the most important products. Packaged food products and frozen foods do not have much market until the urban market develops. Only such food products as ketchup, cookies, and crackers are demanded during the first three stages, and these too on a limited scale. Lipstick, nail polish, and face cream are among the cosmetics with any demand in the initial stages. Of course, there are definite differences between rural and urban customers in the type of goods demanded, both durable and nondurable.

Inasmuch as most exchanges are cash transactions (since consumer credit initially becomes available in the fourth stage), most purchases take place at certain times of the month and year. In urban areas, shopping is generally timed during the first week of the

EXHIBIT 3-1. Perspectives of Marketing in Different Stages of Market Evolution

Market Evolution Stage	Size[1] of Market (% of total Population)	Type of Customer	Central Buying Motive	Principal Marketing Task
Elite Market	Less than 1%	Traditionally rich and powerful people: landlords, big business owners and political leaders	Distinction	Exchange
Affluent Market	2% to 3%	Current and potential professionals in government, business, and education	Achievement	Physical Distribution
Rural Market	8% to 10%	Newly rich farmers	Fulfillment	Demand Creation
Urban Market	15% to 20%	New business (mostly small- and medium-sized) owners and skilled workers	Life Style	Product Development
Mass Market	over 60%	Rural business owners; skilled farmers; semi-skilled urban dwellers	Necessity	Market Information

[1]Each stage includes the proportion covered in the previous stage.

Goods Demanded	Sources of Goods	Role of Price	Marketing Institutions	Communication
Select durable and nondurable goods	Mainly imported	High price to impart status	Import agents and dealers in large cities	Limited print advertising; word-of-mouth communication
Durable goods (scooter, small appliances, gas stove, black and white TV, radio); packaged goods (toiletries, limited cosmetics and snack foods), and some ready-made clothes	Partly imported and partly locally manufactured by companies with foreign joint ventures or licensing	Medium price to develop market at the upper end	Dealers in major urban centers and emerging towns	Increased emphasis on print medium; radio advertising; cinema slides
Select durable goods (bicycles, sewing machines, radios); packaged goods; (soap, face cream, oil, tobacco products); clothes; shoes	Mainly locally manufactured with indigenous technology	Low price to penetrate market	Dealers in satellite towns	Some print and radio advertising; outdoor advertising; intensive word-of-mouth communication
Durable goods (colored TV, stereo system, VCR, camera, car, washer, dryer); variety of packaged goods (toiletries, cosmetics, food products); furnishings, ready-made clothes (mostly standard products)	Mainly locally manufactured by domestic and foreign companies	High price to skim/low price to gain share	Beginnings of new kinds of channels: department stores, supermarkets, chain stores, franchised stores, self-service outlets	Beginning of commercial television; across-the-board increase in other kinds of advertising
Different kinds of durable and nondurable goods in different styles, designs, shapes, and colors	Globally manufactured	Globally competitive price	New kinds of channels get fully established	Television emerges as the primary medium. Intensive use of all other media

month when the salary is received. In rural areas, most purchasing is done during the harvest season.[20]

Price

In Third World countries, government plays a significant role in price determination, particularly of those essential goods consumed by the masses. Despite that, price is, more or less, set by demand and supply forces. For example, dealers may hoard products in short supply rather than sell them at the price fixed by the government, and later on dispose them of at the going rate, usually labeled as black market price.[21]

Further, government's influence on price begins to decline as the market progresses from one stage to the other. Alternatively, it may be hypothesized that government's hold on price is inversely related to the economic prosperity of the country. In terms of the stages of market evolution, beginning with stage four, i.e., the urban market stage, most prices are set by a free play of demand and supply forces. Government's role at that time becomes ad hoc. For example, a poor agricultural showing, perhaps due to bad weather, may lead the government to control prices of food grains, sugar, edible oils, and textile goods. Further, such price controls are short-lived.

In the fourth stage, monopolistic competition begins to have an effect on pricing. As new products/brands are introduced and product differentiation becomes an essential element of marketing strategy, companies set prices following monopolistic competition. About the same time, price haggling and bargaining, typically associated with Third World markets, become less common. As awareness of national brands gains momentum, dealers find it unnecessary to engage in bargaining. In other words, bargaining loses significance as a promotional tool for nationally advertised durable and nondurable goods. This is particularly so at the level of authorized dealers. Small shopowners and/or street vendors may still peddle national brands at bargain prices, but the customer must accept the risk of the brand not being authentic.

In stages four and five prices vary from area to area and store to store (assuming prices are not fixed by the government). Depending on the amount of services that a store provides, the price may be lower or higher. For example, in the absence of consumer credit, it is quite common for local dealers to provide short-term credit to regular customers with payment due at the beginning of each month. Prices in such a situation, commonly noticeable in stage two as urban affluent people (mostly salaried) are living it up, can be expected to be higher than where all transactions are in cash. Similarly, as the urban economy takes off, specifically in stages four and five, suburban shopping centers emerge. Generally speaking, shopping centers in affluent neighborhoods have fancier stores that price their merchandise higher to meet the overheads.

Distribution Channels

Overall, wholesalers play a crucial role as channels of distribution in Third World countries. Most retailers are very small and need wholesalers for financing and for supplying goods in small quantities.[22] Manufacturers find it more practical to deal with a few wholesalers than to work with thousands of mom-and-pop-type retailers.

Channel changes begin to occur during stage two, the affluent stage. As development efforts shape up, off and on disequilibrium occurs in the economy such that inflation is high and the masses find it difficult to meet their basic necessities. To take care of such eventualities, government establishes fair-price shops to distribute essential products at subsidized prices. Such shops, although owned and operated by the government, are like chain stores in the West.

In stage three, the advent of chain stores goes farther as some large manufacturers establish company-owned stores to distribute their products, especially fabrics, general merchandise, shoes, and kitchenware.

Large-scale retailing does not take off until well into stage four when small-sized department stores and supermarkets begin to appear. In stage five, these stores become fully established. At that time, they are much larger in size, offer many more services, and may even constitute a part of a chain.

Such retail innovations as enclosed malls, retail credit cards, mail order/telephone shopping, and so on begin to emerge toward the tail end of stage four, and flourish in stage five. Wholesale and retail margins in the beginning stages are low, but they gradually go up as these institutions begin to offer additional services. This generally happens in later parts of stage two. For example, some stores may start offering home delivery and gift wrapping. However, the services are offered on ad hoc basis and in a disorganized fashion.[23] They may be available to some customers and not to others.

In stage four, the tempo of services goes up partly due to competitive pressures but mainly due to demand by consumers who, by now, are more aware and discrete. But the level of services demanded and offered may not reach Western standards for a long time because the change process is slow; consumer demand increases gradually, and the retailers' response is limited to what is most essential. In other words, retailers as an institution do not develop into professional businessmen until well into stage five.

Promotion

Overall, the tempo of promotion increases from one stage to the next. This appears logical, establishing the fact that perspectives of promotion increase with market development.

Initially, the major emphasis is on print media as in stages one and two. In stage two radio advertising starts, but does not become a major factor. In later stages, as the market develops, television advertising begins (stage four) and gradually occupies a key position (stage five). In stage three, however, word-of-mouth communication becomes most significant. This is because rural customers are less mobile and depend on opinion leaders in their purchase decisions.[24]

Although the advertising industry is likely to become a growth business in Third World countries as their markets evolve, it will never be as open as in the West. This can be explained by two factors. First, Third World countries, based on the experiences of developed countries, will impose controls on advertising for ethical and health reasons. For example, cigarette advertising may be banned; advertising directed at children may be permitted only sparsely.[25] Second, advertising calls for "openness" which may strike against the cultural traits of many Third World nations.[26] Thus, one can expect advertising to be a regulated business.

ENABLING CONDITIONS

As we enter the twenty-first century, there will be a growing demand for products from the Third World, and its ambitions and demands will mimic in most ways everything that has gone before in Western society. Once Third World countries are exposed to products of modern living, people of whatever shade, culture, or origin want roughly the same things.[27] While a microwave dinner is unthinkable for a paddy grower in Thailand today, it will not be in ten or twenty years.

Still, one should approach the Third World with great caution and be prepared to be underwhelmed by it. Although the generalities of income distribution are much alike in many of these countries, the whole history, culture, and disposition of the people are critical to success.[28] The Third World's scarcity of capital will be a factor to reckon with. The infrastructure may be a problem. Excessive control of the economy may be another problem. Many things that we take for granted, such as a transportation system that works or an accounting system that reflects costs, may be absent in many Third World nations.

The pent-up demand in Third World countries is enormous, but one cannot ignore the reality of the enabling conditions that enhance market development and make the demand potential realizable. Exhibit 3-2 groups these enabling conditions into four categories: business conditions, market characteristics, competitive environment, and market infrastructure. Specific factors under each category are listed. The four kinds of enabling conditions reinforce each other, and a deficiency in one area may be partly compensated by excess in another, at least in the short run.

Business Conditions

The first step in the market evolution process in Third World countries is an initiative on the part of leadership to take economic development measures. In this endeavor business conditions operating in the country play a significant role. These include: natural resources, technology, and professional skills.

Natural Resources

Nature randomly endowed different regions of the world with natural resources. The natural riches of a place bestow upon it

EXHIBIT 3-2. Enabling Conditions for Market Evolution in Third World Countries

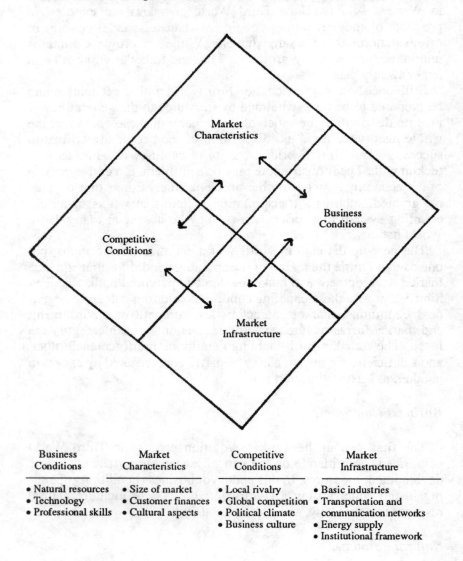

Business Conditions	Market Characteristics	Competitive Conditions	Market Infrastructure
• Natural resources	• Size of market	• Local rivalry	• Basic industries
• Technology	• Customer finances	• Global competition	• Transportation and
• Professional skills	• Cultural aspects	• Political climate	communication networks
		• Business culture	• Energy supply
			• Institutional framework

unique economic advantages. But nations are groups of communities arbitrarily organized, usually without regard to such economic considerations as the abundance or lack of natural resources.

A country rich in natural resources can process its endowments and export them. The most outstanding example of the possession of a resource providing economic leverage is the abundance of oil in the Middle East. Natural availability of minerals in different countries provides them with a base to begin economic development programs. For example, Zambia and Zaire produce two-thirds of the world's cobalt and thus have a natural advantage in this area.[29] Since the metal is important for an essential industry (the aircraft industry is crucially dependent on cobalt, which is used in jet engine blades), its availability within their borders helps them in their economic development efforts. They start with an advantageous position.

Natural resources have a "make or break" effect on Indonesia's economy. Between 1974 and 1986 oil and gas accounted for 77% of her exports, and coffee ranged between 26% and 69% of Colombia's exports.[30]

Natural resources also include climatic conditions as well as a nation's location and size. Location relative to other nations that are suppliers or markets affects market evolution due to the feasibility of cultural and business interchange. For example, proximity to the U.S. has had an important historical influence on Mexico's market development.

Technology

Humanity's 200 years of experience with industrialization and the seemingly insatiable thirst of nations for further economic growth—a desire which dramatically accelerated after World War II—have pointed to a major dictum with increasing palpability. It is that modernization and its concomitant, economic development, are predicated upon an extended application, in both time and space, of scientific knowledge toward productive purposes, i.e., technology.

It has been said that:

> The primary driving force is not investment itself but the "technological multiplier" that technological innovation and

diffusion can achieve: (1) by increasing the productivity or value added of the sectors in which new technology is employed; (2) by lowering the factor costs of those who utilize the outputs of those sectors and releasing their resources for other useful purposes; and (3) by stimulating "responsive innovations" in customers, suppliers, or functionally competitive branches.[31]

Knowledge has to be available before it can be applied. A society which strives toward modernity through industrialization can either generate its own technological requirements or it can import them. One common characteristic of most Third World countries is the dire paucity of technology, a major requisite of growth and development, from domestic sources. They must, therefore, depend on foreign sources to provide technology. However, countries that do have some technology of their own will have a head start in the market evolution process.

In modern times, technology has become so important that it can even overcome natural barriers. Consider the Colombian cut flower industry. Colombia had no special advantage in being a significant competitor in this industry. Yet using U.S. technology, in about ten years the country developed a unique strength to penetrate the European and American markets. In some varieties, the Colombian flowers gained as much as 35 percent of the total U.S. market.[32]

Professional Skills

Professional skills refer to managerial talent as well as skilled blue- and white-collar workers and technical experts. People who bring capital, labor, and resources together to fashion them into a productive organization that must face the risks of an uncertain world occupy strategic positions in the market evolution process. Thus, given the same inputs, presumably a country with superior professional skills will do better than one with weak management. Endeavors to achieve economic growth will result in better and more timely payoff if they are planned, implemented, and controlled effectively. Proper management of economic development efforts is likely to enhance the market evolution process. It is due to the managerial gap that markets have fallen behind and have not evolved smoothly in many Third World countries. The point may be illustrated with reference to India:

> It is only a few years back that the steel industry complained of a power shortage and blamed the power sector; power in turn complained of the coal problems; the coal industry felt that railways were not moving fast enough; then the railways again placed the blame on the coal and power sectors.[33]

The lack of proper management leads to a vicious problem of working in isolation of the other's needs, resulting in inordinate delays, de novo examinations of decisions, and resultant frustration among entrepreneurs. Managers, however, cannot succeed in isolation. They must have a pool of qualified and willing workers to implement their plans effectively and in a timely fashion.

Thus, the market evolves more smoothly in countries where the level of professional outlook is higher; people take their work seriously and are eager to excel. The professional outlook depends on many factors such as opportunities for education, cultural inheritance, and political force. For example, efficiency in China can be attributed to force, while in Thailand and Indonesia, it is an inherited trait.

Market Characteristics

A variety of market characteristics influences the evolution of market. These are: size of the market, customer finances, and cultural aspects.

Size of the Market

The size of the home market of a country facilitates the evolution of market since there is a captive demand to cater. It is the fundamental demand factor that determines the pool of prospective buyers or market potential. Large demand encourages mass production which, in turn, makes it feasible to achieve economies of scale. The resulting reduction in unit cost enables the country to effectively compete internationally. Exports increase, providing valuable foreign exchange for importing technology and equipment not produced at home. In brief, the size of the market permits a country to start within an inward orientation and work toward an outward global orientation.

Customer Finances

While size of the market is a crucial variable, its practical significance depends on the income of the people in the market. In other words, people must have means in terms of income to become viable customers. Market evolves only when a large population is backed by adequate income. As a matter of fact, in Third World countries, the real problem is income, not population. A number of countries–China, India, Indonesia, and Brazil–have large populations but the vast majority live at the subsistence level since they cannot afford anything beyond that. Small wonder, therefore, that the market for a variety of consumer products, considered essential in industrialized countries, is limited in Third World nations.

The real problem is inequitable income distribution. For example, in Third World countries, the top 10 percent of the population receives around 36 percent of the countries' income and much more in such nations as Brazil at 51 percent and Kenya at 46 percent, whereas in most developed countries the top 10 percent do not receive over 30 percent. Sri Lanka, however, is an exception among Third World nations because it has a more equitable income pattern than even the United States.[34] From that standpoint, market evolution in Sri Lanka should progress more smoothly.

Cultural Aspects

Cultural factors affect market evolution through customers' attitudes toward material things in general, product quality, convenience, disposability, and innovations. Further cultural homogeneity of people within the country makes the market evolution easier since that enlarges the size of the market. A study of technology exports from Egypt confirms the importance of cultural ties in expanding the scope of market. For example, 80 percent of Egypt's exports go to Arab countries.[35]

Customers' actions are shaped by their lifestyles and behavior patterns as they stem from their society's culture. Thus, products that people buy, the attributes that they value, the principals whose opinions they accept, are all culture-based choices. For example, religion, an important aspect of culture, influences outlook on life, its meaning, and its concept.[36]

Consumer demands for convenience and time-saving made the evolution of mass market feasible in the U.S. In Japan, consumer demand for a quality product forced Japanese manufacturers to lay major emphasis on quality. Market evolved as the suppliers responded by providing superior state-of-the-art products. Thus, the pattern of market evolution in a country is strongly influenced by its cultural traits.

Competitive Conditions

If business conditions and market characteristics are favorable, the pattern of market evolution is determined by competitive conditions, i.e., the number of firms that enter the market, the speed of their arrival, and the level of resources they invest in their entry moves. Generally, the more intense the competitive activity, the faster the market evolution.[37] Competitive activity begins among local rivals, but should be extended to global firms. In this endeavor, the political climate of the country and the business culture at large play a significant role.

Local Rivalry

Market thrives when firms are forced to outcompete each other. When their survival is at stake, they improve existing products, develop new ones, and lure customers in various ways (e.g., lower prices, extended warranties, better after-scale service), resulting in market development at a faster pace. Firms fight it out by meeting the customer needs more precisely and by overcoming hurdles that may prevent evolution of the market. For example, nonfrill products may be developed to create a mass market. Methods of financing may be worked out to make it feasible for the customers to buy products. Adequate guarantees may be given to boost customer confidence in the market offerings.

An important factor in Japanese success has been the domestic rivalry. In any industry in which the Japanese have established international competitiveness, the number of rival firms has been high, for example, 25 firms in audio equipment, 23 in shipbuilding, 9 in automobiles, 14 in copies, 15 each in construction equipment and television, and 34 in semiconductors.[38]

The market rivalry strengthens the position of some firms while it is harsh on others. As a matter of fact, some firms may be forced into exiting the market. Only the fittest survive. However, for the market to evolve and flourish, local rivalry is nearly always necessary. It drives companies to move beyond whatever initial advantage led to their founding.

Global Competition

One of the most significant market developments in developed countries during the past decade has been the emergence of global competitors and global competition. Coincident with that awakening has been the realization that Third World firms will have to develop the ability to compete with global firms if their markets are to evolve smoothly. This means the competitive activity must be extended beyond local rivalry to encompass firms from all over. This condition has been forced by global increase of international business.

We are heading toward an era where, as far as business is concerned, the concepts of nationality and traditional antagonism between nations and ethnic groups are not useful.[39] In fact, to dismiss such views outright and consider the world's inhabitants as a single race of consumers with shared needs and aspirations is the first conceptual lead toward a pragmatic and productive businessman's world view of the forthcoming era.

Successful local firms must develop the strength to withstand competition from firms from outside. This way they secure their position at home and become active in markets elsewhere in the world. Global competition may force local firms to quit certain fields (i.e., industries), since they find it difficult to compete against outside firms. At the same time, however, in certain other fields they will become a major factor worldwide. Through this give and take, the national market becomes a part of the global market and evolves at full speed on par with markets in developed parts of the world. The country loses some industries but gains global supremacy in some others. The net result is that local firms concentrate in fields in which they have a competitive advantage on a worldwide basis. Encouragement of local firms to compete globally helps in making a market a part of the global market. The global market is served by the firms most competent to do so.

Political Climate

Promotion of competitive rivalry among firms, locally and globally, to a large extent depends on the political climate in the country. Government can improve or detract competition. For example, vigorous enforcement of antitrust laws encourages competition and stimulates innovation. Some governments pursue complete isolation from the world economy but promote competition locally. Markets in such countries evolve very slowly and will have difficulty in progressing beyond the urban market stage. Some governments encourage full-fledged competition which does help in developing the market quickly but basically yields the position to foreign firms. Local firms never mature to be a major factor, even in the home market. The reverse of this is to completely shut off competition by providing virtual monopoly power to state-run companies. Such an alterative is least conducive to market evolution. Inefficiency becomes rampant and the economy becomes static.

Another option is to gradually promote competition as the market evolves. Initially, competition is encouraged among local rivals. Then, on an industry-by-industry basis, global firms are allowed to enter the market. Usually by then, the local firms have gained enough experience to compete with outsiders, first on the home front and then in their own markets.

How far and how much global competition the government might encourage in its market would depend on such factors as:

a. Government's receptivity to foreign business in the country
b. Economic perspectives of the country, whether market-driven or statist/socialist
c. Rationality of the country's regulatory environment

d. Unique strengths/competitive advantages of local firms in selected industries
e. Ability of local firms in selected industries to compete globally
   using their unique strength
f. Amount of red tape or number of bureaucratic hurdles prevalent in the country

Business Culture

A competitive spirit prevails in the economy when there is an
entrepreneur class present in the society. Entrepreneurs take the risk
to get ahead. They are not afraid of challenges and competition does
not scare them. For example, South Koreans compete jealously in
consumer electronics by spewing out new models continually and
by maintaining efficiency improvements to stay competitive within
their quirky, high-cost infrastructure. These manufacturers develop
stringent components and machinery requirements, giving rise to an
equally sophisticated supplier industry. They are true entrepreneurs,
who serve as the backbone of the economy. They continue to excel
in the home market in spite of global competitors. When the home
market gets saturated, they look to exports to grow, and Koreans
have done that with notable success.[40]

Market Infrastructure

The availability and efficiency of infrastructure is an important
determinant of a nation's market evolution. The market-related infrastructure comprises basic industries, transportation and communication networks, energy sources, and institutional framework. Essentially, infrastructure represents those types of capital goods,
institutions, and services that serve different industries in their activities in the marketplace. The quality of infrastructure directly affects a country's economic growth potential and the ability of entrepreneurs to effectively engage in exchange activities.

As market evolves, a country's infrastructure typically expands to
meet the needs of the expanding marketplace. There is some question of whether market emergence increases the pace of infrastructure development or whether an expanded infrastructure leads to
market evolution. Most probably, infrastructure and market evolu-

tion progress concurrently, although at different rates. Companies market their products even with an inadequate infrastructure, but it usually becomes necessary to modify the offerings and other aspects of marketing strategy. When infrastructure does not keep up with market evolution, discrepancies take place in providing adequate service to the customer and future development of the market slows down.

Basic Industries

Basic industries comprise capital goods such as steel, cement, machine tools, telecommunications, computers, and the like. Establishment of basic industries triggers economic activity in the country, laying the foundation of market evolution from the elite to the affluent stage. Thereafter, these industries assist in the movement of large masses from the farm to the plant creating the modern blue-collar worker, i.e., the semi-skilled machine operator, and with him, mass production industry. Concurrently, farm labor is reduced, increasing agricultural productivity. This way rural market emerges. The demographic shift from farm to industry continues and more and more large-scale, basic industries are established in response to rising economic activity, enabling both farm and industrial output to increase manyfold. Related and supporting industries keep the momentum going. Mass production and mass market become an accomplished fact.

Transportation and Communication Networks

Without adequate transportation and communication facilities, market evolution does not progress smoothly. For example, distribution costs may increase substantially, affecting prices upwardly and thus forcing many customers out of the market. Similarly, the ability to reach certain segments of the market may be impaired. In Nigeria, for example, two distinct consumption areas exist, which are isolated from one another due to an inadequate transportation system.[41] The most important element in the diet of those individuals close to the coast is fish. Fish are brought to the market in mid-morning and, if not sold by late afternoon, must be discarded due to spoilage. Thus, a large proportion of the fishing industry output is lost. The diet of people in the interior consists chiefly of yams, which are consumed during approximately one-half of the year. For the remaining six months, the interior population is subject to relative famine due to the exhaustion of the yam supply and a lack of importation of food from any other region. Through the development of a transportation system that provides the means to store and transport fish, the creation of place utility, the population of the interior could be relieved of their dependence upon yams and the economic waste due to fish spoilage could be eliminated.

Communications networks are equally important in the proper market development. Adequate communication networks make the information travel fast without distortion which, in turn, helps in decision making, both by businessmen and bureaucrats.

Energy Supply

Adequate energy supply is basic to any economic activity, be it in agriculture or industry. For a smooth market progression, abundant energy must be available at cheap prices in a manner that does not pollute the environment. In many developing countries, industries do not run at planned capacity due to energy shortage. Even household power supply is cut off due to shortage. In other words, both production and consumption sectors of the economy are affected adversely when energy supply is limited.

Institutional Framework

As the economy develops, a variety of institutions are needed to support expanded activity. Retailers, wholesalers, advertising agencies, marketing research firms, after-sale service outfits, consumer financing organizations, providers of storage and warehousing facilities are the kinds of institutions that support market evolution. These institutions do not appear automatically. Conditions must be created by government and market leaders to assist in the concurrent development of an institutional framework. For example, banks can be encouraged to offer consumer financing. Large-scale retailing can be pioneered by those entrepreneurs who take the initiative to establish basic industries. Government can offer incentives for building storage and warehousing facilities. Without an effective institutional framework, the market will be limited to local economies, concomitant spot shortages, and waste of surpluses.

One significant factor in establishing effective market institutions in developing countries is the influence of borrowed technology. Examples can be found of countries or areas of countries that have been propelled from the eighteenth century to the twentieth century in the span of two decades, mainly depending on foreign technology. Interestingly, the new institutions function side-by-side with primitive arrangements. For example, it is not unusual, as in Pakistan, to find a modern supermarket operating surrounded by a number of mom-and-pop stores.

Having described the enabling conditions for market evolution, it must be reiterated that government plays a vital role in the development of these conditions. Government can influence each of the four conditions either positively or negatively. Government's role in shaping these conditions is based on such issues as policies toward economic controls, education, subsidies, and the like.

CONCLUSION

Markets in Third World countries evolve through stages identified as: elite market, affluent market, rural market, urban market, and mass market. Perspectives of marketing in each stage vary. For example, demand creation is the principal task during the rural market stage, while product development is significant in the urban market stage.

Market evolution from stage to stage is affected by four conditions: business factors, market characteristics, competitive conditions, and market infrastructure. These conditions, individually and as a system, create the context in which a nation's market evolves.

In later chapters, the application of the market evolution model presented above is examined with reference to India. India was chosen for three reasons. First, in the last five years a large middle class, with substantial purchasing power, has emerged there. Second, India's large market potentially holds a tremendous opportunity for American business. Third, India's democratic traditions and sizable merchant class fulfill the basic requirements for market evolution.

Chapter 4

India's Business Scene

India is a pluralistic society of 850 million people. It is an enigma, a country of contrasts. On the one hand, it is the twelfth largest industrial power in the world, and, on the other hand, it is the fifteenth poorest nation in per capita terms. From possessing the third largest pool of scientific and technical manpower, it has the dubious distinction of having the largest number of illiterates and unemployed/underemployed in the world. While it possesses formidable nuclear capability, it struggles with basic metallurgy to produce a needle of consistent quality. Metropolitan and urban India present a picture of an affluent minority with hedonistic lifestyles. It coexists with the grinding poverty of rural India that possesses its own mosaic of light and shade. Whatever horizons one may paint, the enduring reality of two Indias is apparent.

LIFE, LAND, AND PEOPLE

India, a great steaming stew of diverse nationalities, religions, and languages, is in fact much more a continent than a country. Geographically, the large, triangular-shaped nation is separated from the rest of Asia mainly by the Himalayan mountains. The Republic of India, called Bharat in native languages, has an area of 1,269,346 square miles (3,287,593 square kilometers), about one-half that of the United States. It has a warm climate dominated by the seasonal winds known as monsoons. However, because of its size, relief, extremes of elevation, and relation to the oceans, it has many local variations of temperature and rainfall.

History

The multiple faces of India were both molded and produced by five millennia of history. The diversity of natural settings, ethnic types, languages, religious beliefs and practices, dietary habits, and lifestyles of India often bewilder those who come from societies less heterogeneous or that have shorter histories. From ancient times to the present day, people have made their own discoveries of India. More than in any other society, the concept of linear historical time appears meaningless as successive phases of Indian civilization are all present in contemporary India.

The known history of the Indian subcontinent is punctuated by a series of invasions and migrations from the northwest through what are now Afghanistan and Pakistan; only the last major conquerors entered the region from the sea. Six major time periods mark Indian history: the time periods of Harappa (ca. 3000-1500 B.C.), ancient (560 B.C.-A.D. 650), early medieval (650-1210), Mughal (1526-1707), Modern (1707-1947), and post-independence (1947-present).

The Indus Valley Civilization dates back over 5,000 years. From about 5,000 B.C., Aryans speaking Sanskrit merged with earlier peoples to create the classical Indian society. The words India, Hindu, Hindi, and Sind all stem from the word Sindu, which is what the Ayran-speaking migrants called the Indus River. Buddhism flourished in King Asoka's reign (third century B.C.) but declined afterward. The Gupta Kingdom (fourth through sixth century A.D.) was a golden age of science, literature, and the arts. Arab, Turk, and Afghani Muslims ruled successively from the eighth to eighteenth centuries. The Portuguese and the Dutch came to India, but the English ended up with political control.

In the 1930s, Muslims, who had totaled over 20 percent of the population of British India, had concluded that their minority position would be untenable in a nation dominated by Hindus. In March 1940, the All-India Muslim League declared as its goal the creation of an independent Islamic state. India's nationalism, Gandhi's "civil disobedience" to British Rule, and Mohammad Ali Jinnah's advocacy of a separate Muslim state resulted in India's independence in 1947, the establishment of Pakistan, and Gandhi's assassination. The Indian Republic began in 1950 with a constitution that derives many aspects from the American constitution. The appendix at the end of this chapter provides a chronology of important events in Indian history.

Population

In 1990, India's population was 850 million–more than three times that of the United States and about three-fourths of China, the only country with more inhabitants than India. But India's population is growing two percent annually, whereas in China the population growth rate has been reduced to about 1.2 percent annually. India is also more densely populated than China, with an average of 547 persons per square mile (211 per square kilometer). Exhibit 4-1 shows the area and population of different states in India. In terms of population, Uttar Pradesh is the largest state in India with almost 140 million people, accounting for one-sixth of the total population. It is for this reason that India's prime minister usually comes from this state. Areawise, however, Madhya Pradesh is the largest state, followed by Maharashtra.

In 1990, about 25 percent of the population of India lived in urban areas (about 2500 towns and cities), an increase of eight percent since 1951.[1] The remaining 75 percent live in more than 500,000 villages. The drift or rush to the urban areas is obviously revolutionary in its effects on Indian life. With one of every four Indians now living in a town, and since there may be a large turnover, with an even larger proportion acquiring some experience of town life, it becomes rather pointless to think of India as a land of unchanging villages. Many urban dwellers maintain their ties with village life. They take back to the villages new ideas of what is possible and desirable, and the villages themselves thereby change, though slowly. Increasingly, among the mud huts of the drier areas or the thatched cottages of the deltas, there are small brick buildings–local administrative or welfare offices, but most of all schools. The literacy rate lags in rural areas and among women, but for all of India it has risen from 16.6 percent of the population in 1951 to 43.5 percent in 1990.

Whether it is the "pull" of city amenities or the "push" of economic depression in the countryside that has led to the urban explosion is debatable, and there are other factors to consider, such as the

EXHIBIT 4-1. India's Area and Population

State	Area (thousand km)	Population (thousands)		
		1991	1981	1971
Andhra Pradesh	275	66,305	53,550	43,503
Arunachal Pradesh	84	858	632	468
Assam	78	22,295	19,897	14,625
Bihar	174	86,339	69,915	56,353
Goa	3.7	1,169	1,008	795
Gujarat	196	41,174	34,086	26,697
Haryana	44	16,318	12,923	10,037
Himachal Pradesh	56	5,111	4,281	3,460
Jammu & Kashmir	222	7,719	5,987	4,617
Karnataka	192	49,817	37,136	29,299
Kerala	39	29,011	25,454	21,347
Madhya Pradesh	443	66,136	52,179	41,654
Maharashtra	308	78,707	62,784	50,412
Manipur	22	1,827	1,421	1,073
Meghalaya	22	1,761	1,336	1,012
Mizoram	21	686	494	332
Nagaland	17	1,216	775	516
Orissa	156	31,512	26,370	21,945

growing demand for both office and industrial workers. The result in general has been an overcrowding that in many cases threatens to swamp already backward municipal services. In major industrial centers especially, there are huge barrack-like tenements or large areas of utterly unplanned construction. These slums often encroach upon the healthy, planned, if dull, old British "civil lines" (the areas where civil servants, lawyers, or other professional men lived) or upon blocks of new, middle-class apartments. Social differentiation in India's cities may take the form of areas devoted to one "community"—Christians or Parsees—or one caste, as in the villages. In con-

State	Area (thousand km)	Population (thousands)		
		1991	1981	1971
Punjab	50	20,191	16,789	13,551
Rajasthan	342	43,881	34,262	25,766
Sikkim	7	404	316	210
Tamil Nadu	130	55,638	48,408	41,199
Tripura	10	2,745	2,053	1,556
Uttar Pradesh	294	138,760	110,862	88,341
West Bengal	89	67,893	54,581	44,312
Union Territories: Andaman & Nicobar Islands	8	278	189	115
Chandigarh	0.1	641	452	257
Dadra & Nagar Haveli	0.5	139	104	74
Daman & Diu	0.1	101	79	63
Delhi	1.5	9,370	6,220	4,066
Lakshadweep	0.03	52	40	32
Pondicherry	0.5	789	604	472
ALL INDIA	3,287	848,933	685,185	548,160

Source: Information Wing, Embassy of India, Washington, DC.

trast to Western values, the juxtaposition of extremes of wealth and poverty is accepted by both rich and poor as a natural circumstance.

The prevailing impression of the larger Indian city today is one of fantastic crowding of immense and diverse populations, but at the same time of a teeming and vigorous life. Where the street is wide enough to have a pavement, much of it will often be occupied by the stands of craftsmen and hawkers of every description. Traffic is often chaotic, animal transport (bullock carts, horse-drawn carriages, and, in dry areas, even camels) mingling with more modern vehicles. In dock areas there is even a good deal of haulage by men, and this, together with the frequent use of two or three persons for an apparently simple task, can be regarded as a form of disguised relief for India's underemployed population.

Except in the greatest cities, the "downtown" itself is extremely varied in character. The often garishly painted sculptures of the temples compete with the bright lights of the local movies. Big European-style offices and stores may be surrounded by old-fashioned shops whose owners still live in or above them, while the narrow bazaar streets, often so crowded as to be almost impassable by wheeled traffic, are flanked by open booths. The booths of each trade are grouped close together and the atmosphere is pervaded by a distinctive smell of culinary odors. Always busy, the bazaar really wakes up toward the cool of the evening, when it is lit by naked electric lights or oil-fed pressure lanterns.

Religion

India is the birthplace of Hinduism, Buddhism, Jainism, and Sikhism. As a secular state, however, India has no official religion, and religious toleration is guaranteed under the constitution. Hindus constitute about 83 percent of the population, Muslims 11 percent, Christians 3 percent, Sikhs 2 percent, and Buddhists and Jains each less than 1 percent.[2]

Caste System

The caste system, a set of social and occupational classes into which individuals are born, is an important facet of Hinduism and, thus, is a dominant feature of Indian life. Since independence, the government has been attempting to eliminate castes, but caste consciousness remains important in Indian politics, despite the fact that caste discrimination is unconstitutional. "Harijans," the lowest caste, traditionally called the untouchables, who constitute 15 percent of the population, and tribes, who constitute seven percent, are given special protection by the central government.

Education

Education is the concurrent responsibility of the national and state governments, with the national government laying down policy directions and the states implementing them. The system of education is comprised of primary, secondary (with vocational and technical courses), and collegiate institutions. Education is free and compulsory through age fourteen. Literacy has risen from 17 percent in 1950-51 to 43 percent in 1990; in that year 52 percent of all men and 31 percent of all women were literate.[3] Literacy is generally higher in urban areas.

Languages

About 200 different languages are spoken in India and an appreciation of the linguistic divisions provides a key to better understanding of the nation. Four principal language groups are recognized of which the Aryan and the Dravidian are the most important. Hindi (belonging to the Aryan linguistic group) is the official language; English is also widely used in government and business. In addition, fourteen other languages have received official recognition in the constitution: Assamese, Bengali, Gujarati, Kashmiri, Marathi, Oriya, Punjabi, Sindhi, and Urdu belonging to the Aryan linguistic group; Kannada, Malayalam, Tamil, and Telugu belonging to the Dravidian language group; and Sanskrit that provides the root for many of the Indian languages. Sanskrit is no longer a spoken language. Many other languages are spoken by smaller groups and they are either regional variations or dialects.

Cultural Traits

If diversity is the most conspicuous feature of India, ineffable strands of unity are nonetheless unmistakable. They give India a continuity of culture and persistence of traits in its long timespan. Indians value physical purity and refinement of spirit highly. Acceptance of incidents as the will of Fate (or God) is widespread. Many urbanized women are "liberated," but modesty and shyness are traditionally valued. Gandhi's ideals of humility and self-denial are highly respected. Social harmony is important; an Indian will say yes rather than risk upsetting someone.

The basic social unit in India is the family. It takes precedence over the individual. In most families, aunts, uncles, and other relatives live together. The elderly are respected. Upper-class urban families are smaller than most rural families. The Indian government has been trying to promote family planning, and by the early 1980s, there was a consensus that couples could be effectively motivated to limit the number of children they had through family planning. Contraceptive use has increased dramatically. By 1990, roughly one-quarter of India's population was using some form of effective birth control.

Material Life

A nation's material life reflects its economic advancement and the standard of living of her people. One indicator of material life is the overall pattern of consumption. Currently, India's families spend over 60 percent of their income on food, with expenditures on health care being as little as 2.5 percent and household furnishings accounting for only 4.2 percent (see Exhibit 4-2). However, these aggregate figures fail to reveal an important fact of life in India. While a large population lives a mediocre life, a substantial proportion maintains a decent standard of living, and the number of people in the latter group is rising, which potentially makes India a promising market for a variety of goods and services.

India's large population, the physical terrain, climate, and culture are all conducive to the development of a consumption society.

GOVERNMENT AND POLITICS

India gained its independence from the British on August 15, 1947, at which time two predominantly Muslim regions in the northwestern and northeastern corners of the subcontinent became the separate state of Pakistan. (Later, political problems within Pakistan led to the creation of a separate country in the northeastern region, Bangladesh). On January 26, 1950, India became a democratic republic, adopting a constitution that combines British and American principles of government.

The country follows a parliamentary system of government both at the center and in the states. At the center, there are two houses of parliament: the "Lok Sabha," elected directly by universal suffrage on a "first past of the post" constituency system, and the "Rajya Sabha," indirectly elected by state assemblies. The head of the country is the President, chosen by an electoral college of both houses of parliament and state legislatures. The President calls the leader of the majority party in the "Lok Sabha" to form the government. He/she becomes the Prime Minister (i.e., head of the government) and runs the government with the help of a cabinet of ministers appointed by the President on the advice of the Prime Minister. The constitution vests all executive power in the President, but the real relationship between the President and the council of ministers headed by the Prime Minister is analogous to that of the British Monarch, who exercises ceremonial powers, and the British cabinet which actually governs. The country is divided into twenty-five states and seven union territories.

Despite India's enormous problems, it has the distinction of being a true democracy. Since independence, ten general elections have been held, all on time, and all as free and open as in North America and Western Europe, but with the distinction of larger voter participation despite still low literacy and insufficient transport. As much as 63 percent of the Indian electorate cast its vote in the ninth general elections in 1989, and the number of voters reached the half a billion mark due to the lowering of the voting age from twenty-one to eighteen.[4] India has proved that democratic stability need not precede economic prosperity, and that universal literacy is not a precondition for open and fair voting.

Skeptics have often questioned the stability of the Indian democracy since, so far, mainly one political party (the Congress Party) has dominated the government, and mainly one family supplied the Prime Minister. In the 1989 elections, however, for most Indians, the days when the dominance of a single party was acceptable came to an end. Voters were at last willing to trust somebody else with running the country. However, the Congress Party again regained power in the 1991 elections but only as a minority government, and the Prime Minister for the first time came from South India, eliminating the dominance of the Nehru/Gandhi family that hailed from the North. Indian democracy may have come of age.

Many critics view India's political future as bleak. They point to

EXHIBIT 4-2. Consumption Expenditures of Selected Countries

Country	Food and Beverage	Clothing and Footwear	Housing and Operations	Household Furnishings
Industrial market economies:				
Belgium	24.5	6.6	16.8	13.2
Canada	18.1	9.4	19.9	8.4
France	21.0	6.7	16.3	9.5
West Germany	26.4	8.6	18.3	11.2
Japan	25.0	6.6	17.8	7.0
Sweden	24.3	7.9	25.8	7.0
United Kingdom	20.6	8.3	18.5	7.6
United States	16.7	8.3	19.8	6.2
Middle-income countries:				
Mexico	38.4	10.7	11.2	11.7
Philippines	54.6	6.2	12.1	7.0
South Korea	45.5	7.2	9.7	4.7
Low-income countries:				
Bangladesh	n.a.			
India	62.3	9.5	7.0	4.2
Kenya	49.2	7.7	12.6	9.4
Sri Lanka	58.2	12.2	4.3	4.5

n.a.: data not available

Note: For the following countries, expenditures are expressed as percentages of total consumption in constant prices; base year for Belgium, Sweden and the United Kingdom is 1980; Canada, 1981; France, 1970; West Germany and the United States, 1975. The expenditures for the remaining countries are expressed in current prices: Mexico, 1970; Philippines, 1982; South Korea, 1980; India, 1970; Kenya, 1980; and Sri Lanka, 1975.

Source: National Accounts Statistics: Main Aggregates and Detailed Tables 1983 (New York: United Nations, 1986), Table 2.6.

Medical Care and Health	Transportation	Recreation	Other*
9.6	12.4	5.0	11.9
3.5	15.7	11.5	13.1
15.0	12.7	7.9	11.0
2.9	15.7	8.4	8.6
9.9	8.6	10.3	15.1
2.5	15.6	10.3	6.7
1.1	17.1	9.7	17.2
11.2	15.5	9.6	12.8
5.0	9.3	4.9	8.9
2.9	3.3	4.3	9.8
4.3	10.3	9.4	9.0
2.5	7.9	3.0	3.6
2.2	8.4	4.1	6.4
1.6	12.3	3.9	3.2

Other includes expenditures for personal care, restaurants, and hotels.

continued problem of dealing with the Sikh extremists in Punjab and the political turbulence in Kashmir as symbols of a nation in disarray. India sometimes seems like a fragile cloth being rent apart at its many regional, religious, and ethnic seams. And yet the most remarkable thing about India probably is the surprising strength of the social fabric rather than the fraying at the fringes. The fabric holds, in part, because of a tough and large apolitical army (India has the world's fourth largest standing army), a ponderous but omnipresent bureaucracy, and a powerful commitment to political freedom at the grassroots level. But the main source of India's strength is to be found in its very size and diversity. The country is so vast and varied that a genuine crisis in the North Indian city of Amritsar is a genuine irrelevancy in the east Indian metropolis of Calcutta, more than 1000 miles away. News headlines fail to mention that during the rioting after the assassination of Prime Minister Indira Gandhi, most Indian factories continued to make everything from steel and autos to petrochemicals and computers.[5]

To conclude, India is a multi-ethnic nation with a population of over 850 million that represents a multitude of racial, religious, and ideological types and subtypes. It is beset by such problems as widespread poverty, and communal clashes. Yet it is the world's biggest democracy, where an ancient civilization coexists with modern technology.

ECONOMIC POLICY

India has always placed a high value on economic growth for creating a prosperous society. However, its economic policy has been characterized by the pursuit of multiple and sometimes contradictory objectives. These objectives are embedded in two values: self-reliance and social equity. The pursuit of these objectives led to the creation of perhaps the most regulated economy in the noncommunist world. The general guidelines of India's economic strategy are enunciated by the national government's Planning Commission, whose five-year plans establish development priorities, production goals, and guidelines for allocating investments. A large public sector was created to ensure that strategic sectors of the economy remain responsive to state objectives. A comprehensive system of licensing was established to regulate industrial investment and production capacity. Under this regime, a single application to set up an industrial plant had to satisfy as many as eighty-six different enactments and control agencies before receiving approval.[6] Trade policy became dominated by pervasive quantitative controls and some of the world's highest tariffs, and foreign investment and technology transfer have been closely regulated to safeguard the country's self-reliance.[7]

Goal of Self-Reliance

How far has India progressed toward its goals of economic growth through self-reliance and social equity? First, a large infrastructure of growth institutions and a broad industrial sector have been built which would continue to facilitate a more effective strategy of development in the future. Second, economic gains have been large, and today India is the world's twelfth most industrialized nation in terms of output. Exhibit 4-3 depicts India's ranking on various dimensions. India is the largest producer of tea in the world, and the second largest producer of rice. It ranks fourteenth in value added in manufacturing and eleventh in terms of electricity generation. India is the fourth largest user of nitrogenous fertilizers. Economic gains, however, have been largely nullified by the continuing growth of the population. It is for this reason that, according to GNP per capita, India ranks fifteenth from the bottom among the poor countries.

Third, India has done well in developing human capital, unhindered by religion and fundamentalism, which augurs well for stable growth in the future. India has more students enrolled in universities than any other country in the world, about 4.5 million in 1989.[8] Only the United States and the former Soviet Union have more technical and scientific personnel than India.[9] Fourth, while economic gains have not been universally distributed, a substantial middle class is emerging. The size of India's growing middle class exceeds the population of the United Kingdom, West Germany, and France combined.[10]

Fifth, a diverse industrial network has been developed that manufactures practically all consumer goods and a large variety of industrial and high-tech products. Sixth, improvements in agricul-

EXHIBIT 4-3. India's Ranking in the World

	Unit	World Total	India	India's Rank in the World
General:				
Area	million km	135.8	3.3	7
Population	millions	4,998	781	2
Gross domestic product	US $, billions	n.a.	204	12
Value added in agriculture	US $, billions	n.a.	64.5	4
Value added in manufacturing	US $, billions	n.a.	35.6	14
Electricity generation	billion kwh	10,063	198	11
Agriculture and Allied:				
Arable land	million hectares	1,373	165	3
Irrigated area	million hectares	228	44	2
Tractors in use	millions	25.3	0.65	13
Nitro. fertilizer consumption	million tonnes	72.4	6.5	4
Cattle population	millions	1,278	199	1
Production:				
Rice (paddy)	million tonnes	454	78	2
Wheat	million tonnes	517	46	4
Groundnut (in shell)	million tonnes	20.1	4.5	2
Cotton (lint)	million tonnes	16.6	1.3	5
Tobacco	million tonnes	6.3	0.46	3
Tea	million tonnes	2.4	0.67	1

Note: Data generally relate to 1984 to 1987. Figures for India shown here are taken from publications of the United Nations and the World Bank, and may not in all cases tally with those shown elsewhere.
Source: Statistical Outline of India: 1989-1990 (Bombay: Tata Services Limited, 1989) pp. 201-202.

	Unit	World Total	India	India's Rank in the World
Production: (continued)				
Potatoes	million tonnes	285	13	5
Milk (cow and buffalo)	million tonnes	496	39	3
Butter and ghee	million tonnes	7.4	0.66	2
Eggs (hen)	million tonnes	33.8	0.96	6
Fish catches	million tonnes	76.5	2.5	7
Sugar	million tonnes	103.4	9.26	2
Cotton yarn	million tonnes	11.6	1.2	3
Cement	million tonnes	930	37	5
Iron ore	million tonnes	834	47	6
Transport and Communications:				
Rly. passenger	billion km.	n.a.	266	4
Rly. freight tonnes	billion km.	n.a.	217	5
Civil aviation	billion pass. km.	n.a.	17	13
Social Statistics:				
Pupils at first level education	millions	574	84	2
Scientific and technical manpower potential	millions	111	2.6	5
Radio receivers in use	millions	1,776	60	6
Long films production	number	4,150	912	1
Cinema houses (fixed)	thousands	247	12.7	3

ture have made the country self-sufficient in food, and development of the Bombay High field off the west coast has made India 70 percent self-sufficient in oil.[11] Seventh, India's economic dependence on agriculture is gradually shifting to industry. For example, agriculture's contribution to GNP declined from almost half in 1972 to less than 30 percent in 1988.[12] Eighth, India's conservative fiscal policies minimized the problems with its external debt. Its total external debt accounted for a manageable 158 percent of its exports.[13]

Global Comparisons

Despite the achievements listed above, India's economic growth performance compared to other developing countries has been disappointing. India began the 1950s in quite favorable circumstances compared to other Third World nations; it possessed relatively good infrastructure, an ample endowment of natural resources, a large internal market, a good supply of technically skilled labor, an abundance of cheap labor, and a stable political system. Despite these favorable factors, India's rate of growth has been relatively low. When compared with nine other large and diversified developing economies, India's 3.7 percent average annual rate of GDP growth during 1965-80, as shown in Exhibit 4-4, was less than all but one. Its 4 percent average annual rate of industrial growth was particularly laggard compared to the 9.1 percent average for the nine other countries.

India's economic performance showed modest improvement during the 1980s, while other Third World countries suffered from the debt crisis and declines in oil revenues. Its GNP grew at an average annual rate of 4.6 percent from 1980 to 1987. This approached the 4.8 percent average for the other countries listed in Exhibit 4-4. An important factor in India's improved performance was the increase in its industrial growth rate from 4.0 percent to 7.2 percent—considerably above the 5.4 percent average for the nine other countries. Despite these recent improvements, India's growth rate still remains below its aspirations.

India has received relatively low levels of foreign direct investment (FDI). One study estimated that over the period 1969-82 the annual average of gross FDI (i.e., not subtracting repatriations) in

India was $2.9 million.[14] In comparison, during 1979-80, net FDI (deducting for repatriations) in Brazil was $14 billion. In Mexico, South Korea, and Argentina it was $7 billion, $648 million, and $1.5 billion, respectively. Indian industry relied on the acquisition of foreign technologies less than any other newly industrializing country.[15]

Goal of Social Equity

Progress toward achieving social equity has been limited, too. India still has more people living in poverty than any other country, with the possible exception of China. Estimates of the number of people living below India's poverty line are controversial. The debate is complicated by the fact that there are sharp fluctuations in the number of people living below the poverty line at different points in time. It is generally agreed that from the 1950s through the late 1970s there was no statistically significant trend in the relative incidence of poverty.[16] The government contends that the combination of accelerated economic growth and poverty-alleviation programs has lowered the percentage of the population living below the poverty line from 48.3 percent in 1978 to 37.1 percent in 1984.[17] It projects the continuation of this trend so that the poverty level will decline to 25.8 percent in the mid-1990s.[18] Although most economists agree that the incidence of poverty declined from 1978-84, the range of the decline is a matter of dispute. Many contend that government estimates overstate the improvement.

Another body of evidence suggests that India's economic growth has failed to translate into a substantial reduction in the country's poverty. One of the biggest disappointments of India's development regime is the failure of industrial growth to generate enough jobs for the rural poor. Structural change in economic production has not been accompanied by a comparable change in the structure of employment. Although agriculture's share of GDP dropped from 50 percent in 1972 to less than 30 percent in 1988, its share of the labor force decreased only slightly, from 67.8 percent in 1972 to 65.4 percent in 1990.[19] As a consequence, Indian agriculture has had to sustain the livelihoods of a rapidly growing population. Per capita net domestic product (NDP) in the agricultural sector has remained stagnant while that outside of agriculture exhibits an annual growth

EXHIBIT 4-4. Comparison of Economic Performance: India and Selected Other Countries (US $ and percentages)

	GNP Per Capita		Total GDP (%)	
	1987	Average Annual Growth (%) 1965-87	1965-80	1980-87
Argentina	2,390	0.1	3.5	−0.3
Brazil	2,020	4.1	9.0	3.3
China (PRC)	290	5.2	6.4	10.4
India	300	1.8	3.7	4.6
Indonesia	450	4.5	8.0	3.6
Mexico	1,830	2.5	6.5	0.5
Pakistan	350	2.5	5.1	6.6
South Korea	2,690	6.4	9.5	8.6
Thailand	850	3.9	7.2	5.6
Turkey	1,210	2.6	6.3	5.2

Source: The World Bank, *World Development Report 1989* (New York: Oxford University Press, 1989), pp. 164-67.

rate of 2.5 percent.[20] Furthermore, the increase in the number of people dependent on agriculture has placed growing pressure on the land. From 1970 to 1985, the number of operational farmholdings increased from 70.5 million to 89.4 million while the area operated increased by only 0.67 million hectares.[21] The percentage of marginal farmers (i.e., those owning less than one hectare) increased from 50.6 to 56.6 percent.[22] The portion of the rural labor force working as wage laborers rose from 34 percent in 1972 to 40 percent 1990.[23]

RECENT ECONOMIC REFORMS

Reforms of India's industrial policy can be traced as far back as the mid-1970s. While no political leader has been more closely

| Average Annual Growth Rate (%) | | | | | |
| Industry | | Agriculture | | Services | |
1965-80	1980-87	1965-80	1980-87	1965-80	1980-87
303	−0.9	1.4	1.6	4.0	−0.3
9.8	2.4	3.8	2.6	10.0	4.1
10.0	13.2	3.0	7.4	7.0	7.6
4.0	7.2	2.8	0.8	4.6	6.1
11.9	2.1	4.3	3.0	7.3	5.6
7.6	−0.3	3.2	1.4	6.6	0.8
6.4	9.1	3.3	3.4	5.9	7.1
16.5	10.8	3.0	4.4	9.3	7.7
9.5	5.9	4.6	3.7	7.6	6.4
7.2	6.7	3.2	3.3	7.6	5.0

identified with reforms than the late Rajiv Gandhi, most of his reforms reflected an evolution in the thinking of India's policymaking community that began long before his rise to power. Many analysts trace the improvement in India's economic performance since the mid-1970s to the impact of previous reform initiatives. Rajiv Gandhi's identification with reform is in part explained by the fact that his reforms went further and were more systematic than those of his predecessors. He is also distinguished by his fascination with high technology. Rajiv Gandhi enunciated a sweeping rationale for reform, asserting that India had reached a watershed. Deploring the country's high-cost industry with its technological obsolescence and inadequate attention to quality, he declared that India must address its shortcomings through greater efficiency, more competition, and the absorption of new technologies.

Greater Priority for Infrastructure

Since the late 1960s, infrastructural bottlenecks have acted as major constraints on development. Energy demand outpaced supply, leading to crippling power shortages. India's railroads were unable to meet the needs for freight transport. Communications were antiquated and highly inefficient. In recent years, increased emphasis has been placed on investment in infrastructure.

Relaxing Industrial Regulation

Economic reforms initiated under Rajiv Gandhi and further strengthened by the Rao government have brought significant relaxation in industrial regulation. While the measures taken have curbed the intrusiveness of the regulatory regime, they reflect a continuing belief in the need for state intervention to guide the economy. The new measures are intended as much to promote structural changes in India's industrial base–by encouraging development of backward areas, high-tech industries, and economies of scale–as to alleviate inefficiencies resulting from regulation.

Promoting the Development of Capital Markets

Policy reforms creating new incentives for equity and debenture issues have helped to make India's capital markets an increasingly substantial source of investment finance. From 1980 to 1988, market capitalization more than tripled, from $7.5 billion to $23.8 billion. The value of equity traded increased from $2.8 billion to $12.2 billion.[24]

Measures to Improve Technological Capabilities

Concern for improving India's technological capabilities preceded Rajiv Gandhi's rise to power. In 1984, a government White Paper on Technology Policy and the Report of the Committee on Trade Policies recommended measures to increase imports of modern foreign technologies and to provide greater support for indigenous research and development. Rajiv Gandhi's government stressed the importance of India's technological modernization. In pursuit of this goal, he liberalized imports of capital goods, increased funding for research and development, reformed public sector research institutions, and relaxed restrictions on foreign collaboration.

Promoting Exports

Recent reforms of India's trade policies have attempted to remove the disadvantages and disincentives that exporters suffered as a result of the Indian regulatory regime. Measures to curtail quantitative controls and reduce tariffs on the import of capital and intermediate goods have been an important element of this strategy. These policies have been designed to benefit an array of "thrust industries" that the government has selected for export promotion. India's trade reform is predicated on a calculated risk that liberalization of imports in the short run will reduce trade deficits in the long run.[25]

India's economic reforms have important marketing implications. First, deregulation should encourage competition in the market providing alternative choices of products and services to the consumers. Second, emphasis on technology should raise the quality of goods available. Finally, improvements in the infrastructure should encourage the development of new marketing institutions and enhance the level of services offered.

Limits of India's Economic Reforms

Economic reforms in India have brought substantial changes, but the measures taken until now are only initial steps on what remains a long and difficult journey toward a more flexible and efficient economy. The scope for competition and freedom of maneuver introduced by the reforms is limited. Most industrial deregulation has been directed at India's small- and medium-sized units, and many measures apply only to firms willing to locate in backward areas. India's 1,663 largest private sector firms are still restricted in various ways.[26] In most cases, government approval in one form or another remains necessary for substantial expansion and diversification.

If market competition is to efficiently allocate resources, there must be an effective mechanism to weed out the losers. At the same time that economic reforms have augmented competition, India has suffered from the unrelenting growth of "sick" industrial units. These are firms that, after being registered for a minimum of seven years, have accumulated losses equal to the value of their assets. Despite the introduction of measures designed to curb their growth, the number of sick units has risen dramatically.[27] This problem must be tackled.

Future of India's Economic Reforms

The change in governments following the November 1989 and June 1991 elections has not altered the course of India's economic reforms. While inflation had been an important electoral issue, the relaxation of industrial regulation did not stir much controversy. Under India's current Prime Minister, trends toward the liberalization of domestic industrial policy and the promotion of domestic capital markets and exports are continuing. As a matter of fact, the new government appears to be adopting a more liberal stand. It wants to establish a worldwide economy through large-scale liberalization by freeing foreign investment conditions, cutting down protection for Indian industry, and streamlining bureaucratic procedures. For example, in July 1991, the government announced the new industrial policy that permits foreign investors to make a deep thrust into India's closed economy. The policy for the first time allowed direct foreign investment up to 51 percent equity in thirty-four groups of high priority industries without prior government clearance.

CORPORATE ENVIRONMENT

India is an example of the spread of pluralistic democratic capitalism in the Third World, an American ideal. Since independence, the economy has developed in accordance with five-year plans. Under these plans, a diversified, modern, industrial economy with a large measure of state control began to be developed in place of the colonial economy left by the British. Economic gains have been large, and today India is one of the world's most industrialized nations in terms of output. However, economic gains have been largely nullified by the continuing growth of the population, and India still faces major social and economic problems in feeding and providing employment for such a large population.

Private vs. Public Sector

India has a total of about 200,000 companies. In order to enhance the pace of industrial development, India early on decided that the government must play a key role in establishing and running business enterprises. They were especially justified in industries requiring heavy investment and/or those promising slow return, which would not hold much interest for private business. By and large, the public sector enterprises in India are run inefficiently. They operate more as government departments than business enterprises. Many of these enterprises are generating losses and their products and services are of poor quality. One justification for state monopoly is to provide services that the private sector would not otherwise provide or to ensure that these services are priced so as to be widely accessible. Yet public sector pricing in India has become consumer-exploiting, monopolistic pricing of the worst kind. For example, pricing of public utilities is now a mode of taxation.[28] A tool for promoting economic equality has become the captive of a class-based state.

Today India has about 1200 public sector enterprises owned and operated by the central and state governments. They are by and large relatively large enterprises and account for half of the country's industrial production. For example, the 200 companies attached to the various ministries of the central government employ nearly 2.5 million people and produce goods and services worth nearly $30 billion.[29] They manufacture and market goods and services ranging from coal, steel, cement, textiles, watches, lamps, scooters, chemicals, and fertilizers to ships, machinery, machine tools, aircraft, and heavy equipment.

As far as the private sector enterprises are concerned, they are strictly controlled and carefully watched. Even with recent liberalization, there are over 50 different enactments and control agencies to be satisfied by an investor before he can set up a plant; scores of agencies have control over daily operations.[30] Many committees have recommended reduction in controls, but they have not been reduced and the reason is obvious. Originally set up in accord with Fabian Socialism, the controls now create the livelihood of a class of almost 20 million people, mostly government employees, many of whom will lose income if controls are reduced.[31] Controls are maintained in the interest of a class, the bureaucrats, rather than because of ideology. Despite the bureaucratic hassles, a typical Indian firm operates in an environment characterized by tariff walls which protect it from foreign competition. Inasmuch as the domestic demand exceeds supply, it can continue to operate profitably with small scale operations, low levels of technology and high unit costs. Most firms, therefore, do not attach importance to quality products, latest technology, competitive pricing, large scale operations, and targeted marketing strategies. Protected as they are in their market, even private businessmen in India discourage any attempts to open up markets to foreign competition. While they would want fewer controls for themselves, they would not want to face foreign competition.

If the above description makes it sound as if the public sector controls the economy, nothing could be further from the truth. In 1989, 74 percent of GNP originated in the private sector which consists of over 140,000 joint stock companies and millions of smaller private businesses. There are other indicators, too, that private enterprise is vibrant in the economy. A recent study by the Industrial Development Bank of India indicates that after-tax profits in the private sector increased in 1989 by a dramatic 40.2 percent, while the volume of dividend payments was 33 percent higher than in 1988.[32]

Foreign Business in India

There are about 250 foreign companies that maintain branch offices in India. In addition, there are 100 Indian subsidiaries of foreign companies in which they hold majority ownership; about half of these are from the United Kingdom. In addition, India approves about 1,000 collaborations between foreign and Indian companies annually. Some of these collaborations are one-time technology transfer arrangements or licensing agreements, while others are joint ventures to manufacture the product or service in which the foreign partner can hold no more than 40 percent equity.

The U.S., followed by West Germany and Italy, remains India's major foreign collaborator. Industry-wide, electrical equipment, industrial machinery, and chemicals are the three leading industries in which India seeks foreign collaboration. In the latter half of the 1980s, the tempo of foreign collaborations increased significantly, a trend likely to become more important in the 1990s, as a result of sweeping changes by the Rao government.

Indian Business Overseas

Indian companies have set up joint ventures in a number of developing countries and also in a number of industrially developed countries such as the U.K., U.S.A., West Germany, Canada, and Ireland. In fact, according to one study, India has emerged as one of the leading developing nations to set up joint ventures abroad. The same study states that there are about 200 Indian joint enterprises spread over 35 countries, out of which 110 have gone into production and 87 are in various stages of implementation.[33] These statistics are over ten years old and, thus, the number of Indian joint ventures overseas currently must be much larger, especially in light of the liberalization program. Between the private and public sector, the former has been more active in seeking overseas opportunities.

Public sector enterprises, however, are also selectively seeking internationalization. According to government statistics, Indian public enterprises are stated to be involved in some 400 projects in at least 50 nations.[34] Balmer and Lawrie was the first public sector enterprise in India to make direct foreign investment. The company successfully commissioned its barrel and can plant in Dubai (United Arab Emirates) in 1978. Bharat Heavy Electricals Limited has considerably contributed to the installation of thermal power generating capacity in Malaysia and has installed other electricity generating units like hydro turbines in Thailand. It is involved in the manufacture of 120 MW capacity boilers in Libya on a turn key basis, laying of a sub-marine cable from Zanzibar to the coast of Tanzania, and the development of a 544 MW electricity generating plant in New Zealand. Another well known Indian public sector enterprise, HMT, has made significant strides in its internationalization effort. It has set up a subsidiary company known as HMT International Ltd., which is spearheading the parent company's international effort. HMT has entered the U.S. market for machine tools through its branch office and has entered into various types of collaboration arrangements with firms in Nigeria, Tanzania, Kenya, and Indonesia for supplying machinery and providing project consultancy and technical services. In Nigeria it has entered into an agreement with the Federal Government of Nigeria for setting up a machine tool unit. The agreement with the Small Scale Industries Development Organization of Tanzania envisages a supply of machine tools for eight common facility centers to be set up by the Tanzanian organization. In Kenya it has formed a joint venture company for the setting up of a machine tool unit. It has also entered into an agreement with SONELGAZ in Algeria for the supply of machinery and equipment, installing and commissioning the same, and training of personnel both in Algeria and in India. In the nonmanufacturing sector a number of nationalized banks have made efforts at internationalizing their operations by opening branches in foreign cities with significant Indian communities.

India's Foreign Trade

In 1989-90, India's exports amounted to $1.5 billion. In the same year, India imported goods and services worth $2 billion. India's principal exports include tea, iron ore, cotton yarn and fabrics, textile apparels, handicrafts, chemicals, engineering goods, leather manufactures, gems and jewelry, jute, fish, rice, spices, cashew kernels, and coffee. Imports are comprised of petroleum and products, edible oils, chemicals, fertilizers, iron and steel, nonferrous metals, electrical machinery, other machinery, transport equipment, pearls, and precious stones. India's foreign trade, both exports and imports, has progressively increased in the latter half of the 1980s. This trend is likely to continue in the 1990s as the country embraces further liberalization.

The United States is India's largest trading partner accounting for almost 20 percent of its exports and over 10 percent of its imports. The former U.S.S.R., U.K., West Germany, and Japan are India's other major export markets. Essentially, the same countries account for the imports.

INTERNATIONAL COMPETITIVENESS

Competitiveness is the ability of a country's entrepreneurship to design, produce, and market goods and services that are better and/ or cheaper than those of the international competition. Based on a study that assessed how national environments are conducive or detrimental to the domestic and global competitiveness of enterprises operating in various countries, India ranked well ahead of other Third World countries on six of the ten factors, scoring the first or second position. The study covered twenty-two industrialized countries (all members of the Organization for Economic Cooperation and Development except Iceland; Belgium and Luxembourg were treated as one entity), five newly industrialized countries (South Korea, Singapore, Hong Kong, Taiwan, and Malaysia), and five Third World countries (Brazil, India, Indonesia, Mexico, and Thailand).

The competitiveness of national environments was assessed through 292 criteria covering each of the thirty-two countries. The ten factors were: dynamism of the economy, industrial efficiency, market orientation, financial dynamism, human resources, state interference, natural endowments, outward orientation, innovative forward orientation, and socio-political stability. The factors were equally weighted. Exhibit 4-5 summarizes the criteria used for each factor.

India ranked first or second among the five developing countries on dynamism of the economy, industrial efficiency, outward orientation, innovative forward orientation, and socio-political stability. It ranked worst on the factors of human resources and natural endowments, scoring fifth and fourth place, respectively.

India remains the leading nation among Third World countries on the overall world competitiveness scoreboard. Although Thailand is slightly ahead of India, India's large market gives it a substantial edge. Relative to four other developing countries, India is merited with one of the most efficient industrial sectors, backed by competitive banking and financial sectors. Other points of strength include

EXHIBIT 4-5. India's International Competitiveness Ranking[1]

Factor	Brazil	India	Indonesia	Mexico	Thailand	Factor Criteria
I. DYNAMISM OF THE ECONOMY	3	1	4	5	2	Related to the macro-economic environment, it assesses the broad domestic industrial economic setting, incorporating some components of competitiveness.
II. INDUSTRIAL EFFICIENCY	5	2	3	4	1	Measures the success by which economic resources are efficiently utilized. It involves many of the classical indicators of competitiveness: labor costs, productivity, corporate profits, investments, cost of living, and inflation.
III. DYNAMICS OF THE MARKET	1	3	2	5	4	Reviews wealth, structure, and sophistication of markets given that a country's international competition will depend on how intensely its business community is subjected to national market forces, internal national market conditions, and the strategies firms apply.
IV. FINANCIAL DYNAMISM	3	2	4	5	1	Covers many aspects of financial environment such as government debt and deficit spending, monetary policy, variety, volume, and cost of available finance freedom to move capital.
V. HUMAN RESOURCES	2	5	4	3	1	Examines competitive advantages in the skills, motivation, flexibility, age structure, and state of health of the country's work force. Covers spectrum of human resources: population, labor force unemployment, barriers to unemployment, brain drain and training standards, work ethics, salary levels, and health facilities.

Category						Description
VI. STATE INTERFERENCE	5	3	4	2	1	Measures types of state involvement deemed ultimately detrimental to international business competitiveness, namely the public sector's share of expenditure and employment, the fiscal burden, subsidies, and regulatory constraints.
VII. NATURAL ENDOWMENTS	1	4	2	3	5	Has to do with efficient use of natural resources and their possession.
VIII. OUTWARD ORIENTATION	5	1	4	3	2	Factor favors countries which rely on business abroad for economic well being, such as Switzerland, the Netherlands, Belgium, and Ireland. High growth in exports, strong currency, and excellent performance in export-related activities are important.
IX. INNOVATIVE FORWARD ORIENTATION	4	1	5	3	2	Criteria include degree of innovativeness in products and services offered, production techniques, and management. Market forces must be allowed to redeploy resources from declining to new high growth sectors.
X. SOCIO-POLITICAL STABILITY	5	2	3	4	1	Concerns political stability, industrial relations, reliability of judicial system, threats of arbitrary expropriation, crime, general prosperity, and satisfaction of employer.

[1]Ranking 1 signifies highest competitiveness; ranking 5 shows lowest competitiveness.

Source: Adapted from *The World Competitiveness Report 1989* (Geneva, Switzerland: The Economic Forum, 1989).

India's entrepreneurial spirit as well as an excellent ability to scout new technologies to compensate for its poor rating in research and development. Other high marks of excellence include a strong marketing orientation as well as availability of qualified technical personnel. State interference, however, continues to be a strong negative aspect of India's competitiveness.

INDIA'S EMERGING MARKET

India is in the throes of a middle-class revolution that could transform its attitude to business. When India won independence in 1947, its middle class was a bare two to three million and was swamped by a total population of 350 million. Today it accounts for some 200 million people out of a total population of about 850 million, and is growing fast. The rise of the middle class has sparked a boom in consumer durables, once a market confined to a wealthy few.

Characteristics of the Indian Market

There are several reasons for change in India. GNP growth has accelerated to an average of 5 percent a year in the 1980s, compared with 3.2 percent in the 1970s. Growth is now a little more widely distributed, so money trickles down from the rich to the poor, and on the way it irrigates the middle class. Anti-poverty schemes have provided income-earning assets, like cows and sewing machines, to 25 million people in rural areas.[35] Industrial growth and urbanization have accelerated in the 1980s. Rural roads and the green revolution have encouraged industry and services to spread to villages where only the land used to provide a living. That has boosted spending power.

In the 1950s India went in for socialist planning in a big way because the consuming class did not matter or exist. Most of the population was desperately poor, and many (bonded laborers and subsistence farmers) were effectively outside the market. Government policy was aimed, not at catering to the needs of a few rich consumers, but at raising living standards of the poor.[36] So it banned imports and curbed the production of most consumer durables, levying steep duties on those that were manufactured. In such an environment, waste and corruption became rampant. For a long time, socialism yielded neither rapid growth nor social justice. But in the 1980s economic liberalization, together with more enlightened anti-poverty schemes, elevated tens of millions of the poor into the middle class. It is no longer possible even for socialist politicians to claim that television sets are the playthings of the rich, or that all shareholders are fat cats. In consequence, the government no longer curbs but encourages the production of durables, so it is more open to technical collaboration between Indian and foreign companies, and is willing to let in some foreign equity, too. It no longer equates the private sector with evil or profits with sin, and tax breaks are regularly announced to encourage the growth of shareholdings.

Putting it differently, a large consumer market has evolved in India and no government, no matter what ideology it pursues, can afford to curb market needs. Small wonder, therefore, that even the Marxist state government of the state of West Bengal is avidly wooing big business and multinationals.

From the viewpoint of businessmen, both national and foreign, India represents an emerging market in the making. Compared to Western standards, the market has been barely scratched. But a foreign firm needs strong determination to make its way into India. Government polices are changing, but slowly. Many restrictions must be adhered to. For example, international brand names are usually banned because the Indian government reckons they give foreign companies an unfair marketing edge over Indian competitors. Pepsi-Cola was recently allowed to enter the Indian market, but on the condition that it did not call its product Pepsi-Cola. Many companies overcome the problem with a hybrid brand incorporating the name of a joint-venture partner, like Allwyn-Nissan or Swaraj-Mazda light trucks. In 1991, for the first time multinationals have been permitted an equity stake of 51 percent in joint ventures; until then it had been limited to no more than 40 percent. Red tape and corruption are still widespread. Despite these limitations, a company can ignore a growing market of the size of India at its own peril, especially when the potential is unlimited. In addition, as the economic prosperity increases, more liberalization is likely to follow. If the 1991 liberalization program is any indication, Indian economy will be practically deregulated by the turn of the century. The companies that are already in will naturally have an advantage.

Marketing Implications

The middle-class revolution is leading to striking changes in the marketplace. One is stunned by the arrival of a consumer culture among a substantial proportion of the population, more than the total population of many countries in western Europe.

India's middle class is hard to define. Depending on how one calculates, its number could range from 50 million to 300 million. Some economists define the class in terms of purchasing power rather than occupation, since in India the former is a better measure of influence. Earlier only the salaried and business class could afford durables and convenience goods such as processed foods, but an increasing number of workers and farmers can now afford them, too. Television is a useful yardstick: some 33 million households in 1990 owned television sets. With an average of six people per household, that makes a middle class of 200 million. The rate of new television sales suggests that the middle class is expanding by approximately 10 to 12 million a year, if replacement is allowed for. That extrapolation heralds a new marketing era: the consumer as "maharajah."

In the late 1980s sales of durables soared:[37] a decade ago, television sales were just 150,000 a year; in 1990, 5.4 million were sold. Annual production of motorcycles, mopeds, and scooters has risen tenfold to more than two million. Sales of cars have quadrupled to 200,000 a year. Sales of washing machines rose from none in 1980 to $200 million in 1990. Vacuum cleaners are becoming popular, and there is a boom in sales of everything from bicycles to refrigerators, sewing machines, and fans.

The trend is not limited to consumer goods. India's stock market has boomed, too. The country now has an estimated six million shareholders, plus another 13 million investors in mutual funds (unit trusts).[38] These estimates exaggerate the true picture since they blur multiple holdings by individuals. Nonetheless, India's investors now willingly subscribe $4 billion a year to new capital issues, against only $300 million a year in the 1970s.[39] Even life insurance, run by an inefficient state monopoly, is growing at 40 percent a year.[40] As in the U.S., the middle class in India is a democratic slice of society, enormously varied in its tastes and background. Concentrated in the big cities, its members are from various castes and regions. And like the new middle class in many cultures worldwide, they threaten to turn much of yesterday's enduring tradition into tomorrow's fading curiosity. In India social position used to be equated with an English education and a job in the Indian Administrative Service; today it is money that increasingly defines status, even in sensitive matters like arranged marriages. The new consumer boomers arrive with the latest of everything, from foreign fashions and MBAs to car payments and European vacations.

What seems to typify this middle class, and especially its new members, is a furious drive to make up for lost time–to buy the brightest and the best, whether it be a refrigerator, a VCR, or a smuggled microwave oven. And this trend is likely to continue in the 1990s at a faster pace. The most stunning sign is the constant stream of new things to buy, from color television sets (first mass-produced in 1982) to instant noodles (1983) to radio-cassette players (1985), all of which have landed in shops that rivaled those of the former Soviet Union for austerity. Advertising has also exploded across the country, with ad revenues increasing from $298,000 in 1977 to over $100 million in 1990.[41] It fills endless roadside billboards and more than 20,000 magazines and newspapers, and carries images of the good life into the homes of India's 200 million television viewers–130 million more than there were just five years ago.[42] TV creates aspirations, allows people to see the products and choices that are available, and allows competition to flourish.

The consumerist big bang occurred in 1982 with the advent of color television broadcasts in India. Two years later, "Doordarshan," the state television monopoly, began allowing advertisers to sponsor shows. In the five years since, advertising revenues at "Doordarshan" have jumped more than tenfold. Top-rated shows sometimes draw 150 million viewers–a hefty audience for any advertiser.[43]

Video arrived in India only about five years ago, but today there are 100,000 video shops and probably another 100,000 video parlors across the country, exposing the country's poor and middle classes to a wider world.[44] Foreign travel has boomed. In 1990, over three million Indians traveled abroad, compared with 600,000 in 1980.[45] They are bringing back new tastes. To take advantage of the potential market for its clothing, for example, Benetton has opened nine stores in Indian cities this year and has plans for nine more.[46] Overall, India's market, as shown in Exhibit 4-6, ranks tenth largest in the world. In 1978, India's market ranked below Spain and Canada, but continued growth, especially during 1983-88 (155.95 percent), boosted its position above these nations. Before the end of this century, India's market could conceivably be larger than the United Kingdom's market, and may even supersede France.

Future Scenario

India must boost exports to meet its increasing imports and foreign obligations, and upgrade its industry to make it globally competitive. In these pursuits, India will continue to loosen controls, invite more foreign investment, and seek technology. No matter which political party comes to power, the economic realities cannot be ignored. After all, the projected population of one billion people in the year 2000 must be fed, clothed, and housed. It is a tremendous task in itself and becomes much more difficult in the wake of rising aspirations, which television creates. India has many attractions for foreign investors including low labor costs, a big pool of skilled workers, an abundance of engineering talent, and a tremendous depth of management. Slowly India is moving out of hiding to face the world marketplace. As its initial overtures succeed, it will gradually open the doors for foreigners on liberal terms.

Illustrated below are India's efforts to make a mark in the international markets, a forerunner of permitting access to foreign competitors in its own markets.

Maruti Cars for France

India arranged with a Paris automobile distributor to sell the Maruti cars that it manufactures in a joint venture with Japan's Suzuki company. At the end of 1990, about 2500 Maruti cars were sold in France. Although there have been problems of sorts, the

EXHIBIT 4-6. Size, Growth, and Intensity of World's 12 Largest Markets

Major Market	Market Size (1% of World Market)			Market Intensity (World = 1.00)			Five-Year Market Growth (%)
	1978	1983	1988	1978	1983	1988	1988
United States	23.30	20.96	18.08	4.82	4.40	3.99	17.50
Former USSR	14.32	13.16	12.17	2.14	2.03	1.97	9.15
China	3.84	6.64	11.56	0.16	0.26	0.61	333.25
Japan	9.14	9.07	8.10	3.31	3.42	3.29	12.15
Germany	4.92	4.93	3.95	3.55	3.91	3.47	5.63
Italy	3.04	4.06	3.69	3.09	3.35	3.38	10.96
France	3.67	3.77	3.39	3.10	3.38	3.22	9.96
United Kingdom	3.47	3.38	2.85	2.75	2.87	2.70	19.79
Brazil	2.24	2.21	2.58	0.82	0.78	0.88	25.79
India	1.33	1.53	2.44	0.08	0.09	0.17	155.95
Spain	2.30	2.41	2.12	2.64	2.87	2.76	18.33
Canada	2.23	2.02	1.94	4.25	3.81	3.92	22.09

Notes:

Market Size shows the relative dimensions of each national or regional market as a percentage of the total world market. The percentages for each market are derived by averaging the corresponding data on total population (double-weighted), urban population, private consumption expenditure, steel consumption, cement and electricity production, and ownership of telephones, passenger cars, and televisions.

Market Intensity measures the richness of the market, or the degree of concentrated purchasing power it represents. Taking the world's market intensity as 1.00, BI has calculated the intensity of each country or region as it relates to this base. The intensity figure is derived from an average of per capita ownership, production, and consumption indicators. Specifically, it is calculated by averaging per capita figures for cars in use (double-weighted), telephones in use, televisions in use, steel consumption, cement and electricity production, private consumption expenditure (double-weighted), and the percentage of population which is urban (double-weighted).

Market Growth is a five-year average of the growth rates for several indicators: population, steel consumption, cement and electricity production, and ownership of passenger cars, trucks and buses, and televisions.

Source: Business International, July 30, 1990, p. 256.

experiment has by and large been successful. The company hopes to introduce the car in other EC countries by the middle of the 1990s, and export about 20,000 cars in year 2000. In addition, it plans to export another 5000 cars annually to developing countries in Asia, the Middle East, and Africa.[47]

India strictly protects its automobile market, levying a duty as high as 200 percent on imported cars. But as it learns to play the global game, it will be forced to accept foreign cars on a reciprocal basis. Such a scenario is not far-fetched. Companies capable of visualizing ten years into the future can expect a slow but large automobile market developing in India.

Telephones for Export to the U.S.

An Indian company, Bharati Telecom Limited, has entered a collaboration to supply five million push-button telephones for the first time to the U.S. market. The U.S. imports over 140 million such instruments annually and the Indian company hopes to capture one-fourth of this market in the next five years.[48] India's efforts to break into the U.S. market in high-tech areas reflect her endeavors to reduce dependence on traditional exports.

India's Software Industry Goes Global

India has emerged as a global source of software. Its thriving software business sprang up, in part, because the country's low wages, top-notch technical training, and large number of English-speaking citizens made it attractive to U.S. and other foreign companies that wanted to pare software development costs. Satellite dishes link Indian programmers to corporate clients around the world.

Although the industry is primarily devoted to writing programs for foreign clients, a few upstarts have more ambitious goals. They want to become India's answer to Microsoft and Lotus, creating generic packages for a broad international market. For example, Tata Unisys of Bombay has developed a signature verification program that calls up photographs of customers on the screen. Its worldwide clients include such well-known names as Arthur Andersen, Pacific Bell, Bell South, Citicorp, Hong Kong & Shanghai duty-free imports of some capital goods, as part of its export-promotion program. The amount of duties to be dropped is tied to the value of exports produced by the goods. The government also expanded the list of items that can be imported without a license. Additions include edible oils, adhesives, coffee in bulk, high-end personal computers, and some paper and wood products, as well as parts for consumer durable goods.

Hewlett-Packard, Continental Insur-, Bank of America, and IBM.[49] er companies and exports software a tiny percentage of the total interna- India's standpoint it represents a fivefold increase in less than five years, and a tremendous opportunity to become a major software competitor globally.

Consider Tata Consultancy Services (TCS), the largest software company in the country, that has successfully exerted itself in the global market. It has won the contract to integrate the European Stock Exchanges for 1992.[51] It got the contract in a tough competition against Arthur Andersen, one of the largest consulting firms in the U.S. The project has complex dimensions that require three years and at least 200 people to complete it. The end result will be an applications system for the European securities exchange, from the requirements definitions stage to its implementation. The system will make it possible for a transaction to be quoted in thirteen currencies simultaneously for all the EC members. TCS winning one of the biggest projects that has came up in the international market in recent years is an indication of the strides that the Indian software industry has made. This success symbolizes the sophistication that high-tech industry can achieve in India.

CONCLUSION

Trends and events taking shape guarantee better things for India in the 1990s. Gradual liberalization will encourage investment and consumption, leading to overall economic prosperity. There is an even more salient factor that may drive the country's economic growth upward in the 1990s, providing opportunities for international companies that position themselves intelligently. The general turn away from statism and import-substitution policies, and the embrace of economic orthodoxy and market-based policies should provide a powerful impetus for change. Politically, such bold new thinking is not easy to adopt overnight, but there are trends that indicate a gradual shift in attitude among Indian politicians, especially in light of structural changes being pursued in Eastern Europe and the former Soviet Union.

What will this new change in thinking mean for international business? Although there will clearly be exceptions, overall it will mean a greatly improved operating environment in one of the largest markets. Five general benefits to international business brought about by the turn to market-based policies are included in the following paragraphs.

Slow But More Balanced and Sustained Growth

As investment and exports eclipse government spending as primary growth engines, boom/bust cycles will moderate substantially. Budgetary restraints and prudent monetary policies will tame inflationary pressures and produce greater monetary stability. Stable economic conditions will boost exports and check import growth. Balance-of-payment crises that India is currently facing will, as a result, be the exception rather than the rule. Thus, foreign products will be allowed to enter India without much difficulty.

More Liberal Terms for Foreign Investment

However late the realization, the government now knows that India's future economic progress depends heavily on multinational investment to gain capital, technology, and access to foreign markets. This more enlightened approach is already evident and will become increasingly obvious in the latter half of the 1990s. Many of the major markets will open up including such badly undercapitalized sectors as energy, utilities, telecommunications, and financial services, all of which were once ruled off-limits to foreign capital. The Indian government may also grant foreign companies permission to bid for state companies as the country starts its privatization program. This way, competition will be promoted which would challenge Indian companies to set their house in order.

Greater Access to Local Markets by Exporters

The import liberalization trend initiated by the Gandhi government is continuing at a faster pace. Tariff and nontariff barriers are gradually declining, making it easy for foreign firms to sell in India.

Viable Export Platforms

Local price and wage levels in India will continue to be attractive, permitting a wide array of Indian exports–from textile goods to engineering goods, and from construction contracts to software–to compete in global markets. For labor-intensive assembly operations, India's export zones will remain highly attractive options for companies seeking low-cost offshore production targeted for the Southeast Asian and Middle-East markets.

A Generally Less Risky and Volatile Business Environment Than in the Past

Structural economic reform will attenuate risk–especially financial risk–that plagues business in Third World countries. Meanwhile, democratic traditions will continue to be strengthened, limiting the possibilities of drastic political upheavals.

APPENDIX
Chronology of Important Events in Indian History

Period	Description

Ancient India

ca. 3000-1500 B.C.	Harappan culture
ca. 1500-800 B.C.	Migration and spread of Aryan-speaking peoples into subcontinent
ca. 600 B.CC.	Rise of Magadha
ca 550-486 B.C.	Life of the Buddha and Mahavira (founder of Jainism)
326-25 B.C.	Alexander of Macedon in northwest India
321-ca. 185 B.C.	Mauryan Empire
273-232 B.C.	Reign of Asoka
128 B.C.-A.D. 121	Satavahana Dynasty in Deccan
50 B.C.-A.D. 100	Sangam period in South India; trade with Rome; Tamil kings in Ceylon (present-day Sri Lanka)
A.D. 78	Beginning of new Saka era; founding of Kushan Empire in northwest
150	Sanskrit inscription of Rudradaman I; Saka king in western India

The Classical Age

319-ca. 500	Gupta Empire
375-415	Reign of Chandragupta II
399-414	Visit of Fa-Hsien, Chinese Buddhist pilgrim
ca. 500-600	Huns in northwest India; Guptas continue in eastern India; rise of Chalukya power in Deccan; rise of Pallava power in South India
606-47	Reign of Harsha-vardhana of Kanauj

The Medieval Period

711	Arab invasion of Sind
ca. 780-826	Life of Shankara, the philosopher
ca. 899-1300	Chola power in South India, expansion in Southeast Asia
985-1018	Reign of Rajaraja I, Chola king
998-1030	Raids of Mahmud of Ghazni in northwest

Period	Description

The Medieval Period
(continued)

1192	Battle of Tarain, defeat of Rajputs by Muhammad of Ghor
1206	Establishment of Muslim Slave dynasty in Delhi
1296-1316	Reign of Alauddin Khalji, expansion of Delhi sultanate
1325-51	Reign of Muhammad bin Tughla
1336-1565	Vijayanagar Empire in South India
1347	Founding of Bahmani kingdom in Deccan
1398	Invasion by Timur, sack of Delhi
ca. 1400-1526	Independent kingdoms in North India
1440-1518	Life of Kabir, bhakti saint
1469-1539	Life of Nank Dev, founder of Sikhism
1485-1533	Life of Chitanya, bhakti saint
1510	Portuguese capture Goa

The Mughal Period

1526	First Battle of Panipat, defeat of Ibrahim Lodi by Babur
1526-30	Reign of Babur, founder of Mughal Dynasty
1530-39	Reign of Humayun, struggle for power
1539-55	Sur Dynasty in Delhi
1556-1605	Reign of Akbar, consolidation and expansion of Mughal power
1571	Foundation of Fatehpur Sikri
1579	Abolition of special tax on Hindus
1580	First Jesuit mission at Mughal court
1605-27	Reign of Jahangir
1606	Martyrdom of Guru Arjan Das
1616-18	Sir Thomas Roe obtains permission for English East India Company to trade in empire
1628-57	Reign of Shah Jahan; Taj Mahal and other great buildings constructed; Mughal expansion in Deccan
1630-80	Life of Sivaji, Maratha leader
1657-58	War of succession
1658-1707	Life of guru Gobind Singh, tenth and last Sikh guru

Period	Description
The Mughal Period (continued)	
1675	Execution of Guru Tegh Bahadur
1679	Reimposition of the special tax on Hindus
1681	Aurangzeb moves to Deccan, war with marathas
1699	East India Company constructs Fort William at Calcutta
1707-12	Reign of Bahadur Shah followed by gradual disintegration of Mughal Empire into virtually independent provinces
1739	Nadir Shah sacks Delhi
1740-60	Struggles for power in Carnatic and Bengal involving forces of European trading company as well as indigenous forces
1761	At third Battle of Panipat, marathas defeated by Ahmad Shah Abdali
British Period	
Company Rule	
1757	Battle of Plassey, nawab of Bengal defeated by East India Company forces led by Robert Clive
1765	Company awarded *dewani* (power to collect taxes) of Bengal, Bihar, and Orissa by Mughal emperor
1767-99	Four Anglo-Mysore wars
1772-1833	Life of Raja Ram Mohan Roy, social reformer
1775-1818	Three Anglo-Maratha wars
1799-1839	Reign of Ranjit Singh in Punjab–Sikh Empire
1813	East India Act
1829	Law prohibiting suttee
1835	Thomas Babington Macaulay's "Minute on Education"; English made official language
1838-42	First Afghan War
1843	Conquest of Sind by British
1845-49	Two Anglo-Sikh wars
1853	First railroad and telegraph lines opened
1856	Annexation of Oudh by company
1857	Sepoy Mutiny (or Sepoy Rebellion), also known as Great Uprising; marked formal end of Mughal Empire

Period	Description
British Period (continued)	
Empire to Independence	
1862	Indian Penal Code introduced; India High Courts Act
1869	Suez Canal opened
1875	Arya Samaj founded; Aligarh College founded by Sir Sayyid Ahmad Khan (1817-98)
1878-90	Second Afghan War
1885	Indian National Congress (Congress) founded
1892	India Councils Act
1905	Partition of Bengal by Lord Curzon, viceroy
1906	All-India Muslim League (League) founded
1909	Morley-Minto Reforms
1911	King-emperor (George V) visits India and announces reversal of partition of Bengal; transfer of imperial capital to New Delhi from Calcutta
1916	Lucknow Pact between Congress and League
1917	British declaration on Indian self-government
1919	Massacre at Jallianwallah Bagh, Amritsar; India member of League of Nations, Third Afghan War
1920-22	Noncooperation movement under Mahatma Gandhi's leadership of Congress; Khilafat Movement
1921	Montague-Chelmsford Reforms of 1919 inaugurated as part of Government of India Act
1927-28	Simon Commission; All-Parties Conference, Nehru Report
1930	Gandhi's Salt March
1930-31	Civil disobedience movement
1930-32	Roundtable conferences, London
1931	Gandhi-Irwin Pact
1935	Government of India Act
1937-39	Provincial autonomy; Congress ministries
1940	Pakistan Resolution adopted by Muslim league in Lahore

Period	Description
British Period (continued)	
Empire to Independence (continued)	
1942	Fall of Singapore; Sir Stafford Cripps mission; abortive "Quit India" movement; mass arrests
1942-44	Great Bengal famine
1944	Gandhi holds talks with Mohammad Ali Jinnah
1945	Labour government in Britain announces intention of early independence in India
1946	Mutiny in Royal Indian navy; British cabinet mission to resolve political deadlock; interim government installed with Jawaharlal Nehru as prime minister; Constituent Assembly elections
Independent India	
1947	Lord Mountbatten, viceroy, announces plan to partition India (June 3); independence of India and Pakistan (August 15); raiders in Kashmir, military operation (October)
1948	Assassination of Mahatma Gandhi (January 30)
1950	Republic of India adopts Constitution
1951-52	First general election
1953	New state of Andhra Pradesh created
1954	French territories incorporated
1955	Afro-Asian Conference in Bandung; Hindu Marriages Act
1956	Second Five-Year Plan (FY 1956-60); reorganization of Indian states
1959	Dalai Lama enters India from Tibet for political asylum
1961	First Conference of Nonaligned States, Belgrade; India seizes Portuguese colony of Goa
1962	Border war with China
1964	Nehru dies (May 27); Lal Bahadur Shastri elected Prime Minister
1966	Indo-Pakistani wars in Rann of Kutch and in Kashmir
1966	Tashkent Agreement; Shastri dies (January); Indira Gandhi elected Prime Minister

Period	Description
British Period (continued)	
Independent India (continued)	
1969	Congress splits; Indira Gandhi remains Prime Minister
1971	General elections (March); civil war breaks out in Pakistan (March); liberation of Bangladesh; 20-year treaty signed with Soviet Union (August)
1972	Simla Agreement between India and Pakistan (June)
1974	India detonates nuclear device in underground test (May 18)
1975	Emergency proclaimed (June 25)
1977	General elections in March; Gandhi defeated; Morarji Desai of Janata Party elected Prime Minister; emergency ends
1980	Seventh general elections; Janata Party defeated; Gandhi elected Prime Minister
1984	Indira Gandhi assassinated (October 31); eighth general elections: her son Rajiv becomes Prime Minister
1989	Ninth general elections: Viswanath Pratap Singh elected Prime Minister
1991	Tenth general elections: P. V. Narasimha Rao elected Prime Minister

Chapter 5

Market Evolution in India

Market evolves as the country develops. Profound changes occur that affect its people. Incomes change, population concentrations shift, expectations for a better life adjust to higher levels, new infrastructures are built, and social capital investments are made. These changes lead to a new potential market with new attitudes among customers.

The pace of market evolution varies from country to country, depending on how the enabling conditions, discussed in Chapter 3, interact to shape the environment. Traditionally, limited economic activity in developing countries restricted the scope of their market evolution. The emergence of newly industrialized countries (NICs), however, proved that markets in developing countries can evolve as fast as, if not faster than, in developed countries, as their development strategies bear fruit. In other words, how fast or slow the market evolves in a country would be a function of the interaction of enabling conditions.

In most developing countries, adequate conditions do not exist that encourage smooth market evolution. For example, a country may have a small home market or its political climate is restrictive, or the level of technology usage is extremely low. In a way, India is no different than other developing countries. However, it has a unique set of circumstances that have helped in the evolution of a huge market in the midst of poverty.

At the time of independence in 1947, the viable market in India constituted a smaller proportion of the population. It was a predominantly urban phenomenon, supplemented by a thin rural stratum. The purchasing power of consumers was low. They were, by and large, tradition-bound in their lifestyle. And, as a class, they were sold on socialism of one variety or another.

The austere look that India's economic policies had in the initial years, with their emphasis on heavy industry and relative disregard for consumer goods, and the efforts at reduction of inequalities through such means as high levels of taxation and curbs on industrial houses, explain the perspectives of market at that time. All that has changed. A new, booming market has evolved. It forms a much larger proportion of the population.

A combination of factors can be ascribed to market evolution in India. With the gradual freeing of the economy in the mid-1980s, the middle class began to be exposed to consumer sophistication unknown before. Relatively free imports started flooding the market with products hitherto smuggled in and clandestinely sold. The medium of this change already existed in the form of color television introduced in India in 1982.

MARKET EVOLUTION

The Indian market has more or less evolved following the model depicted in Chapter 3. Exhibit 5-1 identifies the stages of evolution, size of the market in each stage, and other perspectives. Starting with a small market of about two million people in the post-independence period, today India represents a market larger in size than the combined markets of France, Italy, and the United Kingdom. Looking at the principal reason behind the evolution from one stage to the other, one wonders if some other measure(s) would have helped in smoother and/or faster evolution. For example, was planned economic development through centralized state planning a necessary first step? Could agriculture be revolutionized first? Should economic liberalization have been the guiding force right from the beginning? While these questions can be vehemently debated, India's initiatives do provide a paradigm which could be adapted to other developing countries in their endeavors to emerge as a viable market.

EXHIBIT 5-1. Market Evolution in India

Evolution Stage	Size of the Market (Number of People)	Duration of Evolution	Principal Reason Behind Evolution	Selected Significant Occurrences Affecting Market Evolution
Elite Market	2-3 million	1947-1955 (Post-Independence Period)	British Legacy	• Awareness of British ways of living • Substantial means to be able to afford imported goods
Affluent Market	12-15 million	1955-1967	Planned Developmental Effort	• Industrialization efforts giving rise to professional class • Spread of professional education • Exposure to Western living through print media, movies, and foreign trips
Rural Market	30-35 million	1967-1983	Green Revolution Program	• Farm technology available at bargain rates from the U.S. and elsewhere • Political commitment to achieve self-sufficiency in food grains • Favorable agricultural conditions in the northern states including availability of determined and hardworking labor force
Urban Market	150-160 million	1983-present	Economic Liberalization Measures	• Diffusion of television • Promotion of commercial television • Availability of consumer credit • Liberalization of foreign trade • Cultural acceptance of conspicuous consumption
Mass Market	–STILL IN THE FUTURE–			

Elite Market

When Britishers quit India, they left behind an elite class of bureaucrats, professionals, landlords, and politicians. Although small in number (about two million), members of this class controlled enormous wealth. Accustomed to Western ways through their close contact with the Britishers, or by virtue of their education in England, they constituted a significant market segment for a variety of durable and nondurable goods. The pre-independence subsidiaries of multinational corporations (for example, Lever Brothers), as a matter of fact, catered to the elite class, in addition to serving the Britishers living in India. More often, however, the needs of this market were fulfilled through imports. While the customers were scattered throughout the country, they were served by select distributors, located in large cities, through personal contact.

Affluent Market

India began its first purposeful stage of modernization by concentrating its efforts in two areas: the production of manufactured goods in substitution for consumer goods imports and the creation of basic infrastructure, i.e., roads, electric power, ports, and education. Agriculture and the modernization of rural life were systematically neglected, yielding back in the 1960s to a dangerous decline in per capita food production.[1]

There was a certain legitimacy in these initial priorities. The development of an economy, at its core, consists in the progressive diffusion of the fruits of modern science and technology. Industry is the most dramatic form which science and technology assumes, and the basic infrastructure is directly required for industrialization. However, although difficult to support, there was also an element of irrationality in pursuing the above strategy. Agriculture was associated with the period of colonialism and/or with excessive dependence on imports from industrialized countries. Therefore, it appeared to be second-order–and even faintly humiliating–business, as compared to industrialization.

The combination of these two factors–rational and irrational–has led to an affluent market of 12-15 million consumers, concentrated largely in a few cities and mainly consisting of professionals, both in private and public sectors, businessmen, and political leaders.

Rural Market

The continued population pressure and the setbacks in agriculture led to the spread of a perception throughout India that the next phase of development must be based on a systematic diffusion of the modern skills out into the countryside.[2] Assuming poor rural infrastructure (e.g., roads), minimum basic education, and also a certain backlog of relevant agricultural science, four necessary and sufficient conditions were identified for an agricultural revolution.[3] First, the farmer must receive a reliable and fair price for his product. Second, credit must be available at reasonable rates for him to make the change in the character of his output or the shift in productivity desired. Third, there must be available on-the-spot technical assistance that is relevant to his soil, weather conditions, and change in either output or productivity. Finally, there must be available in reasonable quantity, quality inputs such as chemical fertilizers, insecticides, and farm tools.

India did a reasonably good job in creating the above four conditions, encouraging farmers to increase their productivity and overall output. The results were phenomenal, especially in the northern belt. Dubbed as green revolution, the agricultural prosperity created a new market of 30-35 million rural consumers. Incidentally, India already had in place another condition–availability of quality incentive goods, which other developing countries may have to create. Incentive goods are consumer goods of good quality which the farmer and his family would purchase in great quantity, or would work harder to get if they were cheaper or if his income were higher. Both subsidiaries of multinational corporations and local companies that were well established to serve the affluent market went ahead to capitalize on the opportunities available in the rural market. A variety of consumer goods, both durable (bicycles, radios, watches) and nondurable (toiletries, tobacco products, textile goods), became a common sight in rural markets.

According to the retail audit carried out recently by a market research agency, close to 50 percent of the demand for selected consumer products originates in rural India. In 1989, rural consumers snapped up over 48 percent of safety razor blades, 48 percent of popular toilet soaps, 44 percent of detergent bars, and almost 42 percent of analgesic tablets from the market.[4]

Of still greater importance is the pace at which demand in the rural segment has grown vis-à-vis the urban area. Between 1985 and 1989, the sales of popular toilet soaps in rural India exploded by nearly 15 percent a year. This is in sharp contrast to the growth in the urban segment touching barely 1.3 percent annually.

During the same period, demand for washing products (including detergents) registered an annual increase of 20 percent in rural India, as against 5 percent in the urban segment. The demand for both dry-cell batteries and razor blades went up by 5 percent every year as compared to a negative growth rate in urban India.

Still more striking is the discovery that the lowest income group today constitutes a significant majority of the consumers for various packaged goods. A survey conducted by the National Council of Applied Economic Research revealed that close to 70 percent of those who bought a select basket of products (comprising tea, coffee, edible oils, toothpaste, razor blades, toilet soap, footwear, washing powder and biscuits) were people whose average monthly income was below $40 per month. This income group accounted for 74 percent of the consumption of footwear and edible oils, 72 percent of washing cake, 71 percent of tea and toilet soap, 70 percent of coffee powder and vanaspati (vegetable oils), 68 percent of toothpaste, 66 percent of razor blades and biscuits, and 60 percent of cold remedies.[5]

Progress in the countryside has been catalyzed by the efforts made by the government in successive five-year plans. In addition, agricultural incomes continue to enjoy exemption from taxation. There are now 50,000 banks in the countryside to tap savings and provide loans.

Coinciding with the rising prosperity, there has been an explosion in the media network during the 1980s. This has helped change the traditional lifestyles of villagers to such an extent that, according to a survey in 1989-90, close to 30 percent of rural adults watch television every week with some frequency. The significant point is that almost as many women as men watch television today. During the first half of 1990, as many as 169 different products were advertised on television, ranging from soap to sewing machines, toothpaste to two-wheelers, wrist watches to washing machines, and bulbs to baby powder. Toilet soaps topped the list with the highest advertising expenditure; toothpaste, two-wheelers, detergents, television sets, and tea are other products advertised heavily.[6] Besides, manufacturers have been adopting other forms of imaginative strategies for communicating their sales messages to the rural audiences.

Urban Market

In 44 years since its independence, India has come a long way. A lot of investment has been made to achieve self-sustained growth in practically every field. While progress has been there, it has been rather slow when compared with the performance of other developing countries. Time and again, government restrictions have been singled out as the basic reason for India's mediocre achievement. To set the economy on a growth path, the government of India, in the early 1980s, started lifting controls, although at a slower pace and in a haphazard manner.

The liberalization measures adopted during Rajiv Gandhi's tenure, however, provided a new boost to the economy. All of a sudden, the entire business climate changed. Overall growth during 1985-90 averaged over 8 percent.

From a marketing standpoint the liberalization dose had an interesting, far-reaching effect. Virtually overnight, an urban market of over 150 million people emerged. Consumers in this market, compared to the rest of India, are better educated, more aware, and show greater willingness to acquire and consume new and varied products. In brief, they represent an acquisitive group with materialistic values similar to those common in the West.

Mass Market

At the end of 1990, India's population was estimated to be in the neighborhood of 850 million people. Combined together, the elite, the affluent, the rural, and the urban markets would add up to about 200 million or so consumers. Viewed in India's context, less than 25 percent of the population represents a viable market. Of the remainᴜɪg 650 million people, about half are below the poverty line while the other half live a subsistence existence. This state of affairs raises an important question: Will India ever emerge into a mass market on Western lines whereby the majority of the people may be counted as consumers for a variety of goods and services? Eventually, of course, the majority will come out of the shackles of poverty and become consumers with discretionary income beyond what is required for sheer survival. Technology, combined with international cooperation and human awareness of good life, will make it happen. This may, however, take several generations. In the perceptible future, the mass market in India will remain a theoretical notion. On the other hand, the number of urban market consumers will continue to increase, providing new and growing opportunities for marketers. Although in the context of India, it is not a mass market (since it represents a small part of the population), considered internationally, even this market is huge. It is likely to become as large as the U.S. market, but with less purchasing power.

MIDDLE-CLASS REVOLUTION

A substantial market has taken shape in India. Currently, it is comprised of over 200 million people, but with continuing growth in the economy and urbanization, it is expected to climb at the turn of the century to more than 300 million consumers. The Indian market has the underpinnings of a market in any advanced country. It includes people from all walks of life: from old monied to nouveau riche, and from white collar workers to skilled workers. What is significant, however, is the fact that 80 to 85 percent of the families in the market belong to the middle class.

The middle class is comprised of families who possess neither family status derived from heritage nor unusual wealth. Their social and economic position is achieved primarily by their occupation, career orientation, and skills. The Indian middle class includes professionals, independent businessmen, corporate managers, professors, bureaucrats, and skilled workers. Summarily, the middle class in India represents the majority of the white-collar group and the top of the blue-collar group. The gradually rising prosperity of these middle-class families has brought within their reach consumer goods that were considered luxuries until recently.[7] For example, a black and white television was meant only for the rich until about ten years ago, but is well within affordable limits of most skilled workers today.

Forces Behind the Rise of the Middle-Class Market

The rise of the middle class in India is an inevitable consequence of the development over the last four decades. India's development pattern in the first 30 years after independence discouraged the manufacture of consumer goods. The intention was to restrict public spending and encourage savings so that the money could be used for developing basic industries. India's policy was, to an extent, successful. The country enjoyed one of the highest rates of savings in the world right into the 1980s.[8] But as years progressed, due to a highly demanding trade union movement, and also through the government's own efforts, workers in the organized sector found their standard of living going up steadily. Between 1960 and 1985, the wages in the manufacturing sector went up by nearly 10 percent each year, in the railways by 8.1 percent, and in the banks by 9.5 percent.[9]

At the same time, the "green revolution" of the 1960s improved the lot of farmers in vast areas of North India. And around the early 1970s, a large number of people, particularly from southern India, began going to the Middle East to work on jobs that paid several times more than they would have earned in India.

The 1970s also saw more and more women going out and seeking jobs. Working wives were no more a phenomena restricted to Westernized families in large cities. For example, in 1983, 7 percent of the households in Bombay, Calcutta, Delhi, and Madras had working housewives. By 1989, this figure had gone up to 13 percent.[10] Two-income households were thus multiplying in numbers every six years or so.

To top it all came the ascendence of the service industry. Like the trend worldwide, the service industry caught on and became a large employer in India as well. This created an entirely new class of white collar workers, reasonably well paid, ambitious, and upwardly mobile.[11]

Slowly and steadily, a sizable discretionary income was being built up through the 1970s. Much of this income still went into savings and gold, largely, as it was proved later, because of a lack of consumer goods to buy.

In the early 1980s, the Indian government, going along with the winds of change blowing across the world, began to ease control on the manufacture of consumer goods.[12] Taxes were lowered in some areas; price controls lifted in others. Several products were de-licensed for manufacturing, and customs duty was reduced on electronic goods. Import of a large variety of components used by the consumer goods industry was allowed for the first time. Travel abroad was made easier. With more people traveling overseas, the goods they brought back began having a demonstration effect. So, while a pent-up demand was building up on one side, the consumer goods industry got a fresh lease of life on the other. The expanding network of TV transmitters made television the most potent and successful purveyor of the message of conspicuous consumption. Prime time TV transmission at the end of 1990 reached 280 million viewers, and its power as an advertising medium is tremendous.[13] Television, without doubt, has made the single largest contribution to the growth of consumer culture in India.

The Rajiv Gandhi government that came into power in late 1984 only accelerated changes that the previous government had already begun. Several industries were totally decontrolled, price controls lifted, imports liberalized, and foreign joint ventures made easier. More importantly, the new leader brought along a modern, urban, yuppie image. Suddenly, it seemed as if one did not have to feel guilty about flaunting possessions. Economic activity under Rajiv Gandhi expanded as never before. The middle class prospered, de-mand went up, and production increased. As shown in Exhibit 5-2, in seven years, starting in 1983, car production went up from 45,000 to 200,000 a year. Similarly, substantial increases took place in the manufacture of washing machines, refrigerators, and other durable goods.

Diffusion of Television: An Example

In 1982, the Indian government decided to go in for color TV transmission and drew up a plan to steadily bring the entire country under the TV umbrella in less than ten years. These initiatives

EXHIBIT 5-2. Production of Selected Durable Goods in India

Product	1983	1990
Cars	45,000	200,000
Two-Wheelers (Motor Bikes, Scooters)	50,000	1,200,000
VCRs	5,000[1]	500,000
Refrigerators	300,000	1,000,000
Washing Machines	10,000	800,000

[1]India did not assemble VCRs until 1986. This figure, therefore, represents imports.
Source: National Council of Applied Economic Research, New Delhi.

generated a frantic demand for color TVs. In late 1982, when customs duty rates were eased to allow color TVs to be brought into the country in time for the Asian Games, 60,000 sets clogged the cargo channels of the Bombay airport.[14]

Since then there has been no looking back as far as television is concerned. As shown in Exhibit 5-3, television ownership in ten years (between 1980 and 1990), increased from a little over one million to over 33 million. Despite the fact that a color television costs about Rs. 10,000[15] (about $600), there are more than 75 manufacturers battling it out in the market to satisfy the seemingly unsatiable demand.[16]

Durable Goods: Order of Priority

Middle-class consumers cannot acquire all the durable goods they prefer at once. They must prioritize their acquisitions based on competing demands on discretionary funds. Unfortunately, no formal studies could be found which provide direct or indirect insights into middle-class durable goods acquisition priorities. But based on interviews with knowledgeable people in India (marketing managers, advertising executives, and marketing academics), a priority order, as shown in Exhibit 5-4 has been developed.[17]

A typical middle-class family in India categorizes durable goods into two groups: essentials and major purchases. Electric fan, gas stove, radio, electric iron, sewing machine, and mixer/blender fit in

EXHIBIT 5-3. Diffusion of Television in India

Year	Number of Units (Ownership) (both black and white and color)
1970	Less than 1000
1980	1.1 Million
1984	3 Million
1988	25 Million
1990	33 Million

Source: National Council of Applied Economic Research, New Delhi.

the first category. These products are concurrently purchased within a short time of the establishment of the household. The major purchases, however, are prioritized as depicted in Exhibit 5-4. Other than Bombay and Calcutta, transportation has traditionally ranked first in priority.[18] A scooter or motorbike is the first durable product that families aspire to buy. This is followed by television. However, in many new families television has overtaken the scooter as the first preference. Particularly in smaller cities with short distances to travel and dependable public transportation, the importance of television as the product preferred first has increased. Television/scooter is followed by VCR, cooler, washing machine, dryer, electric oven, air conditioner, car, and finally, foreign vacation.

CHANGING MARKET BEHAVIOR

As living standards improve, consumer attitudes and consumption patterns change. The emerging Indian middle class is going through a revolutionary change, exhibiting new preferences in what and where they buy.[19] Their purchasing priorities are changing with more emphasis on quality than price, and service is more in demand as a component of a purchase. With economic prosperity, the traditional consumption habits are shifting with convenience achieving importance. In product choices, brand name plays a significant role. From retail outlets, they demand longer hours and convenience of shopping with better service, ease of access, and proximity to home.

Demographics

As mentioned earlier, by the turn of the century, India's middle class is estimated to grow to almost 300 million people. Sixty per-

EXHIBIT 5-4. Middle Class Durable Goods (Major Purchases) Acquisition Priority in India

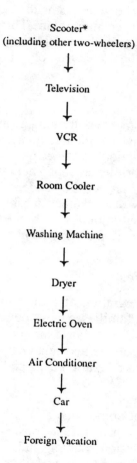

Scooter*
(including other two-wheelers)

↓

Television

↓

VCR

↓

Room Cooler

↓

Washing Machine

↓

Dryer

↓

Electric Oven

↓

Air Conditioner

↓

Car

↓

Foreign Vacation

*Except in Bombay and Calcutta where, due to traffic congestion, two-wheeler vehicles are not popular.

cent of the middle-class population will be below the age of 40 years.[20] Over 70 percent of middle-class families will continue to live in urban India.[21] The young consumer living in an urban area is becoming increasingly cosmopolitan. This is resulting in greater acceptance of regional cultures which manifests itself in the increasing popularity of regional cuisines, clothing, designs, and artifacts across the country.[22]

Attitudinal Change

Middle-class consumers are moving away from being philosophical to pragmatic, from traditional to contemporary, and from Indian to Western in their outlook and vision.[23] Such changes result in large numbers of experimental consumers who are more innovative and amenable to new products and ideas. An inevitable impact is spawning a vast array of consumer durable and nondurable goods, and services: from automobiles to home computers, from home entertainment to international travel, and from ready-to-eat foods to home conveniences.

Growing Liberalization

Through the disintegration of joint families and the concurrent emergence of nuclear families, a new-found *freedom* has emerged in urban metropolitan society. For example, during vacations, rather than going home to parents and relatives, more and more families prefer sightseeing and relaxation trips and special interest holidays like trekking and wildlife.

The freedom from family bonds has resulted in the use of a variety of products at home such as liquor and cigarettes. A more important implication of this trend, however, has been the shifting role in terms of decision making and influence. Of course, the wife/mother becomes an important source of authority. In addition, teenagers and children are also becoming new sources of influence with their attendant demands on manufacturers to fashion products and communication to these target groups.

The Changing Indian Woman

Growth in education, the media influence, and ever-growing numbers of working women are resulting in a quiet revolution among large segments of middle-class Indian womanhood. This has two main implications. The working woman is making increasing demands for personal and convenience products. Personal products range from clothing and footwear to personal care and appearance products of a bewildering variety. Convenience goods–mainly household items–which run the gamut from instant foods to pressure cookers are becoming an integral part of middle India's homes.

Further, there is a need for a deeper and continuing understanding of the emerging Indian middle-class woman. Different from the traditional woman, she has been classified with such labels as *reactionary, self-assured, confident,* and *health-conscious.* However, much more insight is required to get a clearer picture of her needs, activities, interests, opinions, and such aspects as her relationships, self-perceptions, and openness to change. These insights should offer useful information for product innovations and communication focus.

PROFILE OF A MIDDLE-CLASS FAMILY

The contemporary Indian middle-class family is on the threshold of change.[24] While it has not given up many of the traditional values, it is aspiring for modernity. It is not satisfied with just maintaining the current status but seeks to achieve more. While comfortable making friends from other regions, the family would be opposed if the children were to marry outside the community.

Blessed with a good economic life, the middle-class family has a sense of well-being. The family is much happier today than it was five years ago, but the adults, especially the housewife, do worry about the future. The family feels proud of its achievements, but hopes for the future are dependent on children, and this, in turn, would depend on what astrologically the "stars" have in store for the family.

The family is fashion-conscious, spending a lot of time shopping for clothes and jewelry. It cares for good looks and grooming, spending substantial money on toiletries, cosmetics, and health-related products. But the concept of fashionable clothes for the housewife does not go much beyond the "sari"[25] and occasionally "salwar-kameez."[26] In other words, while becoming Westernized, the housewife likes to dress like a traditional Indian woman.

The family enjoys socializing, i.e., formal parties and dropping in on neighbors. At the same time, it must attend "pujas,"[27] and religious ceremonies organized by the community or a friend/neighbor of a different sect. Typically, a middle-class housewife is more of an emulator than a leader. The consumer choices are influenced by her peer group and, to an extent, by film stars and advertising models. She is unlikely to be the first one to buy new brands, except in the area of food products where she likes being innovative. When she does buy a new product on her own, she is not happy until it meets her family's approval.

The middle-class family is more saving-oriented than spending-oriented. Bargain hunting and buying on sale are common traits of the family. But it is willing to pay a little extra for good quality. More important, it is willing to spend extra money on sending children to good schools. The family is fully aware of events in society. Mostly it depends on mass media to keep itself informed about products and services. Interestingly, distribution channels are held in low esteem and suggestions made by salesclerks are invariably rejected. The family is conscious of maintaining good health, but both husband and wife are too lazy to do regular exercise. The wife, however, is careful of what she eats.

PERSPECTIVES OF THE MIDDLE-CLASS SHOPPER: THE HOUSEWIFE IN THE 1990s

The housewife is the principal shopper of the middle-class family. In the 1990s, a variety of changes are expected in her behavior which will affect marketing.[28] There are indications showing her increasing dissatisfaction with the traditional role of a housewife. It is viewed as narrow and constricting, not allowing her a sense of self-identity. Thus, we may expect a shift away from family, to interests outside the home.

The 1990's woman will see herself increasingly as a co-breadwinner who strives for a better standard of living for her family and herself. Besides material gains, she seeks recognition, both personally (self-esteem and self-worth) and socially (recognition from husband, family, and society). She will be more aware, assertive, and demanding. Self-confident, she will be accepted by her family and society at large. This opens up tremendous opportunities for social communication agents, seeking awareness and change in areas such as dowry, education, and inequality.

The trend in the 1980s was growth in nuclear families. Although this trend is likely to continue to grow in the future in nonworking-women households, the young working family of the 1990s may desire the extended family system (with parents and in-laws as support systems, especially with younger children). The middle-class woman of the future will continually strive not to compromise her role as a mother and housewife while at the same time fulfilling professional responsibilities; family first, career after. She will gear her life so that she performs both roles successfully–mother and wife–as well as being a working individual. As ideological pressures and social expectations begin to change, and as the middle-class woman adopts a more nontraditional career, which makes additional demands on involvement and time, she will feel a squeeze on her time with the family. At the same time, the consciousness and need to spend more time with children will increase, with the competitive pressures in the environment mounting. The conflict between involvement with work versus family is likely to increase in the 1990s. The answer may lie in seeking part-time jobs, her own business, or flex-time jobs.

The time pressure is likely to result in new products offering significant time economy. More than convenience, the ability to tailor time to her own needs will be important. Therefore, such products/services as consumer durables, one-stop retailing, prepackaged groceries, and convenient banking hours are likely to grow.

In the area of food, she will be more free-thinking and willing to try and experiment with convenience foods. She will be less critical than the 1980s woman in purchasing semiprocessed, ready-to-make foods, especially if she does not perceive them requiring compromise on taste and freshness. Positioning platforms which offer unique taste with labor savings will be an advantage. She will plan her housekeeping so that she spends less time shopping. She will frequent stores that are located en route from her work or nearby home. She will also increasingly involve her children and husband in sharing household chores. The traditional role/responsibility and division of tasks between man and woman will become more blurred.

For marketers developing new products or services—whether it is tax-saving schemes, purchasing paint for the home, or buying a washing machine—the middle-class woman's opinion will be important. She has money to spend and the freedom of deciding where to spend it. An issue which is a key to many marketers targeting women is that, in positioning of brands or creating advertising messages, should they address the needs of women at large or restrict themselves to middle-class women at the cost of alienating the wider women audience base?

Chances are that the working woman will be seen more and more as a powerful aspirational role model: in the image that she projects; in being seen as an independent, self-assured, and modern woman; in having an individual identity, distinct and separate from her husband's/family's. Her product adoption behavior is, therefore, likely to influence other women.

She will, of course, represent a challenge to the creators of advertising. One of these key areas will be related to identity models which are being reproduced and reflected in advertising today. Should a woman be shown in the kitchen performing traditional roles, anxious to please her husband and in-laws? Should she only be looking immensely satisfied in washing her family's clothes whitest white, or are there other roles or emotions that she should be projecting? For example, can she be shown as a successful woman in a boardroom?

Advertising to women in India today repeatedly focuses on traditional roles: the devoted mother and wife and stereotypical expressions of mother love and care. The answer to the above question, however, seems to lie in role extension, not in role reversal—not in whether women should be shown doing traditional activities—but in how they are shown, what else is shown, who is shown, the style, personality of the model, what image she projects, as much as what emotions and situations are depicted. A recognition of the multiplicity of the middle-class woman's role is crucial—and advertising which is cognizant of this aspect in its positioning is likely to be more successful.

For marketers selling indulgence or leisure products, the middle-class woman of the 1990s will not be as overly self-sacrificing as the woman of the 1980s was. More and more, she will buy herself treats, splurge on new clothes, spend time on leisure–food/drink, watching TV/films on video or in the cinema, travel, go out with friends or family. However, overt appeals of self-indulgence or high living may not work as successfully as providing a rational justification for her emerging behavior.

Self-grooming and personal care are likely to be on the rise. Products which appeal to her need to look good and her heightened focus on her appearance and being well-groomed, without being overly fashionable or stylish, will be successful. An emphasis on discretion, elegance, and dignity will be apparent in all product items–clothes, jewelry, cosmetics, shoes, bags, and watches. Dressing to suit the occasion, wearing enough cosmetics without looking too made-up, is important to this segment.

Existing products will have to fit into a lifestyle of a much busier, more confident woman than existed in the 1980s. More than the desire for convenience, the ability to tailor time to one's own needs will be critical. Implicit in this is a challenge to the media–to TV programs and commercials, newspapers, and magazines–to reflect a new and changing lifestyle. There are challenges for retailers, too. As shopping time gets squeezed and is seen to be less of an outing, the need to adapt to the 1990s middle-class woman will become necessary in the form of more flexible hours, better shelf displays, more attractive packaging, and one-stop shopping.

MARKET OPPORTUNITY

Market opportunity in a country depends on a number of variables such as population, income, consumption patterns, infrastructure, geography, and attitudes toward foreign involvement in the economy. Overall, the Indian market ranks tenth in the world, behind the U.S., former U.S.S.R, China, Japan, Germany, Italy, France, Brazil, and the United Kingdom. Despite its large size, the Indian market for foreign firms remains insignificant. It has been plagued by internal problems and protective controls. However, recent measures have gone a long way in opening the market for firms interested in considering India from a long-term perspective.

With the large domestic market, and assuming technology can be purchased from foreign sources, India can adopt new processes of mass production and mass distribution to emerge as a booming economy. Consider Japan.[29] In 1964, it absorbed less than 500,000 new cars, but took 1.13 million in 1967, 2.38 million in 1970, 2.93 million in 1973, 3.10 million 1979, and 5.65 million in 1989. Where in 1960 there were five passenger cars in Japan per every 1,000 inhabitants, by 1973 the number reached 185 cars per 1,000 and in 1989 it was 320 passenger cars per 1000 people. This expanding market permitted Japan to achieve scale economies based on the newest production technologies, thus reducing costs enough so that large Japanese firms were able to move decisively into world markets.

Given its large market, India has an advantage over other Third World countries offering a viable market opportunity. As a matter of fact, the opportunity in India is much more real than China since, politically and culturally, India is more attuned to materialistic living. From all indications, it appears India has reached a point where economic deregulation will continue to make inroads, as proven by the new liberalization measures adopted by the Rao government. Assuming business firms, both Indian and foreign, favorably respond to the opportunity there, India is a significant market.

While there is a fairly sizable number of families that have bought and are buying consumer goods, in total terms the quantity of the units purchased vis-à-vis Western standards is not that large. That is because the usage frequency is not very high and the penetration is very low. A stage has been reached where aspirations for some people have been converted into reality, yet a large market is available to be served.

An important point to remember is that a barrier has been broken. A middle class of achievers and strivers has evolved. They will continue to aspire for more and more products and services. Further, the number of people entering the middle class is growing at a substantial rate. From all counts, India will continue to be a real boom market for decades, although there may be short-term ups and downs.

MARKET PENETRATION LEVEL

The current levels of market penetration for different goods in India are extremely low, which shows the extent of opportunity on the horizon. To make the point, goods are categorized into three groups–household products, personal products, and durable products. Exhibits 5-5, 5-6, and 5-7 show the penetration level for each kind of good.[30] For example, in Exhibit 5-5, 38 different household products have been identified. Of these, the penetration level of 18 products is low, i.e., less than 20 percent of families buy these products. In other words, such common products in industrialized

EXHIBIT 5-5. Household Product Penetration (Products Used by the Family) in India

PENETRATION LEVEL		
High (60-100%)	Medium (20-60%)	Low (Less than 20%)
Branded Biscuits Bread Cooking Oil Washing Soap Washing Powder Toilet Soaps Talcum Powder Toothpaste	Soft Drink Concentrate Vanaspati Packaged Tea Loose Tea Milk Beverages Detergent Cakes/Bar Ultramarine Blue Branded Scourer Toothpowder Shoe Polish Antiseptic Liquid Phenol	Ready-Made Squashes Tomato Sauce Branded Cheese Noodles (like Maggi) Instant Coffee Branded Milk Powder Baby Food Liquid Soap for Utensils Shampoos Shaving Soap Shaving Cream After Shave Lotion Hair Dye Branded Toilet Cleaner Branded Air Freshener–Solids Branded Air Freshener–Spray Branded Insecticides Branded Floor Cleaner

Sources: Pathfinders (a marketing research firm in Bombay), 1987.

EXHIBIT 5-6. Personal Product Penetration (Products Used by the Housewife Personally) in India

PENETRATION LEVEL		
High (30% +)	Medium (15-30%)	Low (Less than 15%)
Branded Hair Oil	Snow/Vanishing Cream	Perfume
Headache Tablets	Cold Cream	Fairness Cream
Rubs & Balms	Lipsticks	Chocolate Bars
Bread	Nail Polish	Fruit Drinks
	Kajal	Ready-Made Squashes
	Cough/Cold Tablets	Tomato Sauce
	Ice Cream	Branded Sauce
	Aerated Soft Drinks	Branded Cheese
	Soft Drinks Concentrate	Instant Noodles
		Sanitary Napkins

Source: Pathfinders (a marketing research firm in Bombay).

EXHIBIT 5-7. Durable Goods Penetration in India

Products	All India %	Upscale Segment %
Black & White TV	32.5	51.1
Color TV	7.0	25.4
VCR/VCP	1.6	6.8
Cassette Tape Recorder	16.3	34.1
Stereo Systems	3.8	12.5
Mixer/Grinders	17.9	51.0
Pressure Cookers	48.6	86.2
Refrigerators	11.5	39.1
Gas Stove	21.5	55.5
Washing Machines	2.4	7.6
Moulded Luggage	12.9	37.2
Car	1.9	8.4
Scooter	9.6	25.6

Source: Pathfinders (a marketing research firm in Bombay).

countries as instant coffee and shampoos have penetrated less than one-fifth of the households in India.

In comparison with household products, the penetration level of personally used products is much lower (see Exhibit 5-6). Such personal products as sanitary napkins and fairness creams have penetrated less than 15 percent of the families. Even among the high-penetration group for personal products, only one product–branded hair oil–has made significant inroads, i.e., 60 percent penetration.

A caution is in order here. Exhibits 5-5 and 5-6 might have included as many as 25 percent of the families in lower classes. If these families were excluded, the penetration level would be much higher. Nevertheless, the point is made that the penetration levels of different goods in India are fairly low, and as the market continues to evolve, new opportunities for a variety of products would emerge.

Penetration of durable goods in Indian households is equally slim (Exhibit 5-7). Even in the upscale segment, black and white TVs, mixers/grinders, and gas stoves have penetrated about 50 percent of the families. For VCRs, washing machines and cars, the penetration level is still lower, indicating the availability of a huge unserved market.

But things are beginning to change. The emerging middle class represents a viable qualified available market–the set of consumers who have interest, income, access, and qualifications for a variety of household, personal, and durable products. The shopping behavior of middle-class consumers makes one wonder if India is a poor country. Maruti, a company that did not even exist ten years ago, has announced that it is going to double the production of its cars from 100,000 a year to 200,000.[31] In Delhi alone, 100 new Marutis enter the city's congested traffic every day, and twice as many in Bombay. The same is the case with most consumer durables, from scooters to bicycles and washing machines to refrigerators. Briefly, the Indian middle class holds a substantial amount of money that exceeds the national income of a large number of countries. It is a quarter of the entire national income of Pakistan and twice as big as the national income of Ghana.[32] The consumer durable market in India is the biggest in Asia (except Japan); it is even bigger than China where income distribution is more even than in India, and prices are much higher. *Business Week* makes the point:

Indeed, India looks surprisingly good in comparison with China. Ten years of trading with China have taught U.S. Asian-based executives some hard lessons. Unlike China, India allows relatively free repatriation of profits. India also has great private wealth, with 5% of its population, or some 40 million upper-crust citizens, richer than most Americans will ever be. China has only its egalitarian masses.[33]

Interestingly, India is going through a consumer revolution, an all-pervading phenomenon, affecting every facet of middle-class life. Consider the ready-to-wear industry. It started in India in the early 1980s with sales of export rejects and leftovers. In five years it developed into a $1 billion industry. In the southern city of Bangalore the Wear House chain of six stores grew ten times in five years, from sales of $600 a month to over $6000 a month. Their main store, The Big Kids Kemp, with a floor area of 20,000 square feet, is claimed to be the world's largest department store for children's wear.[34]

Food habits, though hard to change, have also been subjected to the onslaught of consumer revolution. Fast foods, noodles, TV dinners, packaged milk, and branded salt are all phenomena of the 1980s. In 1986, Indians drank 220 million bottles of soft drinks. In 1989, the seekers of good life consumed 3,000 million bottles.

India's restrictive environment is slowly being liberalized. Despite being a difficult market to enter, companies who jump on the bandwagon early on will gain a lasting advantage in this burgeoning market.

Establishing Consumer Contact

From all indications, the middle-class market in India is growing fast. At the same time, it is becoming more competitive and the consumer is becoming more discerning. Manufacturers, therefore, are adopting new ways, hitherto unknown in India, to reach the consumers, including direct selling, institutional selling, and telemarketing. For example, up until recently, Reader's Digest Books was the only product category sold in India by direct mail. Today companies peddle exercise equipment to fire extinguishers, colored condoms to bagpiper gold through direct mail.[35]

Apart from direct mail, direct selling has also taken off in India. The unedifying image of the door-to-door salesperson who invariably had the door slammed in his face in mid-sentence is a thing of the past. Companies place well-trained young and confident salespersons to call on customers who have the full backing of a reputable firm, selling a reliable product. Their experience in India shows that direct selling works effectively for products which require demonstration and education on changing habits. For example, Eureka Forbes (Eureka's joint venture in India) has sold products in at least half a million Indian homes since it initiated direct selling in 1988.

Institutional selling is another emerging distribution strategy employed by Indian companies. Cashing in on the consumer financing boom are companies such as Philips. They entice a body of captive consumers–usually the employees of a large company–and offer them their products. The finance, in turn, comes from the mushrooming consumer financing companies such as 20th Century Finance, Classic Financial, or the State Bank of India. According to a Philips' executive, their sales through institutional selling have been growing 15 percent annually. Perhaps the most successful as far as institutional selling is concerned has been Titan watches: over the past three years, institutional business has doubled every year. Evidence of its stupendous success: over 1,500 companies including The Times of India, P&G, Lever, Union Carbide, and Shaw Wallace have bought Titan watches in bulk.[36]

But direct selling and institutional selling are merely the beginning of the story. A large chunk of the vast Indian market can also be accessed through the powerful medium of the telephone. Quick to realize the vast potential of the telephone (in spite of India's poor phone service), more and more companies are increasingly making use of India's rapidly expanding telephone network for selling. There are several reasons why selling on the phone is fast gaining popularity. For one, selling on the phone is easy. For another, its range is tremendous: from small localities to large organizations, it can target them all.

Not surprisingly, a number of companies have sprung up in India that specialize in telemarketing. For example, one of these companies, Magus Marketing Information Support, is experimenting with completely automated telemarketing for office equipment and consumer goods.

Briefly, rising income is creating a generation of eager consumers in India. As a Bombay executive remarks, "Year in and year out, people are becoming better off, more working women, later marriages, fewer children per family, more leisure time, higher expectations, and a propensity to spend on a better life."[37]

But rapidly changing social patterns make marketing to them a complex problem. The economic and social changes now sweeping through India are mixing with the sub-continent's traditional values and lifestyles to create wholly new and complex groups of consumers. The changes are occurring so rapidly–and sometimes so abruptly–that few marketing researchers pretend to understand their ultimate impact. When people shift from a rural to an urban lifestyle, suddenly things happen to them. Their values and motivations change.

Briefly, urban Indians have become serious consumers. A decade of rising prosperity has spread broadly enough to form identifiable markets of millions. For purveyors of consumer goods, the surest bet is that the impact of the trends will be positive, large, and lasting.

CONCLUSION

India's experience shows that economic liberalization exerts a strong influence on market evolution. Other things being equal, liberalization spurs aggregate economic growth and lays the foundation for raising and satisfying consumer demands. In addition, an important lesson which is relevant for other developing countries is that while market evolution directly affects the middle class, benefits trickle down to others down the line. This way more and more people enter the market system. While the middle class expands, a substantial proportion of the population in the lower income groups benefits as well in due course.

Chapter 6

U.S. Business in India

India is a potential growth market for American business because of expanding population, the potential for a rise in living levels based on present low levels of consumption, and the likelihood of renewed economic growth following new liberalization programs of the Rao government. India requires U.S. technology, increased investment, trade, and industrial modernization. From the viewpoint of U.S. business, the advantages for trade and investment in India are persuasive.

Relations between India and the United States have changed considerably in recent decades. The Indian economy has undergone substantial development since its independence in 1947, when it looked to the United States for food grain imports and advice on rural development. Sophisticated institutions now guide the Indian economy, and India, despite its low GNP per capita, has advanced to the point where Indo-U.S. business dealings can be mutually beneficial.

Examination of India's economic reforms is useful in understanding the evolution of Indo-U.S. business relations. They point out India's social and economic priorities, and reveal opportunities for mutual benefit. In the 1950s, India's political and economic philosophy leaned toward more public sector undertakings and state control, though not as doctrinaire a philosophy as in the avowedly communist countries. But since 1985, fiscal and industrial policy measures have been enacted resulting in slowed growth of state-regulated enterprise, encouragement of privatization, expansion of the list of allowable imports, modernization of industries, and reduction of individual and corporate tax liabilities. These new directives have resulted in a buoyant private sector, more consumer products for the

155

well-to-do, and an increased GNP despite the successive years of severe droughts that adversely affected the agricultural production. In summary, the recent economic climate signifies a gradual shift towards a more pragmatic and market-oriented approach than the previous ideologically left-leaning and state interventionist approach of the Indian government.

INDO-U.S. TRADE

The United States is India's largest trading partner, accepting 25 percent of India's exports and contributing 10 percent of its imports. Despite occasional political differences between the two countries, the trading relationship has remained essentially immune from the vagaries of international political issues.

The Growth Pattern of Trade

India's economic liberalization has created opportunities for expanding Indo-U.S. trade. India, for its part, looks to the world's largest market in its drive to increase its exports. Its exports to the United States have grown considerably during the previous decade; from 1982 to 1990, as shown in Exhibit 6-1, they increased over 133 percent. The U.S. share of India's exports has also risen considerably. For example, in 1980-81, the United States accounted for 11.1 percent of India's exports, making it India's second largest market (after the Soviet Union). By 1989-1990, the United States received 19.8 percent

EXHIBIT 6-1. India's Exports to the U.S. (in million $)

	1982	1983	1984	1985	1986	1987	1988	1989	1990
Indian exports to United States	1,404	2,334	2,737	2,478	2,465	2,529	2,952	3,378	3,278
Percentage change from previous year		(66)	(17)	(–3)	(–1)	(3)	(17)	(14)	(–4)

Source: U.S. Department of Commerce, Washington, DC.

of India's exports and was India's largest market. Even so, India remains a minor player in the U.S. market. In 1990, its exports accounted for only 0.7 percent of the total U.S. imports.[1]

India's exports to the U.S. are diversified among a wide range of products, particularly gems and jewelry, garments, chemicals and engineering products, leather goods and handicrafts (see Exhibit 6-2). In trade with the United States, yarns, fabrics, and other non-apparel textile products account for almost 70 percent of Indian textile and apparel exports on a volume basis (only 35 percent based on value). Diamonds have become the single leading U.S. import from India, reaching an estimated $671 million in 1987.[2] Generally, Indian diamond traders cater to the American demand for low cost yet quality gems. This market opportunity has enabled India to emerge as the world's largest exporter of small polished diamonds. India has achieved global competitive advantage in the diamond cutting industry.

For the United States, India's economic reforms have created new opportunities for exports. India's efforts to upgrade its technological base have improved prospects for U.S. exports in an array of capital goods and high-tech industries. Prior to the signing of the Indo-U.S. memorandum of understanding on technology in 1985, U.S. policy constrained the possibilities for American firms to take advantage of opportunities in India. Even since the memorandum was initiated, U.S. firms have been relatively slow to increase their trade with India. From 1984 to 1987, U.S. exports to India declined by 8 percent. In 1988, however, led by substantial increases in transport equipment and cereals, U.S. exports to India grew by 70 percent, and during 1988-1990, they increased 31 percent, despite a large reduction in cereal exports. From 1984 to 1990, high-tech exports rose from 21 percent to 43 percent of all U.S. exports to India.[3]

U.S. exports to India mainly consist of high technology products, fine chemicals, industrial machinery, essential raw materials, and oil drilling equipment (see Exhibits 6-3 and 6-4). These happen to be the fields where demand is expected to continuously rise as India's economy grows and her liberalization program becomes fully stabilized.

EXHIBIT 6-2. India's Exports to the U.S. by Major Product Categories (in million $)

	1983	1984	1985	1986	1987	1988
1. Crude petroleum	818.4	738.3	331.4	1.9	13.5	9.6
2. Petroleum products	48.9	101.4	202.0	259.1	262.1	215.6
3. Textile made-ups	16.8	22.9	30.8	32.3	33.2	44.1
4. Cotton fabric	13.4	40.5	41.5	33.8	80.8	80.8
5. Silk fabric	11.6	19.5	17.9	13.0	12.8	14.0
6. Ready-made garments	221.0	285.2	293.2	344.6	452.0	507.6
7. Luggage & handbags	4.5	8.9	12.5	13.6	16.8	25.3
8. Jute fabric	23.1	15.1	25.4	28.1	28.3	19.3
9. Carpets & rugs	38.8	44.8	60.0	70.8	72.3	73.9
10. Frog legs	2.5	5.3	5.4	5.2	0.5	--
11. Marine products	57.4	45.2	48.1	51.2	60.4	60.7
12. Cashew nuts	74.0	94.4	101.3	133.4	157.0	70.1
13. Coffee	23.6	25.6	38.5	67.2	29.5	14.9
14. Tea	9.0	14.1	10.7	12.7	8.4	9.3
15. Spices & pepper	8.8	18.1	19.2	90.2	51.1	33.9
16. Crude minerals including mica	1.9	5.6	14.6	5.3	3.6	8.1
17. Bone, ivory & horns	0.6	0.5	1.6	3.0	0.3	0.2
18. Gums, resins & lac	17.6	21.7	27.8	22.4	20.7	52.4
19. Plants, seeds, flowers, etc.	17.3	33.5	42.1	26.3	26.7	42.9
20. Crude vegetable material	51.6	68.9	14.6	10.5	7.9	7.4
21. Castor oil	5.6	10.1	7.1	--	--	--
22. Chemicals & related products	20.7	26.3	26.7	29.2	43.3	65.8
23. Leather & leather products	46.7	62.6	67.5	51.4	60.3	72.8
24. Footwear	6.0	12.1	17.8	17.1	30.8	30.7
25. Diamonds	459.1	568.6	503.5	642.9	698.9	997.7
26. Precious & semi-precious stones & pearls	22.4	24.6	18.6	22.7	24.1	28.9
27. Jewelry & related products	9.7	28.0	33.4	31.4	36.7	41.0

	1983	1984	1985	1986	1987	1988
28. Mfgrs. & semi-mfgrs., base metal, NSPF	--	--	23.0	27.6	34.9	41.9
29. Ferroalloys	--	1.6	--	--	--	--
30. Iron & steel bars, rods & plates	3.5	3.2	4.4	3.4	3.7	4.5
31. Iron & steel pipes & fittings	3.4	4.9	12.1	4.9	7.2	24.5
32. Industrial fasteners	1.8	2.3	3.6	2.9	3.2	5.5
33. Hand & machine tools	6.9	8.3	6.8	5.6	6.9	8.6
34. Metal-working machine tools	0.9	1.0	1.6	1.4	1.3	2.0
35. Household & sanitaryware	23.5	30.3	23.3	19.3	23.5	32.8
36. Cast iron articles	12.8	18.3	15.6	20.6	25.7	24.8
37. Pumps, compressors & fans	5.2	7.6	7.1	7.7	8.4	11.7
38. Electrical machinery	1.5	19.2	13.7	11.4	15.1	20.6
39. Lighting fixtures	8.7	10.7	8.6	6.4	7.4	10.6
40. Wood & wooden products, cork	2.9	3.8	4.6	3.3	2.4	5.4
41. Toys & sporting goods	1.6	0.9	0.8	0.9	1.0	1.1
42. Electrical components & parts	8.3	10.8	6.8	5.0	5.5	5.6
43. Parts of office machines & ADP machines	14.0	24.2	15.5	14.2	3.7	5.8
44. Parts NSPF of motor vehicles & equipment	2.8	4.1	3.7	2.9	4.0	7.6
45. Other Commodities	204.2	244.0	313.9	308.2	143.1	212.0
TOTAL	2,334	2,737	2,478	2,465	2,529	2,952

Source: Ministry of Commerce, Government of India

As shown in Exhibit 6-5, five countries (U.S.A., former U.S.S.R., Japan, U.K., and Germany) account for nearly 50 percent of all Indian exports and imports. Unlike many countries, no one nation dominates the trade scene in India. While the U.S. is the leader, it is not so by a significant margin. The Indian marketplace is, therefore, relatively more competitive.

EXHIBIT 6-3. U.S. Exports to India

	1982	1983	1984	1985	1986	1987	1988	1989	1990
U.S. exports to India	1,599	1,827	1,565	1,640	1,529	1,434	2,444	3,026	2,508
(Percentage change from previous year)		(14)	(–14)	(5)	(–7)	(–6)	(70)	(24)	(–17)
Total Trade	3,003	4,161	4,302	4,118	3,994	3,963	5,396	6,404	5,786
(Percentage change from previous year)		(38)	(3)	(–4)	(–3)	(–1)	(34)	(19)	(–10)
U.S. high-tech exports to India	365	361	324	348	451	572	904	1,066	953
(Percentage change from previous year)		(–1)	(11)	(7)	(30)	(27)	(58)	(18)	(–11)
High-tech exports (as a percentage of total U.S. exports)	23	20	21	21	29	40	37	35	38

Source: U.S. Department of Commerce, Washington, DC.

U.S. Trade Deficit with India

A few years ago, the U.S. had a yearly trade deficit of about $800 million with India. In the foreseeable future the balance of trade is likely to continue in favor of India. India is passing through the transition from a highly regulated economy to liberalization which puts great strain on the resources, particularly the foreign exchange balances. Thus, India must limit its imports to essential products. Besides, like the NICs, India to an extent pursues export-led growth which generally discourages imports. As a matter of fact, India, in order to achieve the goal of self-sufficiency, has severely restricted consumer goods imports. The situation, however, will change toward the end of the 1990s as Indian industries enhance their competitiveness and export more. As a matter of fact, the trend is al-

EXHIBIT 6-4. U.S. Exports to India by Major Product Categories (in million $)

	1983	1984	1985	1986	1987	1988
1. Wheat	525.5	43.4	3.6	--	--	223.7
2. Dry milk & cream	--	14.5	0.2	0.3	--	6.0
3. Wheat, flour, meal & grouts	--	--	--	--	--	0.1
4. Preps. of cereal, flour & starch, etc.	41.9	39.5	49.7	43.9	34.0	42.9
5. Nuts & fruits (excluding oil nuts)	4.0	3.8	7.1	2.4	4.1	11.6
6. Rubber–synthetic & reclaims	2.9	4.2	1.3	1.2	0.2	6.0
7. Pulp & waste paper	13.5	21.6	49.9	42.6	38.9	39.8
8. Cotton & other raw textile fibers	8.0	8.8	11.4	8.3	6.4	11.6
9. Fertilizers, crude minerals (excl. coal)	21.3	28.6	21.2	12.9	12.9	10.2
10. Fertilizers & fertilizer material	20.3	214.9	390.6	154.7	45.8	211.5
11. Metalliferous ores & metal scrap	28.6	31.3	79.0	124.8	90.4	129.0
12. Petroleum & petroleum products	13.4	11.3	26.4	11.7	8.1	12.0
13. Fixed veg. oils (soft), crude or refined	35.2	140.1	18.1	19.7	30.6	79.1
14. Organic chemicals & products	38.7	39.0	59.2	52.6	57.5	95.2
15. Inorganic chemicals & products	35.7	56.4	55.8	14.6	14.4	19.4
16. Medicinal & pharmaceutical products	7.7	7.6	12.6	10.4	15.7	30.4
17. Synthetic resins, rubber & plastic material	20.3	17.7	18.1	25.3	32.8	44.9
18. Misc. chemical products	15.4	20.3	18.2	19.7	21.2	24.3
19. Diamonds & other precious stones	8.8	6.5	6.0	6.5	5.9	8.0
20. Iron & steel plates, sheets, bars, etc.	10.2	11.2	11.7	13.8	14.0	39.7
21. Misc. manufactures of metals	10.4	10.7	8.6	11.7	13.4	13.1

Source: Ministry of Commerce, Government of India

EXHIBIT 6-4 (continued)

	1983	1984	1985	1986	1987	1988
22. Steam- & vapor-generating boilers & parts	12.3	23.3	30.6	35.3	35.4	31.5
23. Steam & vapor power units & parts	5.5	3.5	2.7	7.0	6.2	2.4
24. Internal combustion engine pistons & parts	12.0	10.1	13.0	13.7	50.1	85.5
25. Specialized industrial machinery	83.3	113.6	148.4	185.1	132.5	143.6
26. Misc. industrial machinery	57.9	70.7	74.1	76.1	77.8	78.6
27. Metalworking machine tools & accessories	13.8	11.9	15.7	18.6	18.9	18.6
28. Office machines & data processing equipment	67.3	52.7	56.3	85.1	92.8	96.9
29. Telecommunication & sound reproducing equipment	22.2	18.7	25.3	33.1	46.8	39.1
30. Electrical equipment & electrical parts	52.4	56.4	65.9	94.8	95.7	121.2
31. Road vehicles & parts	38.6	35.9	21.2	17.1	38.8	26.6
32. Aircraft, spacecraft, & associated equipment	102.2	80.0	74.7	98.1	111.3	363.4
33. Professional, scientific & control equipment	72.0	69.2	92.9	100.8	107.1	98.3
34. Photo equipment & optical goods	6.7	6.8	11.2	9.0	10.7	12.1
35. Power-generating machinery & equipment	44.5	49.0	61.5	86.2	104.9	128.4
36. Ships, boats & floating structures	141.5	1.0	--	0.1	1.0	45.3
37. Other commodities	233.1	230.8	97.8	91.8	57.7	94.0
TOTAL	1,827	1,565	1,640	1,529	1,434	2,444

Source: Ministry of Commerce, Government of India

EXHIBIT 6-5. India's Major Trade Partners, 1990-1991 (in billion $)

	Indian Exports	Indian Imports	Total
1. U.S.	3.4	2.6	6.0
2. U.S.S.R.	2.1	1.1	3.2
3. Japan	1.9	2.6	4.5
4. U.K.	1.3	2.3	3.6
5. West Germany	1.2	2.5	3.7
TOTAL	9.9	11.1	21.0

Source: Ministry of Commerce, Government of India, New Delhi

ready visible. In 1988, the deficit came down to $508 million, and declined further in 1989 to $352 million, although it again increased in 1990 to $770 million.

There are many indications that support a favorable climate for U.S. exports to India. Indian manufacturers will need plants and machinery to modernize their factories. Similarly, the government's plan to expand phone services and generally to boost the quality of India's infrastructure through computerization and automation of the service sector should create new opportunities. These needs would translate into opportunities for U.S. businesses to export to India goods and services which are on India's priority list: capital goods, electronics, specialized machinery, high-technology products, fertilizer and chemical plants, oil drilling and exploration equipment, vegetable oils, and transportation and telecommunication equipment.[4]

While U.S. exports to India will increase, it is unrealistic to expect a developing country, committed to sustained economic growth, to live on imported goods. Thus, India may continue to enjoy a trade surplus against the U.S. It is neither odd nor unfair if we note that Indians spend over one percent of their income on American goods while Americans spend less than one-fifteenth of one percent of their incomes on Indian goods. In spite of the fact that the two nations are far apart in their economic well-being, the weaker nation should not be expected to engage in trade in absolute terms at the same level.

U.S. DIRECT INVESTMENT IN INDIA

The U.S. direct investment in India has been small. In addition to India being half a world away, restrictions on the private sector and Indian government policies protecting domestic industry caused most U.S. business firms to view India as a difficult country in which to do business. Yet even under such circumstances, many American businesses entered the Indian market, attracted by India's market size, land and labor resources, increasingly self-sufficient industrial base, and stable democratic form of government.

Particularly since the late 1970s, U.S. business has become more responsive to commercial opportunities in India. Gradual changes have made India a more interesting and receptive market. The Indian government now places greater emphasis on increasing production and expanding the role of market forces in resource allocation. New policies have begun to provide for greater access to imports of technology, machinery, equipment, and intermediate inputs to modernize Indian industry.

Level of Investment Activity

India's relaxation of its regulation of foreign investment and collaborations has led to a substantial increase in the presence of U.S. business. From 1957 to 1979, as shown in Exhibit 6-6, the number of U.S. collaboration proposals approved by the Indian government averaged 51 a year; from 1985 to 1988, the annual average was 194. Throughout the 1980s, India had more collaborations with the United States than with any other country (see Exhibit 6-6). For example, in 1988 the U.S. had 191 new project approvals, followed by West Germany (149), the United Kingdom (122), and Japan (71). The U.S. firms are also leaders in terms of equity participation.[5] The value of U.S. investment has also grown rapidly. After averaging $9.6 million during the three years prior to Rajiv Gandhi's accession to power, it rose to an annual average of $35.9 million from 1985 to 1988 and peaked at $65 million in 1988, as shown in Exhibit 6-7. At the end of 1990, the U.S. investment in India was estimated at $350 million. These sums are small in relation to overall U.S. foreign direct investment, but they indicate a growing appreciation of busi-

EXHIBIT 6-6. Approvals for Foreign Collaborations and Investment

	Total Collaborations			Financial Collaborations			Investment Approved		
	All Countries	U.S.	U.S. as Percentage of all Countries	All Countries	U.S.	U.S. as Percentage of all Countries	All Countries*	U.S.*	U.S. as Percentage of all Countries
1957-79	5,706	1,175	21	--	--	--	--	--	--
1980	526	125	24	--	--	--	--	--	--
1981	389	85	22	--	--	--	--	--	--
1982	590	110	19	113	24	21	628	50	8
1983	673	135	20	129	32	25	619	139	22
1984	752	147	20	151	37	25	1,130	89	8
1985	1,024	197	19	238	66	28	1,261	399	32
1986	957	189	20	240	71	30	1,070	295	27
1987	853	196	23	242	90	36	1,077	295	27
1988	926	191	21	282	71	25	2,261	971	43
1989	1,228	265	22	320	90	28	2,588	1,050	40
1990	930	195	21	272	68	25	2,105	842	40

*In millions Rupees
Source: Indian Investment Center, New Delhi

EXHIBIT 6-7. Foreign and U.S. Investment in India (in million US $)

	U.S. Investment	Total Foreign Investment
1981	2.8	13.7
1982	5.7	70.6
1983	14.4	48.3
1984	8.7	109.7
1985	33.5	105.8
1986	25.0	91.0
1987	20.0	98.4
1988	65.0	121.0
1989	95.5	194.3
1990	79.9	132.8
TOTAL	350.5	985.6

Source: Indian Investment Center, New Delhi

ness opportunities within India, especially in the areas of computers, telecommunications, and food processing.

Attractive Industries

As mentioned above, at the end of 1990, U.S. investment in India was estimated at $350 million. The major proportion of these investments has been in chemicals, pharmaceuticals, fertilizer, and electronics. Recent American entrants into the Indian market include Tektronic, General Electric, Digital, and DuPont. Although most U.S. collaborations in India are concentrated in high-technology areas, General Foods has a joint venture to produce freeze-dried coffee and powdered drinks, while Pepsi's joint venture will make soft drink concentrate, along with fruit juice concentrates and snack foods. Hasbro and Mattel have joint ventures to manufacture toys, while Timex will manufacture watches. The Kellogg Company will manufacture and market ready-to-eat cereal products.

Small U.S. firms also have negotiated successful ventures in India. Bry-Air, Inc., a manufacturer of industrial drying equipment, set a record by establishing the first Indo-U.S. joint venture in the small-scale manufacturing sector in 1980.

Due to competing demands in India for foreign exchange, the outflow of foreign exchange for direct investment abroad is limited. According to the Bureau of Economic Analysis of the U.S. Department of Commerce, the value of Indian direct investment in the United States at the end of 1989 was $21 million, largely accounted for by equity in three Indian banks.

Performance of U.S. Companies in India

Overall, U.S. companies have done well in India. This statement is supported by an empirical study on the working of a sample of 34 Indo-U.S. ventures operating in India, sponsored by the Indo-American Chamber of Commerce. The sample included such well-known names as: Corning Glass, Colgate Palmolive, Goodyear, Ingersoll, Johnson & Johnson, Otis Elevator, Pfizer, and Union Carbide. The major findings of the study are examined below.[6]

a. There has been appreciable growth in sales profits, assets, dividends, equity capital, and retained earnings of all Indo-American ventures.

b. Combined sales of all the companies grew at an average annual compound growth rate of 16 percent in the period 1975-1980; gross profit registered a 15.2 percent annual growth; dividends 19 percent; retained profits 17.8 percent; and equity capital 28 percent.

c. Somewhat unexpectedly, growth of net profit after tax (NPAT) was higher at 14.1 percent than net profit before tax (NPBT), 12.9 percent. Financial ratios, such as NPBT/net worth, dividends/NPAT and retained earnings/NPAT fared reasonably well.

d. Assets expanded briskly. Gross fixed assets grew at a higher average annual compound rate (13 percent) than total assets (12 percent)—indicating that Indo-U.S. joint ventures continued to expand despite restrictions imposed by the government and also that some emphasis was placed on long-term productive resources compared with short-term resources or current assets. This latter trend was particularly noticeable in the case of engineering industries, which expanded their gross fixed assets at a 15 percent rate.

e. Sales doubled during the five years, rising from $710 million in 1975 to $1427 million in 1980–an average annual compound growth rate of 16 percent.

f. Companies producing engineering items and consumer products increased their sales by 18.33 percent and 17 percent, respectively, with pharmaceuticals and chemicals recording growth rates of 13.6 percent and 12.6 percent. Companies involved in manufacturing tires and rubber, and chemicals, however, fared poorly, having 3 percent growth.

g. But it was the picture relating to profits that was most revealing. Gross profits grew at an average annual compound rate of 15.2 percent, with companies in engineering and consumer products picking up 20.6 percent and 17 percent, respectively. Gross profit as a percentage of sales was 23.4 percent in 1975 but slipped to 22.5 percent in 1980, attributed to rising costs of materials, equipment, supplies and wages.

h. In absolute terms, net profit before tax rose from $84.8 million in 1975 to $137.4 million in 1980, and net profit after tax from $34.9 million to $62.2 million. The superior rate of growth of NPAT (relative to NPBT) is indicative of the continuous enhancement of various tax concessions.

i. Industry-wise, the lion's share of the aggregate NPBT (62 percent) accrued in the fields of chemicals and engineering industries; in 1975, the share of chemicals was 39 percent and engineering 23 percent. The position was quite different in 1980, with 50 percent of NPBT going to engineering and only 25.6 percent to chemical and allied industries.

j. The return on shareholders' investment, as measured by NPBT/net worth, increased from 46 percent in 1975 to 49 percent in 1980, while the NPAT/net worth ratio during the period averaged 19.5 percent. These ratios indicate good performance in terms of return on shareholders' funds.

k. Dividends for the 30 companies grew at an average annual rate of no less than 19 percent during the five-year period, rising from $16.5 million in 1975 to $30.9 million in 1980.

Earnings retained each year grew by 17.8 percent during the period.

l. While the average ratio of dividends to NPAT was maintained around 50 percent, the increasing rates of profits allowed companies to perform well in terms of escalating dividends and driving for internal capital expansion. In fact, in 1980, companies which declared dividends to the extent of 12 percent or higher on par value formed 56 percent of the sample. One result was that the high dividend payment policy had a direct impact on their share values. Reflecting this, the current market values of the shares of some of the companies in the sample stand at more than ten times the paid-up value.

This goes to show the financial strength of the companies and the buoyancy of the capital market, besides illustrating the long-term growth prospects for joint ventures in India.

m. The net worth of the 30 companies during 1975-80 grew by 12.3 percent annually, rising from $256 million to $455 million. Equity capital increased much faster, by 28 percent, reaching a level of $172 million in 1980 compared with $99.8 million in 1975.

n. The well-known point about India being a reservoir of cheap labor power combined with the advantage of rising productivity is made briefly but tellingly in the study. Wages, salary, and bonuses (WSB) grew during this period to a level of $123 million, representing a 12 percent annual growth rate. But the real point was that for every employee's WSB dollar in 1980, a sum of approximately $12 in sales was achieved, generating $1.12 in profit before taxes and 68 cents in profit after taxes. This compared favorably with the figure for 1975, when nine dollars in sales were achieved per WSB dollar, generating one dollar in profit before taxes and 40 cents after taxes.

o. There may be perpetual cavilling at level of corporate taxes in India, but the specific conclusion drawn about the relevant "burden" of the sample companies in the period 1975 to 1980 is revealing. Provision for taxation rose from $47.9 million to $75.7 million. However, there was actually a continuous decline in the effective tax rate–from 57.96 percent in 1975 to 55.3 percent in 1976, 55.1 percent in 1977, 52.9 percent in

1978, 48.5 percent in 1979, and 48.4 percent in 1980. The reduction in surcharge on tax for the corporate sector in 1981-82 was estimated to bring down the average effective tax rate by another two to three percent.

Financially, Indo-U.S. business collaborations have done exceedingly well in India. At the same time, it is not generally realized that India has an unblemished and quite enviable record of permitting full remission of dividends, profits, and capital. In this respect, India treats foreign shareholders exactly the same as Indian shareholders. Many developing countries encounter periodic foreign exchange shortages and India is no exception. However, a shortage of foreign exchange for the import of capital goods and raw materials has never been allowed to stand in the way of repatriation of capital or remittance of dividends, interest, or other dues. In this way India is perhaps unique among the developing countries.

As far as India is concerned, the collaborations have offered an impressive array of goods and services and have made significant contributions to the Indian economy by providing products from air conditioning and refrigeration equipment to jeeps, from petrochemicals to power generation, from synthetic rubber and tires to electronic equipment, from toiletries to industrial glass and glass fibre, from industrial compressors, machine tools, and hand tools to pharmaceuticals and antibiotics. The list of products manufactured is long and well representative of the demands of a growing economy. In addition, it indicates the considerable benefits derived from product diversification and the import of state-of-the-art relevant technology. In sum, from all indications, the Indo-U.S. joint venture collaborations have been mutually beneficial.

Future Outlook for Direct Investment

Economic liberalization in India continues but at a modest pace. The policymakers remain cautious, in part to avoid risking further balance-of-payments instability. Nevertheless, the policy reforms do appear to be having an economic impact. There has been an increase in domestic competition fostered by liberalized licensing regulations and more flexible import policies. In addition, the Indian government is growing more willing to permit Indian firms to establish joint ventures with foreign firms in order to modernize production and improve quality. While India's economy is characterized by government ownership of a significant portion of the industrial sector, particularly in capital-intensive heavy industries, the private sector is leading the expansion of the manufacturing base. This expansion will continue to offer opportunities to foreign firms both to sell certain products and to establish joint ventures in India, particularly in high-technology areas such as electronics, computers, and telecommunications equipment. With respect to limits on foreign equity ownership, the government now permits 51 percent equity in a variety of industries and up to and including 100 percent foreign ownership in certain high-priority, generally high-technology areas. In addition, the government now authorizes equity ownership by foreign firms in existing Indian firms without approval.

A trend toward more liberal economic policies and a pace of steady economic growth are leading increasing numbers of U.S. companies to explore business opportunities in India. While opportunities abound in virtually any field, the following industries especially look promising.[7]

Telecommunications

With India allocating some $10 billion for communications in its next five-year plan (1990-95), opportunities abound, especially in transmission, components, and microwave/radio technologies.

Electronics

Foreign firms' opportunities have multiplied as a result of extensive liberalization of imports associated with computerization policies and development of an indigenous electronics industry.

Food Processing and Packaging Equipment

Imports of equipment and technology are on the rise as liberalization proceeds and India's industry invests in new capacity to meet opportunities fostered by government policies and changing consumer attitudes.

Mining and Extraction Equipment

New private and public investment for mining development and construction projects, running at $1.5 billion annually, is boosting the market for mining and extraction equipment.

Electric Power Transmission and Distribution Equipment

With nearly one-third ($30 billion) of the current five-year plan's development expenditures aimed at increasing power generation, India should be a major market for imported equipment and technology.

Oil and Gas Field Equipment and Services

In recent years, India has spent over $2 billion annually on equipment and services and will continue to give high priority to this sector.

THE OMNIBUS TRADE AND COMPETITIVENESS ACT AND THE FUTURE OF INDO-U.S. RELATIONS

In May 1989, the United States threatened India with sanctions under the Omnibus Trade and Competitiveness Act of 1988. The Office of the U.S. Special Trade Representative (USTR) specified three key issues for negotiation. It identified India's restrictions on foreign direct investment and the government monopoly over the Indian insurance industry. It also placed India on a "priority watch list" because of its weak protection of intellectual property rights.

Using the Omnibus Trade Act to advance U.S. interests requires considerable political finesse. U.S. negotiators must defend legitimate concerns raised within the American political system, but they must also take into account the politics in targeted countries in order to avoid exerting pressures that might lead to counter-productive outcomes. As noted above, India has made modest progress over the last few years in relaxing its restrictions on foreign direct investment. The public pressure entailed in the U.S. Trade Representative's demands complicates new reform initiatives since they provide ammunition to the opponents of reform. The USTR's negotiations in the area of life insurance may regenerate more anti-American resentment than progress since the Indian government is reticent to curtail the monopoly of the Life Insurance Corporation of India—one of the linchpins of India's social welfare system. In the area of intellectual property rights, the weak provisions of India's Patent Act of 1970 are the primary concern. The Act was specifically designed to facilitate the absorption of new technology by weakening patent protection. It denies patent coverage for products and grants protection only to production processes in areas such as pharmaceuticals, semiconductors, and biotechnology.[8] The Patent Act has facilitated the Indian pharmaceutical industry's efforts to undercut U.S. multinationals in the Indian market and rapidly expand into global markets.[9] American pressure must overcome the resistance of the Indian Drug Manufacturers Association—a powerful lobby, whose membership has reaped immense benefits from the current law.

The high public profile of the U.S. announcement that it would initiate negotiations with India limited the possibilities for progress on legitimate concerns and made negotiations difficult for both countries. The U.S. should avoid overestimating its leverage and sacrificing the positive aspects of Indo-American relations. In the long term, American interests are best served by building support for its concerns within India. This is best accomplished through constructive dialogue and encouraging economic reforms that enhance India's experience with free trade, foreign investment, and the protection of intellectual property.

INDO-U.S. BUSINESS RELATIONS: PARTNERSHIP IN SCIENCE AND TECHNOLOGY

Over the past decade, the importance of science and technology in Indo-U.S. relations has increased considerably. The Indo-U.S. Sub-Commission on Science and Technology has become a vital element of Indo-U.S. relations. The Sub-Commission includes working groups in seven areas: health, medical, and life sciences; physical and material sciences; earth sciences; atmospheric and marine sciences; energy; environment and ecology; and informatics. These working groups currently preside over more than ninety-five projects involving the collaboration of Indian and U.S. scientists.

Although promoting Indo-U.S. cooperation is an important objective of this program, the benefits provided to U.S. science alone are sufficient justification. A recent study of Indian science conducted by the U.S. National Science Foundation (NSF) found that Indians are performing world-class research in chemistry, physics, microelectronics, biotechnology, and materials science.[10] The NSF applies virtually the same rigorous scientific standards to its review of Indo-U.S. proposals as it does to domestic project proposals. The projects are a bargain because the costs of doing research in the United States are much higher than in India. The exchanges have also led to substantial purchases of U.S. scientific equipment and to closer interaction among influential scientific opinion leaders.

Indo-U.S. scientific cooperation is likely to bring even greater benefits over the long term. Scientific discovery is increasingly an *international* enterprise. As expertise diffuses throughout the globe, maintaining contact with the scientific communities of other countries has become essential to keeping abreast of new advances. In addition, problems such as global warming, erosion of the ozone layer, and various other concerns are increasingly global in scope. International scientific cooperation is essential to their solution. It accelerates the development of new approaches, and it spreads common understandings that facilitate apportioning the costs that must be borne to maintain a healthy global environment.

Hopes for expanded Indo-American scientific cooperation may have suffered a setback in October 1989, when the State Department was ordered to establish a special review process for all new proposals for scientific cooperation with the potential for generating intellectual property. The review process must carefully balance American concerns for intellectual property rights with the potential benefits of Indo-American scientific cooperation if it is to avoid creating a bureaucratic bottleneck that would deter the development of new projects.

India's efforts to promote the technological capabilities of its private sector present a second area of mutual benefit. In the past few years, the U.S. Agency for International Development (USAID) has developed some innovative programs that benefit U.S. as well as Indian business concerns. The Programs for the Advancement of Commercial Technology (PACT) exemplifies the new approach. It helps set up joint ventures between Indian and U.S. firms that share interests in developing particular products. PACT provides a conditional grant to support their pre-manufacturing research and development costs. The joint ventures repay twice the original grant after they begin production. PACT was initiated in the fall of 1986 with a provision of $10 million. As of December 1989, it had approved eighteen projects in areas such as computer software, agriculture, and chemicals. These projects augment the technological capabilities of Indian firms. Since many of them are designed to produce exports to third countries, they increase India's exports as well. PACT provides U.S. firms with opportunities to jointly develop new products with access to India's lower research costs. It facilitates their entrance into the Indian market and enables them to accumulate experience in operating in the Third World.

CONCLUSION

The international economy has developed a tier of countries that can be characterized as "transitional" economies. India shares the three basic characteristics of this group. First, it is undergoing a change from extensive to intensive development; economic growth is no longer driven so much by exploiting new resources as by increasing productivity through the introduction of new technologies. Second, India is attempting to rearticulate its economic institutions in ways that promote more efficient utilization of resources. Third, India has achieved sophisticated production capabilities in some sectors.

Transitional economies such as India present both opportunities and challenges to the United States. The opportunities come from the opening up of their economies, their eagerness to acquire new technologies, and their growing capabilities in science and technology. The challenges stem from their growing emphasis on export-led growth and their international competitiveness in certain sectors. Finding ways to establish mutually beneficial relations may be trying at times, since these countries have their own agendas and are not about to allow the United States to impose its will upon them. Nevertheless, these relations will become increasingly important since transitional economies such as India are certain to become more consequential global actors.

In the past, India leaned toward the Eastern Bloc for needed technical assistance. Today, India is leaning heavily toward the Western world for increased trade, expanded investment, and cutting edge technology. With economic liberalization in progress, India should potentially be a very lucrative market for U.S. firms.

Chapter 7

Problems of Doing Business in India

India's colonial past, huge population of 850 million people, zealous concern for self-sufficiency, and self-perception as a regional power put constraints on the extent and kind of business activities that foreign enterprises may pursue in India. Population exerts a strong pressure toward maintaining and enhancing high levels of employment which encourages labor-intensive measures in the economy. The insistence on self-sufficiency does not allow a total freedom of investment for foreign capital and makes protection for native industry obligatory; and the perception of regional power necessarily requires large defense expenditures in the foreseeable future. These factors should temper the comparison of India with the newly industrializing Pacific powers.

India has enacted a variety of laws to pursue its national objectives which foreign companies find troublesome. Interestingly, the problems are not as severe as they appear, particularly in light of the recent liberalization measures. As a matter of fact, given India's difficulties and its large market, the problems vis-à-vis the opportunity in India may be no different than elsewhere.

Geopolitical realities, however, have always stood in the way of establishing cordial political relations between India and the U.S. Unfortunately, U.S. businessmen depend more on biased perceptions and commentaries issued by the U.S. government for evaluation of business opportunities in India than on their own analyses. The problems that multinational businesses frequently associate with India may be grouped in three categories: political/legal hindrances, problems of underdevelopment, and geopolitical differences.

POLITICAL/LEGAL HINDRANCES

Politically India adopts a negative attitude toward foreign investment. It limits equity stakes, bans certain fields, and has labyrinthine licensing procedures. Potential investors are told that "India does not normally resort to nationalization." Not normally, but just on odd occasions. The government considers that the main purpose of foreign investment is to transfer technology; incentives for creating jobs are few. In addition, to invest in India, a company must be willing to "indianize" production. Briefly, a foreign investor faces endless political/legal difficulties in India. In the midst of these difficulties, foreign enterprises should completely write off India. But in recent years more and more U.S. companies–Texas Instruments, Pepsi, Kellogg, Timex–have been seeking entry into India. This is because the political/legal difficulties are partly real and partly hearsay.

Political Instability

When discussing India with an American businessman, usually the first issue raised is political instability. The American is likely to put forth the opinion that the Indian government is a shaky structure prone to unpredictable swings and wide-ranging oscillations in politics and economics.

But the reality is something else. In 1991 India held its tenth general election in which a new government was elected in a fair and free manner. So far, except for a brief period in the 1970s, India's politics have been dominated by a single party. In the last election this dominant party failed to secure majority and now heads a minority government. Minority governments by their very nature are weak since major policy decisions require mutual accommodation which is time-consuming and likely to render the policy ineffective. Despite that, within a month or so of swearing in the government adopted a bold program for deregulating the economy. Briefly, responsible people in India, both within government and outside, feel that in light of changing times, its commitment to the public sector, stringent restrictions on foreign investment, and protection to domestic industries must change. Looking at it differently, India as a democracy is beginning to attain maturity. If the initial steps taken by the Rao government to further liberalize the economy are any indication, India is likely to have more stable, consistent, and globally relevant policies henceforth. It is also relevant to note that India has come to spawn its own MNCs and, as a result, the government is more relaxed about MNC operations in India.

When American corporations look toward other developing countries, China for instance, which is economically positioned in similar situation as India, they accept with equanimity a far greater threat than India has ever been. The 1989 occurrence in Tiananmen Square is a case in point. The interest of the American government as well as the level of U.S. business in China did not change perceptibly despite the atrocities against the political opponents. Yet in India, even an insignificant incident, such as IBM's withdrawal, makes U.S. business raise its eyebrows.

India's value as an established democracy and as a large, viable market is long term. The question is, if American government and business are willing to stand behind and encourage a country that shares American values of freedom and righteousness in her endeavors to uplift herself economically.

Despite her large market, U.S. companies hesitate in exploring India. They are apprehensive about India's investment climate. In reality, these apprehensions are caused by myths which the Indian government has failed to dispel.

Restrictions on Equity Investment

It was commonly believed by U.S. firms that Indian law and/or government policy restricted any and all foreign investment to 40 percent. In reality, there was no such law and no such policy. While the government's guidelines indicated that foreign holdings should be up to 40 percent, this is exactly what it purported to be: a guideline, and was not of inflexible, universal applicability. Whether and, if so, how much investment would be allowed by the government was determined by pragmatic considerations of national economic development and not by a rigid inflexible rule, law, or policy.[1]

The ultimate decision on foreign investment involved an evaluation of various aspects of the project such as the technology brought in, the import substitution, the export obligation, the role of the particular industry in national priorities, etc. On the basis of these criteria, the government evaluated the needs for and extent of investment required. Significant majority holdings were permitted if, for example, the technology was very high, very scarce, and very valuable to India. Even 100 percent foreign ownership was allowed in, for example, 100 percent export projects. Forty percent, therefore, was, in reality, only a general threshold figure on investment, above which were required specific grounds for higher equity ownership.

Clearly, breaking through India's investment barrier has been relatively easy. As *Business International* states:[2]

> The single largest disincentive for MNCs wanting to invest in India is a 40 percent barrier on equity investment by companies based overseas. Theoretically, this limitation prevents majority foreign ownership. Although the new National Front government isn't likely to amend the Foreign Exchange Regulation Act (FERA) and raise the equity barrier to 51 percent soon, some MNCs have found ways to circumvent the regulations.
>
> Contrary to widely held belief, no rules or laws exist that restrict all foreign investment to 40 percent or less: India even allows 100 percent foreign ownership, subject to certain conditions. The 40 percent figure is a guideline MNCs can overcome through several kinds of investments:
>
> (a) *High-technology ventures.* New Delhi permits foreign equity investment of greater than 40 percent in new enterprises when the overseas partner is transferring high or closely held technology. Since "high technology" hasn't been defined, however, it's left to the bureaucracy to determine what qualifies.
>
> In the past, several MNCs have been granted stakes larger than 40 percent by investing in such ventures. In 1988, U.S.-based Halliburton was granted a 60 percent stake in Halliburton Oil Field Services (India) Ltd., which last year began to produce well-completion equipment and cement additives and to perform specialized oil-field services. Two Indian partners—TIL and Dai-ichi Karkarkia—provide equipment and chemicals for the joint venture (JV). Sweden's Kanthal-Hoganas was allowed a 51 percent stake in an iron-powder venture; the technology used is considered proprietary.

(b) *Export-oriented ventures.* MNCs may hold more than 40 percent equity if most of the output is sent abroad. If 100 percent of output is exported, a firm may even win wholly owned status. Gunther of West Germany holds a 63.5 percent stake in Switching Technology Gunther, a Madras venture that began turning out reed switches late last year. Sumitomo has been permitted a 49 percent stake in its JV with the All India Handloom Cooperative Society, which will manufacture garments using technology from Japan's Shuno Apparels.

Other examples include Texas Instruments, Hewlett-Packard, and ANZ Bank, all of which received approval for setting up 100 percent-owned software-development units in Bangalore. In the Santa Cruz Exports Processing Zone, the three 100 percent foreign-owned units—Eastern Peripherals, Semeon Electronics, and Ultratek Devices—will export at least 75 percent of their production.

(c) *Ventures in partnership with the International Finance Corp. (IFC).* On a case-by-case basis, the IFC's equity may be excluded from FERA tenets, paving the way for majority foreign ownership in new JVs. The IFC cannot sell its stake without the foreign firm's approval. West Germany's Unicardan, the first to use this facility, took a 40 percent stake in Invel Transmissions Ltd. The IFC invested 20 percent; the rest was dispersed to the Indian public. Invel manufactures constant-velocity joints for Maruti Cars and light commercial vehicles. Japan-based Mikuni also teamed up with the IFC to launch carburetor and fuel-pump manufacturer UCAL Fuel Systems Ltd. Mikuni and the local promoter each hold 26 percent, and the IFC maintains 20 percent. (The remaining 28 percent will be sold to the Indian public.)

(d) *Ventures in partnership with nonresident Indians of Indian Nationality or Origin (NRIs).* NRIs may subscribe to any firm's new issues, provided they agree not to seek repatriation of capital or income at any time. Thus, a foreign company in partnership with individual NRIs or an NRI trust can get controlling or majority ownership even if its direct investment is limited to 40 percent. Companies such as Schlumberger and Michelin are reported examining this route for their local JVs.

As mentioned above, the 40 percent equity limit was a guideline. But India failed to make the point clear to prospective investors. The new policy, however, has specifically raised the limit on foreign equity to 51 percent to avoid any misunderstanding. As a matter of fact, the new policy goes much further permitting foreign investment, with majority control, in a number of industries which were hitherto forbidden.

Lower Profitability of Investment in India

In some circles it is believed that investment in India is not profitable. Experience of foreign companies, however, shows that investment in India is profitable and compares favorably with the investment in other industrially developed nations. This conclusion is empirically supported by studies conducted by the Indo-American Chamber of Commerce discussed in Chapter 6,[3] and the Federation of Indian Chambers of Commerce and Industry (FICCI).

The study undertaken by FICCI covering 36 Indo-U.S. collaborated companies during 1978-79 to 1982-83 showed that their growth has been good, profits high, remittances comparable, and royalties satisfactory. The following are the major findings of the study:[4]

	1978-79	1982-83	Personal Compound Growth
	(in million $)		
Assets	176.3	567.5	19.71
Equity Capital	73.8	109.4	10.37
Net Sales	840.1	1,589.4	17.28
Net Profit	27.1	58.5	20.56

In four years, net profits of U.S. companies operating in India have increased over 20 percent, while sales grew 17 percent. This shows that between 1978-1979 and 1982-1983 U.S. companies considerably improved their profitability in India. Interestingly, this happened during a worldwide recessionary period.

Restrictions on Repatriation of Profits

India has a unique record of honoring international commitments. Repatriation of earnings by foreign investors on account of profits, dividends, technical know-how fees, and royalties, etc., are freely allowed. India has never defaulted on dividend remittances even during the most serious foreign exchange crisis. Once a collaboration is approved by the government of India, dividend remittances are automatic.

Until recently, the maximum royalty allowed was 5 percent for a period of five years. This has been raised to 8 percent for a period of 10 to 15 years.[5] Tax concessions are provided on royalties and technical service fees. Royalties and technical service fees were taxed at 52.2 percent until 1976. Since then, the rate has been lowered to 30 percent.[6] Special tax concessions are provided to foreign technicians working in India for a period of 48 months.

As in the case of dividends, remittance of royalties and technical service fees is automatic, as long as they are within the initial terms of the collaboration agreement.

Inadequacy of Infrastructure

India's infrastructure has been considered inadequate to sustain foreign investment. Of course, India's infrastructure is no match for the conditions in the industrialized countries. But despite its large population, India has a fairly good infrastructure to support foreign enterprises.

India has one of the best infrastructures in terms of transport, communications, commerce, banking, technical training institutes, trained manpower, supporting services, etc., among the developing countries. India's rail network is the fourth largest in the world. All major cities are linked by air. There are five major ports and five international airports. In addition to regular postal services, voice and teleprinter communication through telephones, telexes, cables, teleprinters, and fax are in service. But the telephone and telex system may not be comparable in efficiency. It is a problem that the government has already started tackling.

Total power output of the country is growing at 20 percent annually. India has a power problem in some pockets of the country today, but the problem will be overcome within the next ten years, as the four super thermal power stations become operational.[7]

India has entered the satellite age in communications, and jet age in transportation. There is a national power grid connected to a chain of super thermal, hydro, and nuclear power stations, and many more power stations are being set up.

Heavy Taxes

It is claimed that heavy taxes negatively affect return on investment in India. In reality, such a claim is more of a perception than a fact. Under the Indian tax laws, there is no discrimination between Indian companies owned by Indians and by foreigners. But the Indian companies are taxed on their worldwide income while foreign companies are taxed only on Indian income. However, the profits of the branches of foreign companies are taxed at a rate higher than the Indian companies for the reason that the dividends in the hands of the nonresident shareholders in such cases would not be taxed in India.

The corporate tax rate in India is 60 percent. But very few companies pay this level of tax. A variety of tax incentives are offered that substantially reduce the tax burden.[8] These incentives are comprised of depreciation, investment allowance, export incentives, tax holiday for select new industrial undertakings of up to 25 percent of profits for eight years, exemption from tax of up to 20 percent of profits for ten years for industries set up in designated backward areas, and amortization of cost of patent rights. With adequate tax planning, companies can cut down their tax burden to less than 20 percent of profits.

Unreliable Business Partners

Indian joint venture partners have been held unreliable, causing problems for U.S. investors through unscrupulous means. There have been rare examples of Indian partners creating problems. On the contrary, able and qualified Indian businessmen can help U.S. companies to develop and grow in India.[9] Of course, the choice of the right Indian partner is important for success.

Different Accounting System

Many U.S. businessmen found the Indian accounting system different and, hence, difficult to comprehend. This is unbelievable since India essentially follows the double entry system of accounting which is most widely used worldwide. There are differences between the U.S. system and the Indian system in the kind and amount of information disclosed and the manner in which it is disclosed, but such differences exist between European and the U.S. accounting system, too.

Additionally, a number of American accounting firms (e.g., Arthur Andersen, Price Waterhouse) operate in India. These firms can help a U.S. subsidiary in India to supply audited financial statements conforming with U.S. norms.

Labor Unrest

Labor unrest in India is distracting for manufacturing operations to run smoothly. Industrial relations in India have progressed along democratic lines, similar to the U.S. and U.K. But inasmuch as India is a developing country, the labor movement is still emerging. Mostly, labor unrest in a democratic society is only vocal. The experience of a single company, if bad on this score, cannot be generalized. Furthermore, there has been noticeable improvement, with the number of strikes and lockouts continuously decreasing.

India, in true democratic tradition, firmly believes that industrial relations not only have to continue but have to be enhanced, and problems between management and labor should be resolved through negotiations.

Inadequate Property Protection

Intellectual property rights (trademarks, patents, copyrights, and design) in India are considered insecure. Here again, there is a problem of perception. There is a highly developed state of the law on the subject in India, providing substantial protection to foreigners, and it compares favorably with other nations similarly placed.

As far as the trademarks are concerned, in the United States the right to a trademark is based on the use of the trademark and belongs to the person who is the first to use the trademark. In India, however, as a practical matter, a trademark generally goes to the person who is the first to register it. Therefore, expeditious and proper registration is the only effective way to protect trademark rights in India. As far as possible, a foreign company should try to ensure that there are no deficiencies in its trademark registration. If a foreign company has a properly registered trademark, in some ways the Indian trademark law gives it better protection than the U.S. law. It is very common in India to get an interim ex-parte injunction restraining an infringer from using a registered trademark or a trademark which is deceptively similar to it. Such a relief is rarely granted in the United States except in the case of counterfeit goods.[10]

It has been frequently alleged that the duration of patent protection in India is inadequate and short. The fact is that, barring some special provisions relating to food, drugs, and chemical processes, the protective period for all other varied, diverse, and numerous fields of invention is reasonable and fairly standard. The period of 14 years applicable to these fields compares favorably with the period in several other countries in Asia and elsewhere such as China (15 years), Malaysia (15 years), Philippines (17 years), Korea (12 years), Sri Lanka (15 years), and Thailand (15 years).[11] Considering the pace at which technology is moving now, the period of 14 years may seem even more reasonable now than it did when the Indian Patents Act was passed.

Regarding the duration of the patent process relating to food, drug, and chemicals, the duration ought to be seen in a certain perspective in which food and drug items which are essential and fundamental to the health and life of the nation are viewed by developing countries. Frequently, patent holding companies have exploited their leverage by charging exorbitant prices. A Swiss firm was reportedly importing a certain patented drug at Rs. 5555 ($278) per kg whereas a Delhi firm was able to procure it at Rs. 312 ($16) per kg. Another patent holding firm was alleged to be charging Rs.

230 ($12) per gram for vitamin B12 whereas the price at which it was available in other countries was Rs. 90-100 ($5-$6) per gram. Still another was alleged to be charging Rs. 60,000 ($3,000) per kg for a drug but it was claimed that, on a warning by the import controller, the price was quickly reduced by the company to Rs. 16,000 ($800).[12] So much and so serious, in fact, was the concern about such pricing policies and practices of patent holding companies in respect to developing countries that even in the United States, a committee of the U.S. Senate (Kefauver Committee) was constrained to make specific mention that the prices of certain drugs and antibiotics in India were among the highest in the world and that India was one of the highest-priced nations.[13]

Further, India is not the only developing country where food and drug products are not patentable. Brazil, Mexico, Greece, Turkey, and even some developed countries such as Austria and Taiwan have no legal provision for patenting food items and drugs.[14]

Another provision of India's Patents' Act that has generated criticism from the American business community is the one that provides for compulsory licensing. This provision, it is argued, is a deterrent to registering patents and transferring technology to India. Such an argument totally misconceives the position of such provisions in patent legislation. Most countries, developed or developing, with the almost singular exception of the United States, have such a provision. This emanates from the basic philosophy underlying intellectual property protection which has been brought out eloquently by the body coordinating the Paris Convention, the World Intellectual Property Organization (WIPO). Among major countries that currently have compulsory licensing in their legislation are Brazil, England, Germany, France, Greece, Switzerland, and Sweden.[15]

The above discussion demonstrates that the concept of the importance of intellectual property in India is established soundly at all levels: statutory, administrative, and judicial. The applicable provisions do, as they indeed must, take into account the felt necessities of the times but this is not done at the cost of the foreign enterprises. The comparisons cited here show that India is not out of step and in fact enjoys perhaps the longest history and experience in these matters in the developing world. Further, the government of India shows a clear intent and willingness to change and adapt in the matter as times and needs require.

Bureaucratic Delays

India is commonly charged with red tape and bureaucratic delays in investment approval procedures. To an extent, this is true. Indian bureaucracy has been the legacy of the British rulers. Bureaucrats are known worldwide to raise questions and create delays even in simple matters. In India, a developing country committed to democratic principles, bureaucracy has played a key role in keeping the government from falling apart, even under the worst political upheavals. While this has been bureaucracy's positive contribution, it has often become an insurmountable hurdle in clearing the affairs of modern industrial enterprises by raising objections and stalling things on minute matters. Political leadership is fully aware of this problem and has taken steps in recent years to reform the situation, especially during the Rajiv Gandhi days, and now by the Rao government. The government has improved approval systems to serve the objective of accelerated industrial development and has cut down delays in the procedures. A "single window" in the Secretariat for Industrial Approval (SIA) is available. The applicant has to submit the application only to this service point which in turn processes the application and issues necessary clearances and approvals. Specific time schedules have been laid down for issuing various approvals as below.[16]

a. Composite proposals (involving foreign collaboration, industrial licenses and import of capital goods)–90 days
b. Proposals involving foreign collaborations–45 days
c. Proposals regarding industrial licenses–60 days
d. Proposals from companies covered under the Monopolies and Restrictive Trade Practices Act and the Foreign Exchange Regulation Act–90 days
e. Proposals from nonresident Indians–45 days
f. Proposals for 100 percent Export Oriented Units–30 days
g. Proposals from existing companies interested in updating the technology (including release of foreign exchange)–45 days

The current government plans to take additional measures to remove bureaucratic obstacles to industrial growth.

Import Restrictions

India's import policy is highly restrictive, which prohibits importation of raw materials, components, and equipment not available in India. This leads to production delays and increased costs. Traditionally, India had pursued a strict policy of import restrictions with the view of (a) utilizing limited foreign exchange on essential things other than on luxury consumer goods meant for the few rich, and (b) encouraging feasible domestic sources of raw material, components, and equipment. India's import restrictions have stood her in good stead in her worst foreign exchange troubles. India never backed out of its commitment to international institutions for debt servicing, and to multinational corporations in the matter of repatriation of profits.

In the 1980s, it was realized that the Indian economy had come a long way and the import restrictions in the current environment were overbearing. Thus, steps have been taken to decontrol imports on a limited basis. While the liberalization measures viewed in U.S. terms are still highly inadequate, they should be examined in the context of Indian economy. A developing country like India, if it were to maintain monetary discipline and manage its economy in a mature fashion, must use its limited resources wisely. It is neither desirable nor realistic to expect India to match import perspectives of industrialized countries. Measures have been taken to liberalize the import policy on a long-term basis to strengthen the domestic production base and to stimulate exports. Import procedures have been streamlined and the policy is kept valid for a period of three years. Raw materials, components, and equipment not locally available can be brought in.

The policy provides additional incentives for export-oriented units. The country has six Free Trade Zones (FTZs). Units operating in these zones have a five-year tax holiday and freedom to import their requirements. The only condition is that the minimum value added must be 30 percent. One hundred percent export-oriented units have all the facilities of a FTZ unit including a five-year tax holiday, and the minimum value addition criterion is only 20 percent.

U.S. investors can now look at India as the manufacturing base for Middle East and Southeast Asian markets.

Risk of Intervention

Often foreign investment in India is considered unsafe due to threats of nationalization. The critics support their view with reference to IBM and Coca-Cola withdrawing from India under undue pressure. The fact of the matter is that, during independent India's brief history of 45 years, no foreign company has ever been nationalized. The threat of expropriation is nonexistent. Even when native banks were nationalized in the late 1960s, the foreign banks were allowed to conduct business as usual.

Up until 1973, India's foreign investment rules were not spelled out clearly, and each project was considered on its own merit. In that year, India enacted the Foreign Exchange Regulation Act (FERA), which regulates, among other things, the level of foreign ownership in Indian companies. The principal motivation behind the Act has been to conserve India's limited foreign exchange resources. The Act required foreign companies to limit their equity to 40 percent. All 900 companies operating in India at that time, other than IBM and Coca-Cola, conformed to the new guidelines and are continuing to operate successfully. IBM and Coca-Cola were the exceptions. But even they are now having another look at India. Other than Union Carbide, due to the tragedy in its Bhopal Plant, no other foreign company with reference to India has received more publicity than IBM and Coca-Cola concerning their withdrawal from that country. It is interesting how facts have been twisted by the foreign press to India's detriment. It became commonly accepted that Coca-Cola left India because the government wanted to know its secret formula and that similar unrealistic demands forced IBM to quit India. The principal concern of India's Foreign Exchange and Regulation Act (FERA) was with the size of equity ownership, not with seeking foreign corporation's proprietary assets. Like the U.S., India is a common law country. Common law is based on precedents. India has always behaved as a mature country fulfilling its commitment with dignity. There was no reason for such a narrow interpretation of a small sub-section in a large Act to scare away prospective foreign investors from India.

On the other hand, India did a poor job of marketing its measures to save foreign exchange resources (vis-à-vis FERA) adequately. India is naive about marketing at the country level, and its bureaucrats are too arrogant to understand the significance of telling their side of the story properly.

Summary

Perceptions are important. Even if eventually found unjustifiable, they constitute important tools in decision making. In the field of investment regulations and practices, as perhaps in many other fields, India has often been judged more by perceived situations than by established realities, more by the uninformed belief of those who have not done business in India rather than by the demonstrated success of those who have, and more by the exception whereby one or two multinational companies (influenced perhaps by reasons of their own global policy) chose to withdraw rather than go by the rule whereby over 8,000 international ventures operate successfully in India.

PROBLEMS OF UNDERDEVELOPMENT

When judging India as a candidate for foreign investment, MNCs should be sensitive to the fact that, as far as the modern world is concerned, it is a young nation that started from a zero base. In 1950-51, at the time of initiating its first five-year plan of economic and social development, India's per capita income at current prices was barely Rs. 375 (about $15). In 1989-90, the per capita income at current prices rose to Rs. 8575 (about $343), while the population has more than doubled. In other words, in forty years per capita income has gone up 23 times, which is not bad. Yet in worldwide comparisons India ranks as a low-income country, and it is susceptible to all the problems that an underdeveloped economy faces: major dependence on agriculture, limited availability of energy, high rates of population growth, rudimentary facilities for transportation, communication, and so on.[17] These facts of life always create problems in what a country should do and can do. In addition, many historical, geographic, political, and cultural factors are intimately related to achieving economic advancement. For example, constant threats from China and Pakistan make it obligatory for India to outlay huge budget allocations for defense. Despite all these odds, India has committed itself to a democratic way which, in the short run, creates its own problems that must be accepted with magnanimity. After all, freedom has a price, too.

Limited Resources

Theoretically, the significance of free trade has been demonstrated for a long time. But the proponents of free trade missed the importance to a nation of becoming reliant, especially when it is vulnerable to its trading partners due to its overall weak position. Economically, India is no match for the U.S., and if it were to fully subscribe to free trade, its limited foreign exchange resources would disappear on luxury imports for the benefit of less than 2 percent of her population. Back in 1989 India was identified as an unfair trading partner under the U.S. Omnibus Trade and Competitiveness Act of 1988. This required India to take concrete measures to liberalize its trade. About the time that India was being pressured under the U.S. law, it was undergoing its worst foreign exchange situation since independence. At one time, the foreign exchange balances were barely enough to meet the basic commitments (for example, maintenance of foreign diplomatic missions) for two weeks only.[18] From India's standpoint it was a matter of survival, while the U.S. was concerned that India was not buying enough American goods. Unfortunately, America applies the same tone and measures to balance its trade deficit to India, a developing country, as to Japan, a global economic power.

False Comparisons

The economic achievements of Asian "tigers" (South Korea, Hong Kong, Singapore, and Taiwan) are often cited as relevant success stories for developing countries to consider in their own economic ambitions. Consider Singapore, for example. More or less liberal policies have worked well for the country, with the city of Singapore emerging as a world-scale financial center in the Eastern hemisphere. But it would be naive to expect that the prescription that worked well for Singapore would suffice for India as well.[19] Singapore is a city state with a mostly urban and educated population of less than three million. The whole country is smaller than New Delhi both in terms of population and geographic area. India has its own problems and ambitions, and they must be considered in the midst of its own socio-economic, political, and cultural realities.

Cultural Adaptation

India in its economic endeavors decided to pursue a mixed economy whereby both state-owned enterprises and private businesses have a role to play. Considering what India had in terms of infrastructure and basic industries, the government had to take the initiative to spur economic activity. At the same time, politically India pursued the nonalignment course. Putting them together, many MNCs concluded that India would eventually become a socialist country. Such a conclusion missed an important trait of Indian culture that attributes high importance to individual freedom.[20] While history will tell how far India's policies made sense, India adapted its polices to become a true democracy, a secular state comprised of people with different religious beliefs and significant regional differences, speaking 16 different languages. In a way, India seeks values similar to those held dear in the U.S., but India must do so in its own way, given its environment and limitations such as large population and limited resources. Despite the agreement in vision that India and the U.S. share, it is a pity that India should be perceived by U.S. companies differently when it comes to making business decisions.

New Information, New Realities

In the last 20 years a variety of new information, mostly based on research in the U.S., has become available that questions many aspects of doing business. New safety measures must be adopted on production lines. Harmful effects of cigarette smoking require that a warning be given to smokers on each pack. Nuclear waste must be disposed of carefully. Television commercials must be regulated to protect customers—for example, children—who are gullible. All this happened in the U.S. and other industrialized countries over 200 years of industrial revolution. But to the developing countries, this information is readily available.

Often, countries like India impose new restrictions on industrial practices, not to be harsh on multinationals, but simply to take advantage of the new information which, fortunately, is available to them virtually free. Developing countries do not have to go through trial and error to seek ways to protect the environment, workers, and consumers. Since they adopt constructive measures instantly, it appears they are being overprotective, but this is not true.

GEOPOLITICAL DIFFERENCES

Presumably, India and the U.S. should be very close to each other since they both share the same democratic ideology and secularist philosophy. But geopolitical differences have always kept the two countries apart. Unfortunately, U.S. businessmen have taken the political rhetoric at its face value, rendering India as an undesirable place to do business. Political outlook has a short-term orientation so that the views change as circumstances desire. But business decisions must be made with a long-term focus. U.S. businessmen are unaware of what India really is, and India has done little to share its true perspectives with them. Thus, Washington analysis becomes the ultimate word on India for making business decisions.

Point of Conflict

India and the U.S. have no basic conflicts of national significance involving the vital basic interests of the two nations. They have no common borders, they have no competition for resources, and they have no trade war barring the recent skirmishes on India being labeled as an unfair trading partner under Super 301. India-U.S. differences are all about their respective attitudes towards problems of Third World nations and how to solve them.

India, on becoming independent, declared itself nonaligned. Nonalignment involves judging each issue on its own merits.[21] It is different from neutralism which means keeping totally silent on various issues. Nonalignment is truly an American concept. George Washington, in his farewell address, exhorted his fledgling nation not to get involved in entangling alliances (the superpowers of his day were Britain and France).[22] India, as a newly independent country anxious to get ahead in the modern world, simply adapted an American concept which late Secretary of State John Foster Dulles called immoral. The real fact is that there is incongruity between American values, beliefs, and their deeds. The concept of liberty, morality, justice, and fairness is selectively applied and practiced in the U.S.

Following her nonalignment stand, India urged the recognition of China in the early 1950s. The U.S. not only rejected India's stand but labeled India as a communist stooge. Twenty years later, the U.S. went all out to accommodate China as a major nation.

India always maintained that the U.S. commitment to autocratic regimes and provision of large-scale military supplies to them would have a backlash anti-American effect. This indeed happened with many authoritarian rulers that the U.S. supported; for example the Shah of Iran and Philippine's Marcos. One need not be surprised if what happened in these countries were to repeat itself in Pakistan in the not-too-distant future. Even though the former Soviet Union has withdrawn from Afghanistan and the traditional cold war between the West and the communist bloc has ended, the U.S. continues to supply sophisticated arms to Pakistan. America's soft attitude toward Pakistan is unjustifiable. Politically, Pakistan's democracy is a misnomer. Philosophically, its commitment to Islamic fundamentalism could be as dangerous as Iran's. Economically, it has not taken any long-term measures to emerge as a self-sustaining free economy. Frankly, the U.S. has virtually nothing in common with Pakistan. Under these circumstances, it is difficult for India to understand how American interests are served through military aid to Pakistan. The effect of America's Pakistan policy on India, however, is highly negative. It creates a heavy pressure on India's fragile resources since a large chunk of the national budget must be allocated to equipping and maintaining the defense forces.

India would like the U.S. and all other countries to pursue their respective national interests; that is the core of the philosophy of nonalignment. But this enlightened national interest should take into account others' interests and not purely parochial ones.

Comparison with China

China and its over one billion goods- and services-starved consumers look like the promised land to U.S. marketers. In recent years, however, many companies are having second thoughts about China. Where foreign investors once saw rosy prospects, they are now dismayed with the problems one runs into in China. In the latter half of the 1980s, one company after another faced such problems in China as meddling bureaucrats, inflated prices, burdensome taxes, unpredictable legal framework, unproductive workers, and more. With the recent clampdown on political expression and signs of a slowdown in economic reforms, American businesses are realizing that China may be a great place to visit, but not one in which to do business.[23]

In the area of trade, disturbing signs suggest that, even as China seeks access to foreign markets, it intends to be protectionist at home. Especially vexing is the frequent Chinese inclination to delay or rewrite terms.

Despite these problems, China still looks attractive to foreign investors, especially U.S. companies. In comparison, India surprisingly appeals less. Across the board, India has much more to offer to prospective investors than does China. India's upper-crust market compares favorably with China's egalitarian masses. Repatriation of profits from India has never been a problem. English as India's commercial language makes communication easier and more convenient. Politically, India is an established democracy. Problems of infrastructure and bureaucratic meddling may be common in both countries, but the overall attitude and alternative ways of solving problems are more flexible in India than China.

Granted, India is a tough place to do business, but compared to China it looks extremely good. Over the years, India's image has been blurred in the eyes of foreign investors since they expected more from a free country than they received. On her part, India has done little to attract foreign investment which it badly needs.

Further, India's political stands have not been well received in the U.S. It is interesting how, for nonbusiness reasons, U.S. investment and trade with India have suffered. If India takes positive steps to welcome foreign investment and U.S. companies adopt a dynamic long-term attitude, India could emerge as one of America's fastest-growing commercial relationships of the 1990s and beyond.

Future Course

The international situation in the Indian sub-continent will be affected critically by the normalization of relations between India and Pakistan. The relaxation of tensions in bilateral relations has a direct economic effect. It is vitally important for India to cut military spending. India's military spending cuts, however, are dependent on the United States not supplying modern offensive weapons to Pakistan. Those supplies are one of the three obstacles to the normalization of Indo-Pakistani relations (along with Pakistan's nuclear ambitions and its support of Sikh separatists in Punjab and Muslim fundamentalists in Kashmir).

Traditionally, India's close relationship with the former Soviet Union has been looked down upon in the U.S. The political significance of this relationship in light of the dissolution of the former Soviet Union has virtually vanished. As a matter of fact, improvements in U.S.-Soviet and Sino-Soviet relations strengthen India's attempts to normalize its relations with China. The Western press has frequently implied that disagreements with China and Pakistan formed the basis of India's adherence to close relations with the former Soviet Union. It seems likely indeed that India's normalization of relations with China and Pakistan (mainly dependent on the U.S. not supplying arms to Pakistan) should lessen the importance of military assistance from the Soviet Union.

But this decline in India's political interest in contacts with the former U.S.S.R. is likely to be replaced under conditions of the growing significance of economic priorities. India's participation in the international division of labor, like China's, is currently characterized by a divergence between the orientation of its imports (the West) and the locus of its export potential (Russia and neighboring countries in South Asia). The emerging economic reforms in Russia should imply expanded prospects for goods and capital imports, especially light industrial products and electronics from India.[24]

As the military factors behind its relations with the countries of Asia diminish, India's geopolitical decisions will relate more closely to a selection of approaches linked to the international economic situation. Hence, India is likely to intensify its economic relations with South Asian countries (relations with these states can develop in combination and balance with traditional political contacts), Southeast Asian countries (primarily the NICs), Russia, Western Europe, the United States, and Japan. (It will, however, be difficult to balance the exports of the OECD countries of the Indian market in the very near future. The prospects are most favorable for those countries that can solve the credits problem. Ideally, commercial exports should be accompanied by a substantial transfer of concessional resources.[25]) These relationships should pave the way for India to slowly globalize her economy. The net effect of this scenario will be an abundance of opportunities for the U.S. and other foreign companies in a growing market.

On the whole, the climate of U.S.-Indian bilateral relations so far has been determined by the development of political, military, and economic relations of the United States with China and Pakistan. In that context, it is a strange logic that underlies arguments that it is in the U.S. interest first to arm Pakistan (and, thus, form a threat to stability on the continent) and then to support the military ambitions of India in an attempt to make it a counterbalance to Pakistan.

Instead, it would seem that India might today be the focus of U.S. economic policy in Asia. It would make sense to open up a new option for India–a choice between its own military and economic expenditures (rather than the old one between different military and political allies)–while creating conditions making the new option more attractive for India.

CONCLUSION

As to the future, foreign investor-host government relations do not grow without reason. They are shaped by external pressures. This has been true throughout history. India and multinational companies have every incentive to work together and will, therefore, be receptive to innovative business agreements to their mutual advantage. The underlying reason for foreign direct investment in India, as is true of any Third World country, is the same as it has always been: it makes good business sense. Today's India is truly emerging into a viable place to do business. The accusatory rhetoric of the past will soon fade into the background as India and MNCs adapt to each other's needs.

Indeed, India's outlook toward MNCs is undergoing a tremendous change. New contractual arrangements, tailored to the times, are appearing. Joint ventures that permit foreigners to hold majority ownership are quite acceptable. A variety of concessions are available to the joint ventures that would have been unthinkable even one year earlier. Some have gone so far as to make financial guarantees in the form of escrow accounts. These accounts ensure that the foreign investor will have access to earnings even in the face of sudden restrictions on hard currency payments. Other incentives include tax breaks and special rates on electricity.

Chapter 8

Strategies for Market Success in India

At the end of World War II, American business held an unassailable position. It had privileged entree to most of the world outside of the communist bloc. A small percentage of U.S. business moved abroad, concentrating first and quite logically on Europe. It later moved into the somewhat mysterious world of Asia, primarily to those countries where American power was most manifest, namely Japan, Taiwan, and South Korea. American skills in management, personnel, accounting, financing, and production were admired and emulated there.

But today, conditions have changed and the world is a tougher place for American business. Indeed, there is now a disturbing skepticism regarding American business capabilities, and nowhere is it more so than in Western Europe and Japan where American capabilities once were most admired. One dominant element for this skepticism has been the slackening, if not irresolution, of American business efforts.

Global market opportunities, however, still abound. But Americans must move fast and be willing to take a longer term view. A buoyant new market is taking shape in India, with a core group of consumers expected to reach over 300 million at the turn of the century. The preceding chapters highlight the emerging shape of the Indian market.

There have been two main disincentives to investing in India which multinationals find most repelling. First, there has been the unrelenting government control. The government favors some kinds of investments and disdains others. The slow-moving, bureaucratic environment could delay project approval for years. Second, India regulated the strength of foreign investment by restricting foreign ownership of equity to 40 percent.

In recent years, however, controls are being relaxed, though slowly. And there are valid reasons that support continuing liberalization. Further, the new policy announced in July 1991 allows direct foreign investment up to 51 percent equity in 34 groups of high priority industries without prior government clearance. In addition, measures have been taken to streamline the approval process.

Decisions pertaining to foreign investment in India need to be viewed in the overall context of opportunity, political stability, fiscal policies, market potential, and the track record of corporate profitability and growth. If one compares India's investment climate with Asian countries, where things are more encouraging, India looks less attractive. But India is a special case and must be looked at on its own. Whatever India's problems may be (such as mass poverty) 25 years hence, India will be an economic giant and a place where companies ought to be.

Because India is different, the classic framework for evaluating foreign investment projects, emphasizing fast pay-off, may not work. This chapter examines success factors in India, strategies that are based on strengths that India offers to foreign investors. Effective strategies for seeking entry into India are proposed. Keys to managing the strategy are prescribed.

WHAT MAKES INDIA ATTRACTIVE

Emerging developments in India recognize the fact that a substantial market opportunity is available to companies in a hitherto difficult place to do business. Measured in both economic and political terms, India is an attractive market to be in, providing long-term growth opportunity. Exhibit 8-1 lists factors that distinguish India from other developing countries as a viable place for foreign investment.

Market Size

India has a consumption-oriented segment in excess of 200 million people, over three times as many as in France, and is expected

EXHIBIT 8-1. Factors That Make India Attractive

- Market Size

- Skilled Labor

- Common Language

- East European Connection

- Diversified Industrial Base

- Capital Availability

- Adequate Physical and Institutional Infrastructure

- Management Know-How

- Democratic Tradition and Political Stability

- Legislative Framework

- Repatriation of Earnings

- Protection of Intellectual Property

- Independent Judiciary

to reach 300 million by the turn of the century. The rising income is creating a generation of eager consumers.

From designer children's clothes to television sets to mouth fresheners to motorcycles to sportswear to milkshakes to toilet soaps to cooking ranges, a market for an astonishingly wide range of consumer goods and durables has exploded nationwide. There was a time when a few exclusive Western-style stores catered to the elite of the society. Today such retail stores are coming up across the country and increasingly match their Western inspirations in service and range of goods.

Skilled Labor

At a time when labor costs are increasing rapidly in NICs, India offers a feasible alternative. As shown in Exhibit 8-2, the cost of a skilled worker in India is one-seventh compared to southeast Asian "tigers."

Common Language

In a land where 16 official languages are recognized, English stands alongside Hindi with all-India status. As a matter of fact, English, not Hindi or any other regional language, is the commercial language of India.

Technical Labor

India also offers one of the most diverse and affordable labor pools of engineers, scientists, and technicians in the world. For example, a low-level programmer earns $3,700 a year, compared with $30,000 a year in the U.S. Research and development managers are available for $16,000 yearly, compared with $100,000 to $120,000 earned by their American counterparts.[1] It is inexpensive technical labor that has attracted Texas Instruments, Inc. and Hewlett-Packard Company to India. Both are doing in-house software development from installations in a southern Indian city.

EXHIBIT 8-2. Asian Labor Costs (1988)

Average Monthly Wage For Skilled Workers	
South Korea:	$633
Taiwan:	$598
Hong Kong:	$544
Singapore:	$547
India:	$ 75

Source: Business Week, May 15, 1989, p. 46 for all the figures except India which is based on India's Planning Commission Estimates.

East European Connection

India has strong economic ties with Russia and the Eastern European countries in the form of trade pacts that allow trade in Indian rupee instead of hard currency. This provides an opportunity for MNCs to enter Russia and the Eastern European markets. As an example, Hasbro was able to sell thousands of toy tanks for former Soviet children through its joint venture in India, Funskool (India) Ltd. To illustrate further, the Russians were extremely captivated by the toy (Hasbro's G.I. Joe Mobat 6000) and they ordered 100,000 units delivered instantly.[2] Granted, the recent changes are likely to make these markets directly available to Western firms, but East European countries will face hard currency shortages for a long time to come, and meanwhile, foreign firms can reach out to these markets through their Indian joint ventures.

Diversified Industrial Base

Since independence, India has developed a manufacturing base in different industries, from steel to engineering goods, from electronic components to chemicals. Thus, to a large extent for component parts and supplies, a foreign firm does not have to depend on imports.

Capital Availability

India's capital market is well organized and shows no dearth of money. Often, stock offerings are oversubscribed by several times.[3] The profitability and investment capability of private Indian enterprises is similar to companies in the West.

Satisfactory Infrastructure

While India cannot match the infrastructure in the industrialized countries, it has satisfactory road, rail, and air transportation networks. Communication networks and services, however, are below par, although there has been considerable improvement in recent years and the government has immediate plans to modernize telecommunications.

Management Know-How

Thanks to early attempts in establishing management education, India has an adequate supply of leadership ability and advanced business know-how among managers. This strength makes itself felt in a variety of ways: the generally good quality of management cadres, the abundance of knowledge of modern management methods and techniques, and a willingness among managers to work hard to take on positions of leadership and responsibility. With talented, hard-working managers, positive initiatives can provide quick results.

Democratic Tradition and Political Stability

What gaps and shortcomings India does have are, to a large extent, made up for by the fact that it is the world's largest democracy, an unusual achievement in the Third World. Individual freedom and right of property ownership are fully honored and commonly enjoyed. India has made many mistakes in various spheres, but its commitment to democracy has given it a stability that augurs well for the future. Currently, India is undergoing unprecedented changes in the government which cynics may consider signs of instability. Actually these changes are pains of political maturity which only go to strengthen India's commitment to democracy.

Legislative Framework

The constitution of legislative framework for economic activity in India is a mixture of American and European practices, with the exception that the public sector has been accorded a significant place in the economy and self-sufficiency is valued highly.

Past attempts to legalize investment and joint ventures have proven to be too narrow to attract external investors. These laws are now rapidly being changed, and the number of joint ventures is increasing.

Convenient Repatriation of Earnings

India has, without exception, kept its commitment to let foreign investors repatriate earnings as agreed. This commitment has been fulfilled, even when India had severe foreign exchange difficulties.

Protection for Intellectual Property

India has adequate laws for protection of intellectual property comparable to other developing countries. There has hardly been a case of gross misuse of copyrights, trademarks, and brand names belonging to foreign firms.

Independent Judiciary

The Indian judiciary is independent of the executive. The law does not discriminate between Indian companies and foreign companies. There have been some major disputes, but many of these have been settled in favor of foreign companies.[4]

Summary

India serves as a model and an engine of development in South Asia, indeed, along the entire Indian Ocean rim. It serves as an engine in a very real sense. It will be a source of the capital and the technology required for growth, and it will be the region's major market.

Currently, India is digesting the most profound industrial changes in three decades. At times one notices the transition problems in this great leap, creating the impression that India will revert back to past controls. But the newly liberated Indian economy has become so vibrant that turning back is no longer an option. To fully complete the transition, India needs foreign technology and investment.

BUSINESS FOCUS

One common problem with the multinational corporations is applying the same criteria for evaluating investment opportunities in the developing countries as they apply in industrialized countries. They conveniently forget that the environment in the two groups of countries is totally different. As a matter of fact, conditions vary significantly from one developing country to another. For example, compare Mexico and India. India has a big population problem which Mexico does not. India has potentially hostile neighbors,

Pakistan and China, while Mexico's northern neighbor, other things being equal, could provide major stimulus to her economy in various ways. On the other hand, India has a large market with substantial purchasing power, available to be served. India has the third largest pool of scientific personnel in the world. On these measures, Mexico is weak. Thus, in order to win out, the foreign investor should look at opportunities in different nations from a different angle.

Sequencing Intentions

The secret of success in India lies in sequencing the business focus. The sequence comprises three steps: transferring technology, building export strength, and grooming the domestic market.

Technology Transfer

In a variety of industries requiring low technology, India has established substantial strength to serve the domestic market. However, as a matter of policy, the country has decided to slowly become globally competitive. For this transition, India needs foreign technology. While the country relies heavily on Russia for defense technology, it clearly prefers Western and Japanese alternatives in commercial fields.

Japanese companies have been quick to realize and respond to India's need and have established front-line positions in a number of industries. The best known Japanese case is Suzuki Motor Company's $25 million investment in India's automaker Maruti Udyog Ltd. A number of Japanese motorcycle makers have Indian joint ventures. Mitsubishi Electric Corporation, Hitachi Ltd., and Toshiba Corporation have licensed color TV picture tube technology to Indian companies. Fujitsu Ltd. has plans to manufacture fiber-optics equipment in India.[5]

A number of European firms have also established ties in India. West German chemical maker Hoechst, France's Rhone-Poulene, and Britain's Imperial Chemical Industries PLC have joint ventures to produce insecticides. France's Alcatel manufactures telecommunications equipment in India, while Britain's Rank Xerox Ltd. produces copiers.[6]

Major U.S. technology transfer deals in India include Du Pont Company's $100 million deal to manufacture nylon yarn and fabric,[7] General Electric Company's joint ventures to produce computer-controlled machine tool devices, semi-conductors, lightning arresters, and others.[8] A number of U.S. firms including Texas Instruments, Inc., Hewlett-Packard, Digital Equipment, Motorola, and Tandy have software operations in India.[9]

Traditionally, U.S. companies have been behind in their quest of the Indian market. On the other hand, India's main hunger is for U.S. technology. This dilemma can partly be explained by the fact that in the last two decades, thousands of Indian businessmen who were educated in the U.S. are more familiar with American technology than they are with Japanese or European technology. In addition, over one million Indians living in the U.S., including many scientists and high-tech entrepreneurs, act as a major conduit for American technology.

As has been mentioned above, a special attraction for technology-transferring companies in India is the fact that English-speaking engineers and skilled technicians are conveniently available for a relatively low salary. Interestingly, technology-related projects encounter little bureaucratic hassle, with government clearances taking about ninety days compared with years for projects lacking technology edge.[10]

To conclude, the trick to doing good business in India is to transfer meaningful technology so that India can make its own products.

Export Development

Successful globalization of the economy requires liberalization of imports which, in turn, must be supported by a sustained level of exports. Since the mid-1980s, India has adopted a liberal posture for the import of essential items. The government hopes that import liberalization should help in improving the quality of Indian products to world standards, manufactured at competitive prices. In other words, liberal import policies should expose Indian companies to a competitive environment and should encourage them to produce quality products which may be exported, enabling India to keep the trade deficit at a manageable level. If exports are not realized, India could end up with a huge trade deficit leading to an insurmountable foreign exchange crisis. Thus, exports are a lifeline in India's attempt to open its economy to global competition.

Foreign companies interested in India should purposefully make it their business to help the nation in its export drive. As is true for MNCs transferring leading edge technology to India, the government provides a variety of encouragements to exporting firms including tax concessions, a simplified system of drawback facilities, international pricing of rubber, steel, alloys, and other items, exemption of profits derived from export business for tax purposes, and others. Usually, foreign subsidiaries in India have taken a lukewarm interest in promoting India's exports. This is partly explained by the fact that the domestic market is large enough for them to do a lucrative business leaving little interest in exporting. As an empirical study on the subject notes:

> The present study does not reveal any statistically significant difference in either export performance or industry characteristics of export of FCEs (foreign controlled enterprises) and their local counterparts in Indian manufacturing. In view of the captive access to the information and marketing networks of their parents, affiliates of MNEs are generally considered to be better placed to tap international markets than their local counterparts. However, the decision to export from the host country, being an important aspect of the global strategy of the enterprise, is not taken on the basis of advantages alone. In a large economy with a sheltered and growing home market, such as India, inward-oriented marketing strategy appeared a far more attractive option for MNEs than using it as an export platform. Hence, they seemed to have opted for it in the same way as their local counterparts.[11]

Grooming the Domestic Market

India is unique among developing countries since it has a large domestic market. The market represents a large pent-up demand that in the past could not be filled. A variety of regulations and controls discouraged the import and manufacture of consumer goods. In addition, the market is fast expanding.

The strength of the domestic market may be illustrated with reference to the automobile industry: since Suzuki Motor Company's joint venture with Maruti Udyog Ltd. started manufacturing cars in India, passenger car sales increased from 45,000 in 1983 to 200,000 in 1990, with the company cornering a 60 percent share of the market.[12]

While estimates vary, India's middle-class market comprises about 200 million consumers. Although a large majority of these consumers are urban dwellers, they are geographically spread throughout the country and some actually live in rural areas in agriculturally prosperous states.

As examined in Chapter 3, the market development in Third World countries is an evolutionary process marked by different stages. The strategic thrust, the international levers, and, consequently, the key decisions required to serve the Third World markets vary at each stage.

The dynamic character of the market implies that strategic priorities should be tailored to the stage of evolution. The market in India has evolved into an urban market, the fourth stage. This market offers a huge potential for practically all kinds of consumer products. However, the market must be segmented using an appropriate scheme depending on the product or service. Further, a tremendous marketing effort is required to create acceptance for new kinds of life-enrichment and convenience products.

Take the case of frozen foods. Consumer response to frozen foods varies significantly between the U.S. and Switzerland. Swiss consumers, though equally as affluent as U.S. consumers, prefer buying fresh vegetables and foods. For them, frozen foods are a safety factor for emergencies and stock-out situations. Now consider India. Traditionally, not necessarily by choice, day-to-day buying of fresh product has been routine. The question is if–with the availability of deep freezers–frozen foods will find a place in Indian homes. The answer to such a question requires consumer probing and understanding.[13]

India's urban market may be compared to the U.S. market after World War II. On one hand, the consumers are hungry for all products that add to their standard of living or "keeping up with the Joneses"; on the other hand, many products may not fit into the Indian cultural milieu. Further, India's resource limitations may restrict the market for such goods as paper products. By the same token, emerging environmental concerns may desire restraint in introducing many products.

Briefly, the Indian urban market represents a country market spread over a wide territory and surrounded by 600 million-plus people who do not belong to this mainstream group. To adequately serve this market, a firm needs to strengthen its market knowledge and formulate relevant strategies.

Putting Sequencing into Practice–An Example

PepsiCo's venture in India serves as an illustration of the working of sequencing strategy in practice. PepsiCo has agreed to transfer appropriate technology to undertake complete integrated manufacturing of a variety of food products in India. In addition, PepsiCo would export 50 percent of the production of the Indian company with a view to achieving export earnings of an amount, during a ten-year period, over five times the outflow on dividends and payments for imported machinery and engineering services, and would, thus, provide India a net gain through exports. In the short run, it would appear it was a sell-out strategy on Pepsi's part. But the company looks at it as an investment into the future. It has claimed, for example, that in twenty-five years or so, India could emerge into the company's five major markets worldwide.

The sequencing strategy does not mean that exporting must precede development of the domestic market. Both the export market and the domestic market may be entered simultaneously. As a matter of fact, in some cases it may be desirable to postpone entry into export markets until the product has been perfected in the domestic market. Maruti-Suzuki cars were exported for the first time in 1988, almost five years after they were introduced into India.[14]

Industry Selection

Although a growing number of industries and product areas offer opportunities in India, there are industries for which the market is limited, for example, consumer goods like textile products or industrial commodities like cement or steel. When we weigh India's perspectives, four kinds of factors, as depicted in Exhibit 8-3, are significant in delineating attractive industries.

Not every company must, should, or can succeed in India; but no company can any longer afford not to weigh the pros and cons systematically in the light of a realistic evaluation of the market opportunity and of its own prospects of success. At this juncture, the crucial question is what industries and product areas, based on the factors identified in Exhibit 8-3, appear to offer a viable opportunity to India.

Technology Gap

In many areas, India has a technology gap, and the country is anxious to fill that gap. It includes both low technologies and emerging, new technologies. A variety of industries likely to help India in closing the technology gap are welcome. For example, normally India does not show much interest in consumer products, but in the interest of seeking plastic molding technology, Mattel Corporation was permitted to manufacture and sell its toys in India.[15]

Infrastructure Need

Infrastructure development must precede market evolution. For example, cars without roads do not make sense. In the last 40 years,

EXHIBIT 8-3. Factors Depicting Attractive Industries

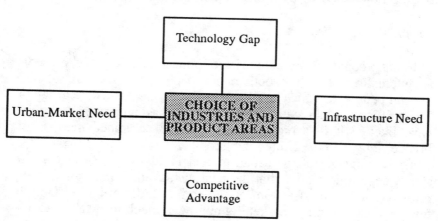

India has invested heavily to upgrade its infrastructure and yet it is barely tolerable. Thus, for market evolution to become self-sustaining, continual investments must be made in improving and developing the infrastructure. Consequently, products and services likely to enhance India's capabilities in the following areas would be welcome: transportation, telecommunications, information processing (e.g., monsoon monitoring), energy generation (e.g., oil exploration), population control, education, and support facilities (e.g., ports, financial institutions, repair and maintenance organizations), and material development (e.g., exploration of new sources of strategic metals).

Competitive Advantage

A country is a desirable global platform in an industry if it provides an environment yielding firms domiciled in that country an advantage in competing globally in that particular industry. Thus, areas in which India provides a competitive advantage to MNCs in their global operations should be attractive. Mainly, India offers two strengths which MNCs can utilize to seek competitive advantage. These are technical manpower and skilled labor, both available in abundance and at unbelievably low salaries and wages. A number of U.S. companies have established operations in India to develop software utilizing the computer talent. However, India's skilled labor has not been used by foreign enterprises on any large scale.

Urban Market Need

Usually countries are either rich or poor. India, however, presents an interesting case. It is both rich and poor. In the midst of 850 million people, of which half barely survive, there is a core group of 200 million people with substantial purchasing power. Scholars have likened India's middle market to the combined markets of France, Italy, and the United Kingdom.

The emergence of the urban market is attributed to a slow but steady economic growth that India has achieved, to the right to own property, and to the freedom of choice that India provides. Only a few years ago, India's market did not mean much for MNCs. However, in the mid-1980s, India reached a threshold level where it realized it had to liberalize its economy and slowly buy and sell globally or stagnate in a vacuum. India chose to seek liberalization. Although liberalization moved slowly, it generated endless needs for consumer products. The growing market is ready for a variety of products which consumers seek as they become prosperous. Alternatively, products that add to the standard of living, either as status symbols or in the form of convenience, have a good potential in India.

Ideally, India is a suitable place to establish businesses that promise to narrow India's technology gap, assist in improving the infrastructure, serve the growing needs of the affluent, and utilize the competitive strengths that India foremost offers to make a mark in the export markets. Solar energy is one such industry. India lacks photovoltaics, the most advanced form of solar energy technology, and for this reason it is unable to use solar energy on a mass scale. Solar energy could go a long way in meeting India's growing energy requirements. Such products as air conditioners will meet a definite need of the market and can be produced cost effectively on a mass scale using inexpensive labor. India could, in effect, emerge as a major producer of solar-powered air conditioners and other large appliances, and compete globally.

In practice, industries and product areas that satisfy at least two of these factors should be considered attractive for establishing business in India. In this way, a number of industries and product areas appear suitable for foreign investment in India. For example, the large appliances industry meets market demand and can utilize inexpensive labor. The consumer electronics industry is attractive since it provides India with new technology and, at the same time, meets the market need. Shipbuilding is also attractive since it requires an abundance of labor and helps in improving infrastructure.

ENTRY STRATEGY

Alternative strategies are available to companies interested in entering India. Careful analysis is needed to delineate the right strategy. Consideration must be given to both external and internal factors in making the entry strategy decision.

Strategy Determinants

Entry strategy is dictated by two factors: ease of entry and India's attractiveness from corporate strategic perspectives.

Ease of Entry

Measured in Western terms, India will never be a "true" liberal economy. Full free play of demand and supply forces with minimum government control is culturally not feasible in India. Indians do require a central authority to be the final arbiter of what should or should not be done. Liberalization only means that government decisions duly reflect the dictates of demand and supply conditions. In other words, the government will continue to call the shots but not on the basis of political idealogy; instead, market forces will be the key determinants.

Essentially, ease of entry will mainly depend on the following factors: *product group* (products needed for the masses such as pharmaceuticals or for improving the infrastructure, or those with high-technology content or export potential are likely to be acceptable easily), *political clout of local competitors* (local competitors with political connections will make entry difficult), *timing of entry* (in politically difficult times entry will be more difficult), and *urgency of need* being served by the product.

Corporate Strategic Perspectives

A company may have high or low interest in entering India in light of its global strategy. For example, in pursuit of cost effectiveness for a business involving high labor content, a company may find India a strategically sound place to establish business. On the other hand, India may figure as one of the several countries that the corporation is interested in entering. Thus, the strategic significance of India in the eyes of the corporation serves as another consideration in choosing entry strategy.

Entry Modes

Exhibit 8-4 identifies four alternative strategies for entering India.

EXHIBIT 8-4. Alternative Entry Strategies

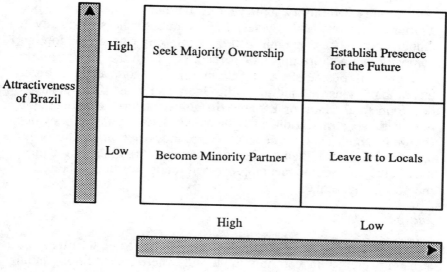

Seeking Majority Ownership

In the case of a business where entry is relatively easy and India figures prominently as a desirable place to be, the company should seek majority ownership through a joint venture. Of course, a wholly-owned subsidiary, even when it is permitted, may not be politically desirable. In this regard what is true of Japan applies to India as well. Based on current Indian regulations on foreign investment, this strategy will fit high-technology industries, or industries where as high as 75 percent output is earmarked for export. From the corporate viewpoint, India will be suitable to locate a world scale plant for manufacturing such standard products as consumer electronics, appliances, toys, etc., or high-technology operations requiring engineers and technical personnel such as industrial chemicals, glass and glass products, office equipment, and fabricated metal products.

Becoming Minority Partner

Becoming a minority joint venture partner is a preferred entry alternative for businesses where India's attractiveness is low, even though entry barriers are minimal. As a minority partner, the foreign company can acquire up to 49 percent equity in the joint venture. The kind of businesses that fall in this category include high-technology industries and those that India badly needs to pursue its developmental plans or enhance its infrastructure. However, the multinational corporation, in light of its global strategy, does not find India significant. Some examples of industries where this alternative makes sense include: personal computers, oil drilling equipment, electronic components, processed foods, synthetic fibers, and medical equipment.

Leave It to the Locals

Leave those businesses to the locals where the foreign firm has no strategic interest in entering India and where, in addition, India makes entry difficult. The steel industry, bicycles, sewing machines, textile goods, and footwear, illustrate such businesses. Basically, these are low-technology businesses. Indian companies have gained substantial strength in many of these industries and, as a matter of fact, they have started expanding in global markets, especially in developing countries. Foreign firms may not find these businesses lucrative.

Establish Presence for the Future

From MNCs' perspective, there are many businesses where India offers good opportunity. But India makes entry in these businesses difficult. Foreign companies may either ignore India or establish a meager presence to be on the spot to take advantage of the opportunity that may eventually emerge. Although India is fast liberalizing its economy, in many fields entry may remain difficult for a long time. However, as Indian companies gain strength in these businesses to become global, India would open its own market to foreigners. Assuming normal progression, in about ten years time currently forbidden fields should selectively be accessible to foreign enterprises. Thus, the wait for India to open up to foreigners might not be a long one. The idea of liberalization has finally taken root in India after four decades of a planned economy and state-sponsored socialism. There is near unanimity that India will continue to liberalize. Meanwhile, by keeping financial involvement in India low, but contact with India high, a foreign company can take a low-cost gamble on the possibility that India would eventually open up.

Industries in this category mainly include different kinds of consumer goods and services for which India is a substantial market. Some examples are different kinds of packaged goods (food products, toiletries), fashion goods, leisure goods, low-technology durable goods (furniture, furnishings), and services (insurance, education). Also included in this category are a variety of commodity-like industrial goods, from chemicals to electronic instruments. Currently, the market is being serviced by local firms, either in the public or the private sector. The quality of their products, while tolerable, lacks comparison with products manufactured by companies belonging to the industrialized world. It is this strength that offers foreign firms an opportunity to occupy a significant market niche in India through product differentiation.

OPERATIONAL STRATEGY

After making a successful entry in India, foreign enterprises are often surprised by the congeniality of the operating environment. In most industries, they initiate their business with some form of technological advantage. Time after time, the MNCs are able to establish a comfortable position by creating the market, understanding their competitors' responses, and learning to deal with the environment. Thus, the problem as far as India is concerned is not so much staying in as getting in.[16]

Despite the fact that sustaining a position in India is not difficult, foreign enterprises must compete in an unfamiliar environment. They must develop both the competence and capability to serve the market and earn a respectable return, while at the same time remaining responsive to the needs of a developing country. Such managerial perspectives have the following major components.

Get in on the Ground Floor

Countries in need of economic development invariably promise favors to the first entrants. The early arrivals often have their pick of partners, suppliers, and distributors. They may receive tax incentives and other inducements. Thus, getting in early can yield enormous advantages. Companies, however, must do their homework far ahead of time to be among the early entrants.

India is not different from other developing countries in this respect. The country has a potential need for a variety of technologies. Yet economic constraints and socio-political realities do not permit opening the opportunities to multinationals instantly. But only multinationals have what India needs. In the long run, therefore, the field will open up and the companies that have done their preparation well ahead can take advantage of the opportunity as it emerges.

It had been known for a long time that India would need to make major investments to modernize its automobile industry. Yet it is only ten years ago that it seriously decided to do so. Toyota and other Japanese car companies sent advance men to India 25 years ago just as the country was beginning to modernize its industrial sector. Because of the close relationship they built with the Indian bureaucrats, the Japanese were able to elbow aside General Motors and Italy's Fiat, both of whom had a limited collaboration with two different Indian companies at one time.[17]

A company that seriously considers India as a potential market should invest heavily in manpower to build relationships with government functionaries, to scout out the best potential partners, and to understand the business environment. The next step should be to build a corporate image and even to create brand awareness to stimulate demand ahead of its market introduction. For example, Hitachi and Toshiba began to advertise their wares in India years before the products were actually available on store shelves.[18]

Be Locally Responsive

Although a company in a global business cannot adapt its product to each developing country market (since the available market may not be substantial enough to justify such adaptation), it must still be responsive to local market needs. The point may be illustrated with reference to Unilever's experience.[19]

Careful scrutiny showed that women in India relied on soap to wash clothes. The company, therefore, developed a detergent bar that could be used by hand. The company uses local raw materials when possible to reduce overhead and stimulate local industry and, thus, local markets. For example, it slashed the cost of importing chemicals from Europe by altering its detergent formula to make use of abundant nearby stocks of soda ash. To overcome a costly local shortage of palm oil, company scientists adapted a number of previously neglected indigenous oils for use in the manufacture of soaps. This eliminated the need for imports, lowered the cost of manufacturing, and helped to support the local economy and Unilever's markets. The company's aim is to raise the overall standard of living, thus stimulating demand for the company's products. Although the perspective is long-term, Unilever's experience in India shows that the pay-off can be immediate.

Choose Industrial Location Diligently

India has 25 states. Of these, four states–Maharashtra, Tamil Nadu, Gujarat, and West Bengal–occupy a dominant place in India's industrial economy accounting for almost 50 percent of the factories.[20] While these states have a well-developed infrastructure, they are overbuilt, resulting in overcrowding and overpricing of real estate. Potential investors may find that three emerging states provide the ideal location for new factories. These are Western Uttar Pradesh, Haryana, and Rajasthan. Closer to New Delhi, these states offer a variety of concessions to new enterprises. From the viewpoint of a foreign firm, other things being equal, a suburban location within driving distance from Delhi is probably the best place to locate a factory in India's current political environment. Of course, if a business is dependent on an essential heavy-to-haul raw material available in another state, it must locate itself closer to the source of raw material. Similarly, a firm may find it good business to be closer to customers concentrated in a particular state or region.

Meet People You Ought to Know

Doing business in India depends on contacts and personal chemistry that help build trust. The most influential Indians are often not chief executives of big corporations, but people behind the scenes. It is these people you ought to know about. Some of these people are famous, others are hardly known outside their home state. Long before you are ready to consider forming a joint venture in India, it is good to develop contacts with a core group of influential people there. Later on, when the time comes to strike business—from finding a potential business partner to seeking government approval—these contacts will stand you in good stead.

Let Them Have It Their Way

The government should not be seen exclusively as creating roadblocks for MNCs. When a foreign company does become susceptible to political risk in India, it can employ a number of responses to salvage its position. If the MNCs' managers are flexible and imaginative in responding to government demands, the consequences could be surprisingly favorable. Encarnation and Vachani found that new product lines and markets, risk diversification, and higher earnings are among the benefits MNCs operating in India enjoyed in the wake of the country's "hostile" equity laws.[21] Some companies, for example, negotiated for manufacturing licenses and other concessions in exchange for "Indianization." Others successfully sought entry to new markets, hitherto forbidden.

Essentially, a company has three strategic options to choose from in response to political difficulties in a developing country like India. These responses are to adapt, to withdraw, or to take counteractive measures.[22] When India imposed new restrictions on MNCs in the mid 1970s, IBM decided to withdraw, because the company could not live with the restrictions imposed by the government on freedom of strategy in product development, pricing, and other areas. Nestlé, on the other hand, accepted India's infringements in return for continued presence in the market.

Brown Boveri, however, opted for the third choice, counterproposal, which amounted to making a new move to gain a competitive advantage based on the company's strengths and the needs of the host government. While the choice among the three options depends on the bargaining power of the company in respect to the bargaining power of the Indian government, generally speaking the counterproposal route is most beneficial. It lets the host country have its way, but at the same time offers enough offsetting inducements for the MNC.

In a democratic country like India, with all the problems of underdevelopment, government must at times make moves to pursue its political objectives. Strict measures against MNCs have a lot of publicity value and, therefore, the government does not mind using them. But the government is fully conscious of the needs of foreign companies and generally makes a positive response to counterproposals.

Invest to "Test the Waters"

MNCs often spurn building a manufacturing presence in markets with apparently good growth prospects simply because the absolute size of the market is considered too small to justify the investment. India has often been considered such a market by many foreign MNCs. Despite the vast population, its level of industrialization and widespread poverty often mean that many high-end consumer goods, as well as a wide variety of industrial products, cannot be profitably produced and sold locally by MNCs.

However, Uniroyal Chemical has found a way out of this dilemma. It approached the Indian market from another direction, employing methods normally used to "test the waters" prior to large-scale investment in other countries. Companies have often combined licensing, joint ventures, and small equity stakes as a prudent first step before making major direct investments. But some companies, including Uniroyal, are finding these techniques useful in tapping markets where they have no plans for eventual full-scale operations.

India currently imports 2,000 metric tons (2,205 U.S. tons) per year of ethylene/propylene (ETP) rubber, valued at $3 million, for use mainly by tire makers. Most foreign ETP producers find the size of this market just not big enough to warrant local production, especially given the fact the country imposes no barriers to imports of this product. Uniroyal has decided otherwise. Through a combination of techniques, it is attempting to capture the market.[23]

Licensing

Uniroyal, which already exports small quantities of ETP rubber to India through a local agent, agreed to license production technology to a newly-established ETP rubber manufacturing venture, Herdillia Unimers. The plant, located near Bombay, began operation in 1990, turning out 10,000 metric tons (11,025 U.S. tons) of ETP rubber per year. Uniroyal ended its relationship with its local agent, turning over its existing accounts to Herdillia Chemicals.

Equity Investment

In the past, licensing is where Uniroyal's involvement would likely have ended (heretofore, the company has only licensed its technology in Asia). Now, however, to demonstrate its commitment to developing the India rubber market, it has taken a 10 percent equity position in Herdillia Unimers. Another 45 percent of Herdillia Unimers is owned by Herdillia Chemicals, and the rest is publicly owned. (Herdillia Chemicals is itself no stranger to U.S. investment; it is 22 percent owned by U.S.-based Hercules.)

Uniroyal believes its new domestic tie, along with an aggressive sales effort, will eventually give it a larger share of a much bigger pie. In fact, Herdillia Chemicals is confident that the new plant's output will help expand the domestic market to $10 million a year by 1992 and $15 million by 1996.

According to Herdillia Unimers executives, the venture will use a multi-pronged strategy to develop the market.[24] The initial focus will be on educating potential customers—plastic, tire, automobile, cable, conveyor belt, and hose manufacturers—about ETP rubber. To do this, the plant will send a team of rubber technologists to meet with companies, present samples, and read papers at technical seminars. All of the targeted industries are seeking to upgrade their production techniques, and it is believed that Uniroyal's advanced U.S. technology should prove appealing.

Make the Most of the Brand Name

In the past, regulations made it tough for MNCs to market their products under foreign brand names in India. But the recent relaxation of rules has made the use of foreign product names in India convenient. As a result, these days Indian shops prominently display such well-known consumer goods labels as Van Heusen and Benetton (clothing), Chesterfield and Rothmans (cigarettes), Raymond Weill and Titan (watches), North Star and Adidas (footwear), Oil of Olay (cosmetics), and Barbie (toys). This trend is equally visible in the case of high-tech and industrial products. As has been said:

> There is an incorrect perception that India does not allow use of a foreign brand name unless it is used in conjunction with the Indian licensee/joint venturer's brand name, i.e., if the foreign company's brand is "ABC" and the Indian company's brand is "XYZ," it is believed that the foreign company cannot use ABC as its brand unless it uses it as "ABC-XYZ." This is not the case except in the electronics industry. What is true is that the Indian government generally does not allow royalties to be paid for foreign brand names. The Indian government believes that only royalties and profits being repatriated for productivity-increasing technology are justified. Since brand names do not increase productivity per se, the Indian government is reluctant to allow payment of royalties for them. Foreign companies may not consider it fair to allow use of their brand names without receiving any royalty. However, they should keep in mind that there are many other ways of structuring compensation for use of their brand names.[25]

Inasmuch as among status-conscious middle-class Indians foreign brand names are held in high esteem, the MNCs should identify their products with the international brand names. In this regard, the following suggestions are helpful.

Pursue Public-Sector Partners

Pierre Cardin (PC) established a link with the Indian Tourism Development Corporation (ITDC) to market its clothing and accessories lines under its international brand name. Association with the state concern cut official friction and facilitated the opening of retail outlets at most ITDC hotels.[26] In addition, PC's boutique in the New Delhi International Airport's duty-free shopping complex generates foreign exchange.

Explore Export-Processing Zones (EPZs)

Foreign companies setting up shop in EPZs agree to export at least 75 percent of output (and hit 30 percent value-added levels). In exchange they are permitted to sell the remaining 25 percent output locally, often under the foreign brand name. Coca-Cola is likely to use EPZs as a route to local brand name sales in India.

Franchise

Licensed retail outlets are rapidly gaining favor in India. The law is silent on using brand and trade names on outlets, so chains like Benetton and Mothercare can open local shops under original names. In a clever variation, Playboy franchisees (licensed by Fashion Sport) operate under the name Rabbit Show, allowing for a close association with the original brand. Products sold in outlets may be marketed under the name brand or a locally coined one.

Coin a Compound Label

If you cannot market under your original brand name, add a locally derived word or suffix. Multinational companies already pursuing this route include Maruti Suzuki (cars), Carriers Aircon (air conditioners), L&T Honeywell (dot-matrix printers), and Wilkinson's Wiltech. Ties between the foreign firm and its local compound name can be reinforced through well-placed advertisements.

A Rose by Any Other Name May Smell as Sweet

Adopt an Indian label, then gear promotional campaigns toward educating local buyers about its foreign-brand roots. Japanese firms have mastered this technique, particularly in electronics: now most Indians know Orson is really Sony and Videocon is National.

Ads may highlight the names of collaborators or make the point more subtly. Sony, for instance, tells its Indian customers, "In case of a problem, please take your Orson TV set to the nearest Sony service center." This approach is ideal when your products basically are assembled kits, and foreign brand names on service centers are often as reassuring as they are on products.

Don't Count Your Chickens Before the Customer Bites

A big name does not necessarily translate into sales. The list of failed foreign branded products in India is long and distinguished: marketers of Tang, Close Up, and Double Cola all found that a well-known foreign name is no substitute for product quality, proper positioning, reasonable pricing, and effective distribution. Expensive locally produced foreign name brands, especially consumer products, often fail in the face of smuggled and imported counterparts.

Shop Around

Most of India's major cities now have surprisingly well-stocked "customs notified" shops that legally sell foreign goods. Given only marginal price differences, most buyers prefer foreign goods. MNCs setting up local operations should consider this when forming local tie-ups; most firms that pick inexperienced partners in the belief that their name would work wonders encounter disaster.

Keep Control in Your Hands

As has been established above, forming a joint venture is probably the best route to enter India. Depending on a variety of factors, you may have a majority or minority interest in the venture. In any event, however, you must keep control of the venture in your own hands.

The safest way to ensure the control is to insist that the chief executive (usually called managing director in India) of the joint venture will be an employee of the parent company. That does not mean that you need an expatriate to go to India. Rather, you should hire and train a native of India in the U.S. who is interested in returning to India permanently to take over as the managing director of the joint venture.

There are over 250,000 professionals from India who make their home in the U.S. A great number of them work for U.S. companies, some of whom look forward to relocating in India if a challenging opportunity presents itself. One of these people with an MBA could be hired to head the joint venture. A person willing to take the risk to return to India will work hard and will always be loyal to his or her U.S. employer. Fully equipped with the parent company's ways of doing business, he or she will be its person on the spot in India making sure that adequate and timely information is channeled to the home office.

In dealings with the joint venture partner and in making business decisions, he/she will invariably keep the parent company's interests in mind. At the same time, both inside the company and in the external community, he/she will be a local person. Briefly, such a person will be a good bridge between a large Western company and a traditional, emerging country. He/she will possess a good feeling for the Indian market that an expatriate American rarely develops, even with long experience, and such an individual mollifies the government's concern about a foreigner controlling the business. At the same time, such a person is more American than many native-born Americans would be by virtue of his/her U.S. education and long stay in the U.S. as an employee.

Of course, to keep the person fully motivated, it is desirable to periodically invite him/her to headquarters for training and indoctrination. As a matter of fact, the person should be made a part of the corporate staff currently assigned to India, and may indeed be transferred to a subsidiary in another country if experience and background could be useful there.

Utilize Local Capital

Joint ventures formed with foreign companies in India have little difficulty in raising money locally. Experience shows that frequently stock offerings by such joint ventures are oversubscribed to several times the value. It is, therefore, prudent to disperse partial ownership among the Indian public and raise capital locally. While it has never been tried, to the best of my knowledge, conceptually, it is feasible to make a stock offering to overseas Indians and raise capital in hard currency.

Keep Majority Ownership Even When the Law Limits It

As mentioned earlier, the new policy permits foreign equity up to 51 percent in a large number of industries. But even where this is not feasible, the foreign company can maintain majority ownership by taking two Indian partners. For example, PepsiCo owns 40 percent of its joint venture in India, while a private Indian company (Tata) has 35 percent ownership, and a state-owned company (state of Punjab's Agro-Industries Limited) has the remaining 25 percent share. Between India and PepsiCo, the former has the controlling interest. But between companies, PepsiCo has the majority. Theoretically, the Indian partners can always get together to the detriment of PepsiCo, but such an eventuality is rare.

Be Patient and Shoot for the Long-Term

A company has to be extraordinarily patient to be successful in India. Even if you make a false start, don't lose patience. It may take years before turning a profit, but you will do well if you persist. Benetton's experience is relevant here.[27] They studied the Indian market for several years before opening their first store. Initially, their executives informally strolled the Indian fabric shops to get a quick feel if the country had a ready supply of patterns and designs of different fabrics in the volumes the company uses. They also chatted with other garment manufacturers that have been active in India for a long time. Later the research became far more detailed and encompassed everything from per capita income to political risk analysis. While gaining knowledge of the market, they also developed a variety of contacts at all levels. It was a long and hectic process but three years of hard work paid off as their first store in Bombay met with instant success and paved the way for additional outlets.

Handle the Payoff Problem

India is no different from other Asian countries–China, Indonesia, the Philippines–where some sort of payoffs are necessary to get things moving. American companies, however, are prevented from making such payoffs under the Foreign Corrupt Practices Act, the U.S. law that governs the business conduct of American citizens and companies abroad.

However, the problem of payoffs is not as great in India as it may seem. First, the Foreign Corrupt Practices Act, enacted in 1977 following revelations that many large U.S. companies had given bribes to foreign officials, is aimed mainly at stamping out efforts by Americans to win business with such payoffs. The law specifically okays payments to officials to "facilitate" routine government action, everything from processing visas and licenses to providing water, electricity, phone service, police protection, and mail delivery. Second, India's democracy is in many ways similar to the U.S. While some people have been involved in payoffs in the past, recent revelations and public outcry on the matter have made Indian politicians and bureaucrats very cautious about them. As a matter of fact, it would not be an exaggeration to say that with India's free press and emerging political maturity, no high-ranking person can survive long for accepting a payoff. (In the aftermath of the Bofors payoff scandal involving the Swedish firm for making illegal payments to some Indians during Rajiv Gandhi's tenure as Prime Minister, a matter that contributed heavily to Gandhi's defeat.)

Of course, small facilitating payments in insignificant amounts are legally permissible in American law and they surely make life in India easy. Thus, American executives should not hesitate to offer such a facilitating "fee" if circumstances so require.

CULTURAL TIPS:
HOW TO ACT ONCE YOU GET THERE

Doing business in India is different.[28] There are sharp differences in style and behavior that divide India from the West and Southeast Asia. For this reason, sometimes conducting business there becomes difficult. But two things help. First, because Indians are so widely scattered in the U.S., U.K., and other countries, a passing knowledge of India's struggle for independence from the British gives you some common cultural perspectives of the society. Second, everyone you meet will probably speak English. Further, you can avoid serious blunders and make a good impression as long as you heed the following aspects.

Dress

The foreign visitor, particularly the one arriving from temperate zones, will find India warm to hot and humid. Nights cool off, but daytime weather will generally be uncomfortable. Tradition and formality, therefore, do not control business attire in India. The climate and the casual disposition of the populace set the tone.

Acceptable work attire includes slacks, a short-sleeved shirt, and a tie. Suits are worn only when visiting senior government officials and during semiformal evening events. Tuxedos, dinner jackets, and smoking jackets need not be part of a travel wardrobe. "Bush shirts" are acceptable daytime wear nearly everywhere.

Very lightweight shoes, even semi-sandal types, can be worn during normal daytime work. Socks, however, should be of a subdued color. Many visitors to India have found it necessary and comfortable to change clothes before lunch and again before dinner. This practice generally necessitates use of local laundry facilities. One-day laundry service is conveniently available. Cherished or fancy items should be reserved for handwashing back home, since Indian laundries use harsh detergents.

Women must remember that India is predominantly a Hindu country but with a lot of British influence. Lightweight clothing is acceptable, but rules of modesty should be observed. Revealing clothing should not be worn.

Manners

Refined behavior is demonstrated through respect for elders and superiors. Positive emotions are emphasized by courteous and friendly behavior; coarse and unrefined behavior is demonstrated by venting one's negative feelings. A display of anger, even the use of blunt or harsh words, is in poor taste.

Some specifics deserve mention. Respect is demonstrated through physical gestures. When in the presence of superiors or respected elders, the visitor will properly sit straight, with his feet on the floor. Any tendency to relax is out of place in such circumstances; an artificially rigid posture should be maintained. Generally, overall physical restraint is called for. Vigorous gesturing, ebullient expressions, and loud laughter must be repressed. Backslapping is a mode of contact that the Indians find particularly objectionable. Such behavior will be viewed as aggressive at worst, and impolite at best.

Special control is necessary when using hand language. Pointing at someone or something with the index finger should be avoided.

The left hand is private to the Indian. Interpersonal transactions, therefore, are all completed with the right hand only. Consumption of food and drink must be accomplished with the right hand.

India is the apotheosis of the "after you" societies. Whenever possible, the visitor should wait until invited to engage in a particular act. Certainly if given food or drink, he will properly wait until asked to commence.

The importance of hospitality is recognized by accepting offers of food or drink. The offering need not be consumed entirely, but it must be tasted. Glasses and cups will be refilled if they are drained to the bottom.

Indians have great national pride. Any criticism of their national philosophy or their accomplishments will offend them.

Titles

In general, academic credits rank just after top political titles. For Indians, a professor is superior to a doctor. Next in line are other meaningful political titles, followed by military ranks. Then come business positions, and last, religious positions. Entire title pyramids are used in correspondence or on business cards. In verbal address to people who have earned formal status, however, only the most senior title is necessary.

The chief executive commonly bears the title of managing director. Some chief executive officers have adopted the title of president. More often, however, this title describes second echelon people, akin to vice presidents. Next on the corporate ladder are directors, who may be functional or operational department heads. Below this level, meaningful decision-making input and clout are lacking.

Here and there the title of manager crops up. General manager could be either a top-of-the-company or a top operating division title. Ordinary managers would be akin to directors. But the use of titles does not stop here. Engineers are called by their professional rank, as are lawyers, accountants, and for that matter, anyone who has earned a university diploma.

Perception of Space

Space is at a premium in India. General behavior patterns, consequently, are geared to avoiding potential difficulties due to overcrowding. Indians also have another way to cope with their tightly packed society: they simply overlook inadvertent invasions of space. In this way the personal and public privacy of the individual is preserved.

Proximity in India connotes friendliness and warmth; physical contact and touching are crucial components of good relationships. That a seat for two holds three, therefore, is a normal and congenial condition. Foreigners, however, are excluded from this friendly huddling. Only after they have been admitted into the extended family, should they consider expressing warm feelings through physical contact. The difference between familiarity and belonging deserves particular notice. Indians strongly object to people who try to create quick and superficial relations by feigning friendship. They find this kind of commercial familiarity vulgar and intrusive. Acceptance into warm, personal relations takes time; a formal stance is appropriate in the beginning.

Granting or yielding space is a sign of respect. People in positions of power should be given room. Space goes with status and visitors should respect this old custom. The foreign businessman should go out of his way to create a respectful distance between himself and dignitary.

Women in Business

The outlook that women should stand beside men, not behind them, bridges India to the West. Like contemporary U.S. women, women in India can be found in senior (though few top-level) positions. The male visitor should treat them with just a little extra courtesy, yet without overt chivalry. Flirtatiousness is totally out of order. A handshake is correct only when the woman initiates it.

The established male visitor should strongly weigh the company of his spouse when traveling in India. Since social life, especially an occasional big event, is so important to relationships, the foreign woman can participate in several ways. She could sponsor special parties for women only; she certainly would become the hostess for all mixed events.

Social Contact and Entertainment

Although the social side of business has not been a tradition in India, it is rapidly becoming one. Both lunch and dinner invitations with business people are now commonplace. The visiting foreigner may certainly take the initiative and, even after only perfunctory contact, attempt to invite Indians to lunch. However, he/she should be careful not to invite a practicing Hindu to a meeting where luncheon/dinner includes nonvegetarian dishes or a Muslim to such an event during *Ramadan*. Such events are best staged in one of the big hotels and should definitely not be ostentatious. Generosity and hospitality are appreciated, but lavish entertainment has been harshly criticized in recent years.

Visitors should remember that social events are not extensions of work activities. They are social, and designed for personal contact; they must not look like high-calorie arm twisting. Any business talk during social get-togethers should be initiated by the Indians. Untimely work conversation is likely to make them feel uncomfortable. Indeed, conversation during business entertaining might well center on personal or local issues.

Indian food is richly spiced. The foreigner will discover a delightful cuisine, rich with new vegetables. Coconuts and peanuts are often used for subtle flavorings.

Western visitors should view water and ice with caution. The local water and, therefore, the ice, may cause severe gastric distress. Bottled water is the only solution.

The guest of honor or the most senior person at the table should begin the meal. Should this honor be offered the visitor, he should refuse twice and only then, after repeated urging, start to eat.

Most modern Indians consume alcoholic beverages. The foreign visitor, however, should not offer liquor to practicing Muslims.

Whiskey (scotch, bourbon, and Canadian) and gin are on the acceptable list, as is beer. Indian beer is good.

When the entertainment schedule includes a dinner, the foreign host should invite the Indians' women partners. Some of the time wives will actually join such affairs. Big receptions are a well-known and less intense way of mixing social and business perspectives. Women are always part of such events.

In better restaurants and hotels a 10 percent gratuity will be included in the bill, the size of which may stagger the foreign host. Entertainment in India, especially if it includes live music, is very expensive. The European custom of adding small change to the bill is normal practice.

Tipping taxi drivers also suffers from nighttime expense account inflation. The normal tip must be doubled.

Invitations to the home of an Indian are less frequent. Should this gesture be extended, the visitor can recognize with pleasure that he has been truly accepted.

All events are likely to start a little late. To have Indian guests arrive 30 minutes after the agreed on hour is normal. If invited to a home, the prudent guest will arrive about 20 minutes behind schedule.

Gifts are widely appreciated and accepted. They need be neither impressive nor expensive. Almost anything from golf balls to nice desk pen sets will leave a pleasant reminder. It is wise to give these tokens of friendship sometime after most business has been conducted.

Image Enhancers/Taboos

The visitor should present a neat, well-groomed, and clean image. Liberal amounts of hair, whether on the face or on the head, will detract from that image.

The foreigner should project a quiet, conservative air of well-being, an aura that might be termed "solid." Solid professional knowledge goes hand in hand with a solid academic background. Both are recognized and appreciated. A visitor who makes an articulate, informed, and authoritative presentation will be respected.

NEGOTIATING IN INDIA

Negotiations in India need to flow according to a pattern. They should start at the top in order for participants to establish the necessary personal base. Next, the process is likely to move to an expert and operating level. Generally top-level decision makers detach themselves from the nuts-and-bolts activity of detailed presentations and negotiations. Once at this stage, the foreign firm may also resort to technical experts. Indians are not adamant about matching equal status people during business discussions, but only senior-level foreigners are likely to gain access to their counterparts in India. Since transactions proceed at a measured pace, foreign image makers can return to their home offices during the protracted negotiating process.

Last, the issues under discussion need to go to the top again. Decisions are ultimately made at this level, and the foreign company ought to have a senior representative on the scene when discussions move back uphill. Last minute concessions or details may need immediate resolution, and the absence of on-the-spot decision power may cause new and frustrating delays.

Closing negotiations may require two steps. Final action is, of course, necessary at the corporate level; further negotiations, however, may also be necessary after the Indian company has reviewed matters with national bodies such as the Reserve Bank of India, an appropriate ministry, or a planning body. These agencies may insert new and different conditions into working agreements.

Procedure

Discussions in the English language will be deliberate. Indians prefer not to rush, but to let matters develop slowly, without pressure. Other sources of delay include the occasional lack of technical expertise at the working level and the Indian negotiators' need to check with other levels or to develop a measure of consensus within their own ranks.

The content portion of negotiations, like the process, should also proceed at a slow pace. Therefore, anything pictorial is likely to enhance presentations. Reliability and after-sale service will be perceived as more important than labor-saving efficiency. Price is important and will be discussed at great length.

The local perception of facts is novel: facts are degrees of probability in India. Therefore, inefficiency and unclear decisions have their reasons. Behind vagueness lie compromises and accommodation. In the end, reality is what people think, how they act, and how they interact.

Negotiating in India requires an understanding of several predominant local methods and preferences. Successful negotiations are devoid of pressure and confrontation. Visitors should remember, however, that the "tikhai" or "accha" word (both meaning "all right" in Hindi) actually means "yes," "no," or "maybe." When Indians say "yes," it does not mean that they agree or that they have promised to do something. At best, it suggests "I understand"; at worst, "I hear you talking." Saying "no" is crude. A "yes, but" is an indication that an issue is meeting with resistance. Nonverbal messages such as distressed facial expressions or other gestures may also show a negative reaction, and visitors must carefully monitor and understand such messages.

Preservation of the dignity of each participant in negotiations is another major concern. Each person has a place in life, and this place, however humble, must be respected. Indians are highly sensitive to any loss of face. Such a loss can occur easily during business discussions. Appearing ill-informed, being proved wrong, being overruled, or even being brusquely corrected may cause the Indian shame. A good method of avoiding such embarrassment is to tell the Indian what is required and then ask them what they suggest. The visitor should seek continuous clarification and feedback; he should avoid disagreement or, worse, argument.

The time may come, however, when the foreigner must stand his/her ground and be assertive. But he/she must be assertive in the Indian way, without ruffling feathers. Otherwise, the Indian will end up feeling socially alienated.

During deliberations a local representative can once more prove to be invaluable. Many times, after facts have been presented, that person alone will complete the touchier aspects of the agreement.

Issues

Bids submitted to state corporations or projects will ultimately be evaluated on their price, terms, quality, delivery, and reliability; on the offerer's reputation, experience, and sales service; and on the confidence the offerer and his agent have generated. Absence of local service, in the person of an indigenous representative, may deflate even the most competitive presentation.

Quotes to Indian enterprises should be in both Indian rupees and U.S. dollars. They should also feature c.i.f. (cost, insurance, and freight) terms and give a close estimate of duties due in India. The last item can be very substantial, since India often uses protective tariffs in place of import licenses. Recent developments suggest, however, that these tariffs will be gradually reduced.

Credit will be a central component of the agreement. Letter of credit (LC) procedures are designed to discourage all but the strong from engaging in foreign trade. Irrevocable LCs with built-in terms are generally not allowed. A substantial deposit, 25 percent of the value of the transaction, is due at the time the LC is opened. This deposit should be in the settlement currency, and it may easily cost one to two percent per month in maintenance.

Buying in India, however, is easy. But the selling pressure is often so low that agreement is impossible to reach. Frequently, vital data will simply not emerge. Or a bargaining stance on the part of the potential customer may seem to indicate a lack of real interest. Only competent intermediaries can clear the path through passive selling attitudes.

Last-minute communications with India are haphazard. Indeed at one point India's postal service was counted among the worst in the region. Special delivery and international mail handling, however, have improved. The cautious foreigner should mail from a major hotel and take urgent pieces directly to the post office.

A massive telecommunications program costing well in excess of $10 billion has been in progress. The satellites are in place, and service is rapidly improving. Local telephone service is available and usable in major centers and between all major towns throughout India.

Wire services can be good. Telegrams can be dispatched from the mail departments of major hotels and from the telephone and tele-graph office attached to the main post office. Top flight hotels and an increasing number of businesses can also make telex/fax connections.

Sense of Time

India's senior managers understand the industrialized and organized importance of time. This comprehension, however, has neither become a way of life nor gained the support of the masses.

Visitors must be patient and consistent. Whenever dates, schedules, and deadlines are important to agreements, the visitor should explain why. When critical time points are involved in a contract, the visitor must determine the likelihood of the host's performance. Because Indians find "no" hard to say and talk more often in terms of probability, friendly, supportive, and continuous communications will provide a useful window on reality.

Indians regard the dark hours of the day belonging to the next day. A Western Thursday night, therefore, is Friday for them. When evening dates are involved in local transactions or in social contact, the foreigner should specify both the calendar date and the weekday.

Decision Makers and Decision Making

Decision making in India is a two-sided operation. On the one hand, the entire process is a moving transaction: deliberations gain clarity and support as they move toward the final authority. On the other hand, decisions require consensus. Fast decisions, consequently, are not yet the rule, although they are not impossible to secure. The Indian formula governing the decision-making process involves the acceptance of hierarchical status and the approval of decisions made by superiors who, after all, know best. The foreigner, however, should refrain from any personal pushing or display of impatience. The individual or his/her agent will be called if more help is required.

Business visitors should not assume that intermediaries have their hands in every transaction. Yet when deliberations near completion, a critical point is at hand, and from time to time expeditors or influence peddlers make their appearance. Their real utility is always hard to estimate. Nevertheless, concepts such as buyers' commissions, rebates, transaction fees, or special sales commissions do crop up, often at sensitive junctures near the end of negotiations. Foreigners should detach themselves from these facilitating transactions, which should remain part of an intramural game.

Reaching the Agreement

Working level negotiators indicate in several ways that agreement in principle has been reached. Most commonly they suggest that the visitors put in writing the issues as hammered out. This step will give the Indians time and opportunity to review the proceedings and ultimately pass recommendations uphill for approval. When good relations exist between the visitor and the local decision maker, the host may suggest that the foreigner take the agreement upstairs himself. Neither of these steps indicates that a firm "yes" is at hand. But both mean that operating people will support the pending contract. Final approval may not even come from the chief executive of the enterprise. As mentioned earlier, he may have to review major agreements with national regulatory and planning bodies. Usually, however, consent of the powerful top-level managers of one of the major enterprises is equivalent to firm agreement.

When negotiations are not going well and no agreement is at hand, the Indians will retreat. They abhor conflict or the appearance of being negative. When the visitor cannot reach his Indian contact by phone or cannot make a new appointment, the negotiations have gone badly and are likely to fail.

If negotiations are proceeding smoothly and agreement seems near, formal documents should be drawn up. This practice has become commonly acceptable. Indians frequently deal with each other on the basis of trust. But today's sophisticated, educated, and urban Indians understand the Western need for written documents. Contracts in India serve several purposes. They are confirmations of confidence and outlines of mutual obligations. They are also instruments that assure cash flow and financial gain.

All agreements are subject to formal contractual details. The local civil code, modeled after England's patterns, will have a bearing on performance under contract. Further, customary law will affect all business transactions.

Indians, like many other Asians, prefer to regard contracts as parameters rather than as airtight working tools. They view efforts to be perfectly clear and beyond question as simplistic: truth, after all, has many facets. When the time comes for interpreting agreements, the Indian capacity to accept opposites may test the foreigner. The foreigner will discover that rules are firm, but they can sometimes be bent.

In the case of a stalemate, arbitration is vastly preferable to legal action. Despite the existence of established, formal arbitration procedures, however, this approach is still inferior to continued efforts at a direct resolution between the concerned parties. A return to "never mind, it will all work out" signals that matters have improved.

Connections

Access to the small group in charge is difficult to achieve, but essential for all but trivial business transactions. As a result, intermediaries bloom in India. At the top of the pyramid is the Prime Minister and the inner circle of ministers, bureaucrats with the rank of secretary, and the heads of big state and private corporations.

Internal communications among these people are personal, effective, and based on mutual obligation. The careful visitor should keep track of who is rising to power and who is in decline. This knowledge is particularly important when a company is forming a joint venture in India. An alliance with partners on the decline spells doom for the fledgling venture.

A second group with power includes a number of professional government administrators or technocrats. Many members come from old, well-placed, and influential families.

Most leaders and their "bridge builders" have one common characteristic. They belong to the 85 percent of the citizens who pay no taxes and they guard the interests and affairs of the thousands of enterprises that enjoy this same privilege.

Two lubricants facilitate progress. One is mutuality: equally potent members of the hierarchy exchange favors. The second is cash payment, which currently seems to be going out of fashion.

CONCLUSION

India provides unprecedented market opportunities. For U.S. firms, the emerging Indian market holds both a threat and a promise. The threat is dramatically increased competition from both local companies and those from other nations. As for the promise, there is the growing market of more than 200 million consumers. In the last ten years, as India began its time-bending leap into the twentieth century, millions of her people began an equally rapid transition from rural to urban, from agrarian to industrial, from feudal to contemporary society. With more of India's population traveling to the urban areas to shop every day, the demand for goods and services–from the most basic household commodities to sophisticated technical devices–is soaring. In coming years, as rising incomes continue to bolster the spending power of India's middle class, the opportunities for shrewd marketers will be unparalleled.

Foreign enterprises can play a significant role in serving the Indian market. But they find the conditions in India intolerable and efforts unrewarding in the short term. India, on the other hand, feels that it offers a good mix of opportunities and incentives which MNCs have not fully valued. The U.S. foreign investment process is too often distorted by diplomatic and geopolitical concerns. While such criteria are important, other factors should weigh more heavily than they now do. For the purpose of true mutual understanding, it is necessary for MNCs to place themselves in the position of a developing country and to view the situation from the viewpoint of India, her circumstances and conditions. For this reason, foreign enterprises may make the following efforts.

Accelerate Direct Investment to Produce High Value-Added Products

Instead of limiting ventures in India to so-called "screwdriver" operations, foreign direct investments should be such as to offer advantages to both the investor and India. For example, new value-added operations should be created by increasing the ratio of local procurement of parts and components. In addition, such ventures should contribute to local economic expansion by developing new markets.

Set Up Local Research and Development Centers

Despite efforts to increase local procurement of parts and components, any MNCs which do not have a local base for research and development that draws upon local Indian talent and capabilities will have difficulty in becoming accepted as an "Indian" firm. Given this, it is important for MNCs to encourage technology transfers and to establish research and development bases in India having a high degree of technical excellence.

Localize Management

By employing local personnel, promoting them into the management team, and giving local ventures a wide range of discretion in management, MNCs must make every effort to localize, in name and substance, their business ventures in India. It is through such efforts at localization throughout the entire spectrum of business–development, production, and marketing–that MNCs can efficiently operate a business that is much better suited to the consumer needs and market characteristics of the Indian market.

Collaborate with Local Business Firms

MNCs should enter into a greater number of collaborative working relationships with local firms whereby their competitiveness will be enhanced. Specifically, any tie-up which takes advantage of the relative strengths of both parties (e.g., in design of technical aspects) will not only be able to contribute to the stimulation of competition and the revitalization of local economy, but will, in the long run, help the venture compete in global markets.

Make Efforts to Expand Indian Exports

twentyThe Western markets offer a highly attractive marketplace for a variety of Indian products. It is earnestly hoped that Indian business firms will step up their efforts to export to the industrial-ized countries the kinds of products that truly match the needs of their customers so that their share in the hard-currency markets is improved. On the other hand, MNCs should positively contribute to this end by improving market access for Indian goods to their own subsidiaries.

Reduce the Investment

U.S. companies should worry more about controlling the busi-ness than owning it. Thus, U.S. firms should choose entry arrange-ments that demand relatively modest financial commitments but offer added momentum.

Pursue a Phased Sequence

India's greatest needs in her present state of economic develop-ment are to enhance her technological capabilities and boost ex-ports. A foreign firm should enter India fully sensitive to her needs and make positive responses in fulfilling them. The reward for the firm will be the access to a large market on very favorable terms.

Firmly Control the Business

Even as a minority partner, a foreign firm can control the opera-tions in India. A good way to achieve this objective is to recruit an Americanized Indian to serve as the chief executive of the joint venture. He can handle the downstream activities in India best fol-lowing on the managerial style and traits of the American parent. Further, such a person will insure corporate control on technology and major investment decisions by providing timely information and developing important contacts.

Chapter 9

India's Policy Initiatives: Need for New Outlook

The current era is truly revolutionary. When it ends and the new one begins after the present transitional period, there will be many new faces among the leading world economic players. India could be one of them, depending on how well it acclimates to a global environment.

Countries pass through different phases in their endeavors to internationalize their economies: phase one of import substitution, phase two of export-based international business activities, and phase three of foreign direct investment. The role of government diminishes as the country successfully moves through the three phases. India has been slow to realize that the ornate straitjacket of state regulations hinders economic growth and development. The results of the modest deregulation of trade and financial markets, cuts in taxes, and decreased control over industry during Rajiv Gandhi's tenure as Prime Minister amply demonstrated the positive impact of economic liberalization.

Despite India's past economic blunders, the country has come a long way in uplifting the economic living of millions of her people. Today it stands at a phase where foreign direct investment could play a significant role in growth and development. At this juncture, it will be disastrous for India and her people if politics slows down its steady movement toward further liberalization. India will be left behind China, Brazil, and other Third World countries of her size and stature in the economic race.

Indian leaders must recognize that socialism is a worn-out and discredited approach to development. Particularly in the case of a mature economy like India, only freer commerce is her best hope of wealth, social development, and stability. The full economic potential of a country can only be realized in an open economic environment in which private capital and market forces can freely interact.

No matter which political party is in power, India needs new policy initiatives to revitalize her economy and upgrade living standards. In order to achieve stable and sustained growth, India should seek to make her economy a part of the global economy through deregulation and liberal policies in all phases of economic life. Initial endeavors of Prime Minister Rao in this direction are praiseworthy, but the momentum gained must be sustained.

ATTITUDINAL CHANGE

Unfortunately, most Indian leaders, whether they be in politics or business, have no concept of how the world is moving. They think it is the seventeenth century and that every investment, like the East India Company, is going to come into India and take over. India's ambivalence toward foreign investment is deep-rooted and bound in a skein of cultural and political threads. Indians are by nature wary of the outside world and terrorized by the type of rapid change endured by such countries as South Korea and Singapore.

But in a modern world, such an attitude of fear and concern does not make sense. Today's MNCs do not represent the edge of exploitation. They represent the availability of greater choice and greater satisfaction. Therefore, comparison of a modern multinational enterprise with the East India Company is senseless.

India's distrust for all things foreign must stop so that technology and investment from abroad can be encouraged. She must move with the times to seek a respectable standard of living for her vast population, expected to reach one billion people by the turn of the century. It is only through global linkages and international partnerships and cooperation that India can significantly grow and develop. Such linkages and cooperation require right impetus, right strategy, and a close working relationship between business and government.

Concept of Modern Multinational Enterprise

Today's global corporations are entirely different from the East India companies of the past. They are nationality-less and do not bear any special allegiance to a country *per se*. That applies even to the country of their origin. It is because today's consumers have become less nationalistic. True global corporations serve the interests of customers, not governments. They do not exploit local situations and then repatriate all the profits back home, leaving each host country poorer for having been there. They invest, they train, they pay taxes, they build up infrastructure, and they provide good value to customers in all countries where they do business. This is not altruism on their part. Nor is it a calculated effort to win good press that will stop as soon as attention moves elsewhere. This is simply good–in fact, essential–business, their mainstay.

If governments need not be so fearful of these foreign-based companies that they erect barriers against them, that does not mean their obligations to their people have ended. They still have the responsibility, now more important than ever, of educating those people and of providing first-class infrastructure for the businesses that will employ them and provide them with goods and services. They must make their countries an attractive location for the global companies to want to do business and invest and pay taxes there. Even better, they should nurture their local companies to grow into the global arena. A small Delhi suburb, Noida, has attracted several foreign companies, for example, Timex Corporation and Zurich-based Orell Fussli. If the township does not support them, these companies will look elsewhere.

By and large, multinational corporations do not seek to exploit local resources to strike private deals with governments for licenses to operate within their borders. What they come looking for now are good markets and good workers, and they bring, in exchange, not private deals for officials, but the promise of a better life for the people. These are worthwhile promises to which governments must be ready to respond.

The foreign label attached with these companies is meaningless. As a matter of fact, instead of being a problem, it is an advantage. It means that the host government need not provide them tax credits, subsidies, or special support for research and development.

Role of Multinational Enterprises in India

India must integrate its industry into a global economy to be in tune with the times. Worldwide barriers are breaking down, and

India clearly cannot remain on an island of its own. The quickest way to achieve global success is through the forging of strategic alliances with multinationals who need the kind of support that Indian companies can provide in terms of manpower, skills, services, and infrastructure.

The government of India and Indian businessmen must look at multinational enterprises differently. They should not be concerned about the global power of these enterprises, but should work to combine their strengths with the strengths of the Indian companies to the advantage of both. In addition, allowing MNCs access to the Indian market can, in turn, provide multinational firms access to other markets, both in industrialized and developing countries. Further, the investment resources of multinational companies can be used to develop India's own resources, especially natural resources, and thus supplement the lack of capital in the country.

No matter how one looks at it, it is apt and important for Indian companies, in both the public and private sectors, to work with multinational companies in the achievement of their own goals. Frankly, MNCs are ready, willing, and capable and have much to offer to India. But India must do her homework by becoming clear in her objectives and her strategy. This way, Indian firms would be able to negotiate from a position of strength.

Change Agents

It is hard to let go of old beliefs. They are familiar. We are comfortable with them and have spent years building systems and developing habits that depend on them, like a man who has worn eyeglasses so long that he forgets he has them on. We forget that the world looks to us the way it does because we have become used to seeing it that way through a particular set of lenses. Today, however, we need new lenses. And we need to throw the old ones away. The above analogy adequately describes the mindset of Indian leadership. They are comfortable with the way things are as long as their political ends are served well.

However, time is running out for India and, unless the people at the helm change their perspectives in keeping with time, they will have difficulty in meeting their obligations to people. They must realize that in the interlinked economy, it does not matter who builds the factory, who owns the office building, whose money lies behind the shopping center, or whose equity makes the local operation possible. What matters is that the global corporations, one way or another, do business within a set of political borders and act as responsible corporate citizens. If they do this–no matter what their home country–they will treat the people fairly, give them good work to do, and provide them with valuable products and services. If they do not, the people will neither work for them nor buy what they produce.

But to fully comprehend what today's multinational company is and how its strengths and resources can be utilized to further India's growth and development, Indian leaders need a cultural change. Broadly speaking, this change must take place at four levels simultaneously: among political leaders, bureaucrats, businessmen, and intellectuals. At each level a different kind of institution/group is likely to succeed in producing the desired change. International agencies, especially the World Bank and the International Monetary Fund, can be most effective in changing the outlook of the Indian political leadership. Although, it would be a slow process, bureaucrats would bow to the wishes of their political bosses as long as they know the bosses have done their homework and they mean business.

Interestingly, many Indian businessmen do not like the idea of India going global. They support economic liberalization so long as it makes their lives easier, but they disdain competing against foreign companies. Their rationale is understandable. India is a large and growing market and, in the absence of foreign competition, firms can succeed with sub-standard products and services based on outdated technology. They do not want their hold on the market to be loosened. This narrow outlook serves them well, at least in the short run, but it stands in the way of national progress and of providing higher living standards to India's masses.

The attitudinal change among Indian businessmen can be brought about through the efforts of select business leaders who are aware of global perspectives and are willing to subordinate their firm's interest to India's interest at large. These leaders must become crusaders of global business thinking among their colleagues. It will be an unselfish act of contribution to society. Indian business leaders

–J. R. D. Tata, G. D. Birla, and Jamuna Lal Bajaj–have in the past taken initiatives to pursue national interests and there is no reason to believe that India lacks business leaders with national vision today.

Finally, intellectuals (academics, journalists, religious leaders) can be converted to a new outlook toward global business and to India becoming a part of it through the efforts of overseas Indians. In recent years, millions of Indians have migrated to other lands in search of a better economic life. A big proportion of these people, especially among those settled in North America and Western Europe, are professionals. These people can play a crucial role in bringing about an attitudinal change among intellectuals in India, formally and informally–formally through their writings and lectures, and informally via individual conversations and group discussions.

An important group in India that can take the lead in this endeavor consists of faculty and alumni of the institutes of management. Most of these people generate and support ideas, values, and viewpoints that favor economic liberalization and global competition. Just a few concerned faculty and students, probably with the help of private business, can conduct research, write papers, hold seminars, and, thus, systematically, infuse a new thinking at all levels in the society.

A caution is in order here regarding the role of international institutions in influencing the attitudes of political leaders. It does not mean Indian leaders are unaware of what is good for their country and, therefore, international agency professionals are needed to advise them. But in a democratic country, if an aspect is susceptible to becoming a political issue, opponents are quick to take advantage of the situation. In the mid-1980s, India adopted limited liberalization due to the vision of Rajiv Gandhi, which resulted in substantial rewards for the country. India achieved unprecedented industrial growth during his term as Prime Minister. Despite that, he himself began to shy away from further liberalization to please his political allies who were not quite willing to give up socialist thinking. In other words, political realities required him to downplay economic liberalization.

But this intermittent attachment to liberalization, global competition, etc., is wasteful. Businesspeople, Indian or foreign, always wonder what may or may not happen. It has been clearly proven that state control of economic affairs is unproductive and wasteful. Communist countries, the hard-core proponents of economic centralization, have given up and are swiftly seeking capitalism. India's own experiment with public sector enterprises has been discouraging. Thus, in the emerging world, there should be no argument that economic liberalization is the way to seek the good life and prosperity. As India's commitment to democracy is irreversible, likewise economic liberalization and globalization of the economy should not be political issues subject to debate. This means all political parties and their leaders should accept economic liberalization as a standard national objective. It is in this endeavor that international agencies can assist India. For example, they can persuade and convince political leaders belonging to different parties, by virtue of their professional status, that economic liberalization should not be a question mark in India's endeavors to seek economic advancement.

IMPROVING PERCEPTIONS

Misunderstandings about India among Westerners are the natural outcome of mistaken perceptions of India. Very few people in India have made any effort to make their country understood. Indians continue to think that if they patiently wait long enough and complain softly, eventually the world will understand them. Indian leaders do not understand that today's global society is radically different from the colonial days. People do not usually come to a tacit understanding without pressure being exerted visibly. When someone has something to communicate to someone from another culture, he or she must organize the facts and try to persuade the listener in a logical way. He or she must also realize that it is necessary to be prepared to counter new and unforeseen criticisms aggressively.

Further, today's global economics are such that simple confrontations, with a winner and a loser, have been replaced by more complex situations where ties must be the objective and cooperation the primary tactic. Thus, Indians must learn to communicate so that their rigidity conquests do not become Pyrrhic victories.

America Is India's Largest Trading Partner

India is a poor country and is no match for the level of trade that the U.S. conducts with industrialized countries. But meager as its trade is, the U.S. is her biggest trading partner. The perception of many Americans that the former Soviet Union is India's close ally is not supported by the facts, at least in the economic arena. But Indians do not communicate. They do not get the facts necessary to substantiate or refute what other nations claim about India. India accepts the accusations and images thrust upon her and silently hopes the world's anger will subside.

U.S. exports to India have increased from $1.6 billion in 1982 to $3.0 billion in 1989. Looking at these figures from the viewpoint of a country with a per capita gross national product of $335, this is a tremendous increase. If India explains to foreigners that this increase could not have been achieved without liberalization of import policy, at least a few of them would be forced to acknowledge that India has not been as closed an economy as they thought.

Creating an Overall Positive Image

By and large, India is held in very low esteem by Americans.[1] An average American thinks of India as a backward country with mass hunger, disease, and poverty. American mass media is partly responsible for this impression. Usually, they portray India in a negative fashion. For example, in the 1991 elections, despite inadequate means of communication and transportation, 310 million people cast their vote, but the media did not highlight that fact; instead, it chose to emphasize that 30 people died due to clashes between opposing parties. As a matter of fact, most news on India in the American press is concerned with some sort of problem. Besides, the American public knows little about India and forms its opinions on hearsay.

As a matter of fact, India is held lowlier than China. Even since the Tiananmen Square incident, as many as 22 trade missions have been sponsored to China by various U.S. organizations. In comparison, during the same period three trade missions were organized to India. Even among American academics, it is not unusual to hear someone say that an Indian scholar will have difficulty communicating in English, much like a Chinese or a Korean.

The bottom line is that there is a big gap of awareness about India among Americans. India must take the initiative to bridge this gap. A well-planned program must be formulated and implemented to make the U.S. public know what India truly is. The program need not be limited to traditional mass media advertising, but may include lectures and seminars delivered by Indian immigrants in the U.S., films and videocassettes made available by Indian diplomatic missions, and the encouragement of American universities to establish study-abroad programs with Indian universities.

Catering to Special Interests

The forces behind "American" pressure on India are quite different from what the Indians conceive them to be. Special interest groups speak in America's name, but they are not America. There is no one American public. Different groups within the U.S. government and in different states hold differing views.

Why is it, then, that when one of these groups speaks up, India begins to become defensive as if it has a guilty conscience? There is no reason for India to quake and tremble every time a lobby against India in Washington makes the newspaper headlines. India should be responsive, but it is more important for her to make a greater effort to find out exactly what is at stake, who stands to gain when a lobby calls for India to open a market or allow Amnesty International to visit Punjab, or accept the importance of U.S. aid to Pakistan for stability in the region.

Pressure can be met by counterpressure. When the congressman from California questions India's tough measures to stop terrorism in Punjab (in order to appease his Yuba City, CA, constituents, which include a large Sikh community), India should approach Pepsico, who has a major investment in the Punjab state, to support her stand.

It is not intended here that India should manipulate American public opinion. What it should do is try to inform relevant and friendly parts of it. Unfortunately, India does not do that. Its communications and public relations are nonexistent or, at best, naive. More important, it does not communicate with audiences that are directly concerned. The result is that those who should be lending a hand in their own interest stand idly by as opponents of India make most of the news headlines.

India must learn to reach the small group of people and try to convince them as individuals. "America" does not listen or think, but Americans do. By the same token, India does not simply mean "Indian government." Indian businessmen and natives, particularly U.S. residents, have an equal responsibility to communicate India's position to American people.

Communicating with U.S. Businesses

While the view, held by many potential foreign investors, that India is unduly restrictive towards foreign investment and technology may be exaggerated, it is desirable that any misapprehensions and mistaken impressions in this regard are corrected.[2] This is not merely a matter of clarification of guidelines or procedures. What may be necessary is to change the image of the country and to introduce major modifications in the arrangements for handling individual proposals, which, in turn, may require removal of several perceived bottlenecks in policies and practices toward foreign investment and technology. Closer links with foreign technological developments may also be developed through investments and participation by Indian companies in selected niche sectors in the United States or elsewhere. As has been said:

> Though a leading reason for India's low inflows is the difficult operating environment for foreign business, investor perceptions of a country's commitment to foreign capital are no less important in determining investment flows. In the case of India, the perception would appear to be negative. Statements in both India and the International Press, pronouncements by policy-makers and senior officials in government, and the seeming arbitrariness of investment policy all give investors the impression that they are unwelcome in the country. That perception, whether well founded or not, is what keeps investors wary of investing in India.[3]

In order to correct that negative impression, India must demonstrate a clear stand in favor of foreign investment and market itself more effectively abroad. The rules and procedures affecting foreign investment should be clearly spelled out, preferably in the form of an investment code and implementing regulations. Priority sectors and types of projects in which investment is welcome should be specified. Specific guidelines would help prospective investors in making the right kind of proposals and could also help to speed up and clarify the approval process. The primacy of perception issues is a leading theme that India needs to work on.

STRATEGY FOR GLOBALIZING THE ECONOMY

India could be a significant player in the world economy, and fairly soon, if it were to decide to join global competition and to modernize the economy. India has all the potential. It is the third largest economy in Asia and the twelfth largest in the world. It has the third largest pool of scientifically trained manpower, an experienced and highly sophisticated managerial class, a tradition of medium-scale entrepreneurship, and a reasonably well-developed infrastructure. India's large and active stock market has a level of capitalization higher than that of any of the newly industrialized countries (NICs).

Despite this, however, India receives far less in foreign direct investment (FDI) than its much smaller, newly industrializing Asian neighbors.[4] During the period from 1981 to 1987, Malaysia received a total of $1.28 billion in FDI, Thailand $3.87 billion, and Indonesia $9.5 billion, whereas India received just $0.5 billion. During 1985 and 1986 alone, China received $9.6 billion. Moreover, despite recent liberalization, inflows to India dropped from a low $194 million in 1989 to $133 million in 1990. It is yet to see how far the 1991-92 liberalization efforts will go.

The low inflows are worrisome because there is a real danger that India might be left behind technologically and its competitiveness gap might increase. Indian policy makers must make a concerted effort to present a new perspective. A national strategy for globalizing the economy should be formulated, thus paving the way for an increased inflow of direct foreign investment and technology in India in the 1990s, enabling the country to become a global competitor in selected fields.

Meaning of Globalization

Globalization refers to a broadened view of markets and competition. For an economy to become global, its companies must learn to compete across national borders against companies with varying strengths and cultures. Doing business in a global economy requires a lot of new learning, including how to find the right country in which to build a plant, how to coordinate production schedules across borders, and how to absorb research wherever it occurs. Managers must learn what sort of people to hire, how to inculcate a global mentality in the ranks, and when to sell standardized products instead of customizing them for local markets.

Globalization strategy will enable India to become a global economic force delivering higher living standards to its citizens. In selected industries, India could achieve global leadership, emerging as a market leader. Profits from these industries could be utilized to buy new technologies for other industries which may next be groomed to enter the world arena. The global strategy permits companies in the industry to achieve *reduced costs* (through gaining economies of scale from pooling production or other activities, moving to lower cost countries, exploiting the flexibility of a global network, and enhancing bargaining power with governments, unions, and suppliers), *improved quality* (through focusing resources on a smaller number of products and programs), *enhanced customer preference* (through increasing global availability, service-ability, and recognition), and *increased competitive leverage* (through combining global resources and using more locations for attack and counter-attack).[5] The net outcome of the globalization strategy will depend on how well Indian companies are able to achieve the above benefits.

From the viewpoint of a developing country, economic globalization is a two-step process. Step one requires initiatives on the part of the government. Step two involves companies in the country responding to the government initiatives.

The Role of Government

To globalize her economy, India should formulate a strategy on the basis of the following outline:[6]

a. Carefully select several priority industries with which to establish global preeminence.
b. Improve and build the infrastructure to support these industries.
c. Encourage domestic rivalry among companies in these industries.
d. Separate import-substituting industries from export-building ones, and do not regulate the latter in the same way as the former.
e. Continue to remove complex licensing processes and regulations on industries because these tend not only to stifle entrepreneurship, but also to become sources of corruption.
f. Encourage companies to seek strategic alliances with global companies to enter markets in advanced countries with a view to establishing brand identity.
g. Encourage foreign investors. There is nothing wrong with initially seeking foreign help to become a global competitor. This means India must give them relatively unregulated access to the local market. In return, India can expect them to build state-of-the-art operations, whose profits can be taxed after they establish world-class competitiveness.
h. Encourage companies to further expand globally, both in developed and developing countries, on their own, using their own brand identification.

India can be a major base for industrial sourcing; it can provide seasoned industrial entrepreneurs to be associated with multinational firms, and it commends itself in many other ways for strategic alliances and cooperation with MNCs. This is different from constantly forcing multinationals to work in such a way that the focus is only on the Indian domestic market. Multinationals are used to working with constraints from all over the world and the foreign exchange resource position of India is a constraint which is well understood internationally. It is unlikely, therefore, that there will be difficulty in negotiating strategic alliances based on India becoming a partner, although a junior partner, in the international playing field.

A message out of all this is that foreign collaborations and foreign investment have to form a part, an essential component of India's global strategy. A second issue which needs to be clearly understood is that while scale is extremely important, this does not preclude small firms from becoming global players because small firms are nimble footed, flexible, lower cost, competitive, and could participate effectively in the international and global marketplace.

In looking at global strategy, it is also necessary to look at the pattern of foreign collaborations which, in the past, have been focused on specific products or a group of products. This limits the partnership scope and potential. It is necessary to move away to a concept of broad-based collaborations which cover the entire range of products and services of a foreign company, including its research and development activities and services. This will encourage Indian companies to develop flexible collaborative partnerships as long as there is adequate reporting to the government. In any case, all remittances of foreign exchange in terms of payments, royalties, technical fees, and dividends are routed through the Reserve of India and, therefore, full information would be available with the government. The present system of application forms and licensing and approval arrangements in India would need to be adapted to enable such broader-based collaborations to be framed and implemented.

Whatever else is done to promote globalization, nothing will be achieved unless there is a surplus of production in India in excess of local demands. Therefore, one important component of industrial strategy must be to build such surpluses, strengthen the buyers' market, and do this across the board in all industries including commodities. Apart from escalating competition and sharpening the competitive capability of industry, it would have a very stable influence on prices and serve as the foundation for global activity. This way, Indian industry would be able to use its domestic base, the local growth, to fuel its globalization drive and use multinationals as partners and vehicles to achieve a global role.

Today, the Republic of Korea has a 2 percent share in world trade. India's share is approximately 0.5 percent and if, by the year 2000, India is to achieve a 2 percent share (the same as Korea has today), then a great deal has to be done in terms of building production, exports, and international competitive capability.[7] All this can be achieved because the basic infrastructure is there, both in terms of men, machines, and money, as well as the expertise and the resources.

Role of Business Enterprises

Companies in select industries that a developing country initially decides to globalize should consider the entire world as the potential market. They should decide where to compete, how to compete, and when to compete in the global market. Global strategy requires companies to seek *(a) global market participation:* i.e., selecting and investing in countries on the basis of global strategic importance as well as the attractiveness of the opportunity in an individual country; *(b) global products and services:* i.e., designing and producing products with global needs in mind; *(c) global location of activities:* i.e., creating one global network of different business activities; *(d) global marketing:* i.e., adapting the same brand name, advertising and other marketing elements in different countries; and *(e) global competitive moves:* i.e., integrating actions against competitors into a worldwide plan instead of fighting separate country battles.[8]

Indian industry should make a positive response to the government measures and consider integrating into the global economy. Although exports have increased in recent years by as much as 40 percent and more, by no means is India a global economy. It is only the beginning of the road, moving from exporting to becoming international and then, finally, global. If the objective of globalization is to be reached, a transformation is required within Indian industry, starting with a very strong commitment from top management to assume a global role, building capabilities to be able to enter global markets using the domestic market as a base, and using strategic alliances and foreign collaborations as part of this overall development.

If Indian industry is to become a global player, it has to look at its own growth process differently. First, instead of short-term business planning to take advantage of market situations, firms will need to develop a long-term strategic approach to the domestic and international markets. Second, the past distance between government and industry will need to be bridged and both must adopt common programs and strategies. Third, because of the large domestic market, Indian industry has been essentially focusing on the internal market, and this must change. Finally, the position of being reasonably satisfied with the way things are has to give way to a new ambition and aggressiveness to operate in the global market, compete, and win.

It has often been claimed that Indian companies are unable to compete with multinational corporations with their all-around strengths. Both government and industry in India support barriers to protect domestic firms against the advantages that MNCs have. The experience of a number of Indian companies, however, shows that even smaller domestic firms can successfully compete with the mighty corporations as long as they pursue sound business strategies.[9] As shown in the appendix at the end of this chapter, Indian companies have been able to outcompete such well-established firms as Lever Brothers and Colgate Palmolive.

Selecting Industries for Initial Thrust

In selecting the industries, India should aim at taking the labor-rich portion of secondary industries away from the industrialized West. This can be achieved by importing key components from the latter, adding labor, and then exporting the final assembled product back to them. For example, in the semiconductor industry, India could (a) import semiconductor microchips (after the ions are implanted and diffused on silicon wafers in the "clean room"–a capital-intensive process); (b) put them through the labor-intensive operations of bonding, assembling, and packaging; (c) use these and other critical components (which may have to be imported) to assemble such products as watches, television sets, and video players; and (d) export these finished products to companies in developed countries under their established brand names. Initially, India does not have many options beyond assembly, because taking over other value-added segments is full of difficulties. It will require expanding operations to upstream products like components and devices, or to downstream activities like marketing and distribution of locally branded goods. Establishing upstream industries would require a lot of management resources, particularly capital and engineering power. Consider the microchips example again. One of its upstream businesses is the silicon single-crystal process, which is such a technologically sophisticated industry that there are only a half-dozen effective global companies. Another element here is the "clean room" environment, typically costing $100 million or more and requiring a very disciplined and skilled work force in order to achieve a yield high enough to be competitive. Even South Korea and Taiwan have had difficulty in competitively entering this field.

Thus, even if India could enter the semiconductor industry, the more profitable segments such as high-speed 64K and 256K memory chips, charged couple devices, and gallium-arsenide semiconductors are well beyond her reach. It is a constant catch-up game. In the process, if India is not very careful, it could end up producing only "engineered commodities" whose profit potential is marginal at best.

Another alternative is to move downstream. However, profitable downstream operations mean establishing a premium brand with its own distribution. Who has heard of any brand name goods from India in Western markets? Perhaps the best known brand so far is only *Bata*. The reason we do not hear about them despite her "dynamic" growth stories is that India is still, to a large extent, an exporter of components and subassemblies for other manufacturers. It produces goods to the specifications of MNCs. Few Indian manufacturers even know about the customers' needs and desires in major markets overseas. India lacks the product design capability to develop unique and appealing products and, thus, is hardly able to claim premium prices for them. India's products are positioned as "low-end" or "price-line" goods in the mass merchandising channels of the advanced countries. These channels take a very large margin of the profit. For example, in color televisions, a typical factory shipment price–the amount of money which a country like India would get–would be anywhere between 15 to 25 percent of the list price in the advanced country. So unless Indian companies can establish their own distribution networks for their brands, there would be a very small profit potential left for them in the current marketplace.

An "own brand" strategy is not only expensive but also risky. Experiences of Japanese companies are relevant here. Panasonic and Sony undertook multibillion dollar projects to establish their brand name. Other brands such as Toshiba, Sanyo, Sharp, Hitachi,

Pioneer, Seiko, and Casio have all spent hundreds of millions of dollars on the media and on dealers' cooperative programs to promote their brand.[10] As a matter of fact, it may not be an exaggeration to say that establishing a brand name in a country like the U.S. is far more expensive than building the production plant to make the product. Based on the experience of numerous companies, it appears that in order to establish the threshold awareness necessary to participate effectively in the global brand name race, a firm needs to invest a minimum of $100 million over five years.[11] If it cannot afford this expense, it might as well remain a supplier to original equipment manufacturers.

Realistically, very few companies in India have the capital and human resources to make that investment in either time or money to take over more value-added segments that promise higher returns. Tata, Birla, Bajaj, and HMT are attempting to become global in select businesses, in the developing regions, and by taking advantage of low labor costs. These are good niches for them in that they can be the lowest-cost provider of these kinds of products and services in the world. But it is very difficult to use this route to increase India's global presence to any significant level. Most companies in India are still buying blueprints and working on licenses from the companies in advanced countries rather than becoming the primary general contractors for macro projects which produce high value-added plants.

But in the long run, India cannot remain a manufacturer of private brands for global companies from the West. To move along, therefore, Indian companies, with the help of government, must make strategic investments in research and development, production, and marketing to take over the value-added segments of the business system and claim higher prices. Domestic rivalry among Indian companies and competition from foreign companies in the Indian market should be a great learning experience for Indian companies aspiring to be global champs. Outside India, the first move may be made in developing countries (i.e., Malaysia, Thailand) where there will be only limited competition from global firms. But the ultimate destination should be markets in advanced countries (both Western countries and the newly industrialized countries). Indian firms may initially form strategic alliances with global companies to enter the advanced markets. Eventually, however, they must stand on their own to market their products under their own brand names.

Adopting Pro-Globalization Policies

In order to foster economic globalization, India must create a positive business culture and environment. The starting point should be to liberalize the industrial sector to enable the free market forces of supply and demand to yield the right motivation and regulate signals of growth and efficiency. This will require the government to take a variety of measures vis-à-vis industrial and trade policies.[12] While the exact policies will require review and contemplation at different levels in the government, the policy changes will need to be carefully sequenced over time, in order to ensure a smooth and sustainable reform process. The policies should aim at creating the "enterprise culture" that would lead firms to take risks and seek profits, within the market discipline of a competitive environment. These policies can be dealt with at three levels: (a) international competitive policies, (b) local competitive policies, and (c) production factor market policies.

International Competition and Trade Policies

The single most important step to globalize the economy is to reform trade policies to give the industrial sector an outward orientation and bring in the pressures of international competition. Despite the reforms during Rajiv Gandhi's tenure and those initiated by the Rao government, India still follows protectionist and interventionist trade policies with a pronounced anti-export bias. In addition to limiting competition, these policies distort price signals, lead to excessive bureaucratic interference in resource allocation, and encourage nonproductive activities.[13] Better trade policies can lead to substantial supply responses and export growth through their positive effects on resource allocations that better reflect dynamic comparative advantages across sectors. In recent years, major trade policy reforms have been undertaken, among others, in Chile, Korea, Morocco, Thailand, Tunisia, and Turkey, and India could learn from their experiences.

In a trade reform package, realistic pricing of foreign exchange is a key ingredient in maintaining the international competitiveness of a country's exports and import substitution industries. Overvaluation of exchange rates discriminates against exports and import substitution industries, and almost inevitably leads to quantitative import restrictions and controls that are cumbersome, distort demand, and ultimately lead to inefficiencies and low capacity utilization. A recent statistical study of developing countries suggests that, in some economies, for every 10 percent by which an exchange rate is overvalued, total export growth is, on the average, reduced by 1.8 percentage points per year, and GDP growth by 0.8 percentage points.[14] Exchange rates should be realistic and dynamically stable in real terms over time. They should reflect, or be periodically adjusted in line with, differences between local and international inflation and other economic fundamentals. There are two exchange rates systems: managed exchange rates and independently floating exchange rates. India follows the managed exchange rates system, under which the rates are determined by the Reserve Bank. The exchange rate, pegged to a basket of currencies, and devaluations reflect the difference in inflation—and, therefore, competitiveness—between India and its trade partners. India must consider following the second system, independently floating exchange rates, under which exchange rates are market determined, thus avoiding the need for the government to decide on devaluations. Many developing countries using this system have weekly auctions of foreign currencies, where rates are determined by supply and demand. The periodicity of the auctions depends on the amount of foreign currency available; if the amounts are large, auctioning could become permanent. One advantage of an auctioning system is that when an exchange rate is substantially overvalued, the auctioning will help in establishing the correct rate.[15]

A second area relating to trade policies is tariff reform. Quantitative restrictions on imports, high import tariffs, and high effective rates of protection yield a substantial anti-export bias by making production for the local market much more attractive than production for exports. India has attempted to provide a free trade status to exporters by allowing duty-free imports of raw materials and intermediary products, and by providing large export incentives. Experience has shown that this strategy is unlikely to succeed over the long term if tariffs remain high.[16] Such a system cannot have the flexibility and dynamism required in today's industry where demand patterns are consistently changing. The only long-term alternative is to liberalize trade. Effective liberalization of tariffs requires (a) replacing quantitative restrictions and quotas by tariffs; (b) reducing the variance of protection by establishing maximum and minimum bounds to nominal tariffs, for example, a range of 40 percent maximum, 5 percent minimum; (c) lowering the average for nominal tariff rates to the 10-20 percent level; (d) simplifying administrative procedures to facilitate trade; and (e)establishing transparent and temporary anti-dumping mechanisms to provide an escape valve for legitimate protection measures. The tariff reform program and its timing should be announced in advance, to enable private entrepreneurs to adjust their production facilities in consonance with the reform program. The experience of developing countries implementing tariff reforms such as Bolivia, Chile, Korea, Mexico, Morocco, Tunisia, and Turkey illustrates that, even with a strong political will, tariff reductions will take a number of years to be implemented and the management of the process needs to be closely coordinated with the management of public finances, given the revenue impact of tariffs.[17]

A third policy area relating to trade involves the desirability of formulating an explicit export development program. Even if a country has reasonable industrial and trade policies, some degree of anti-export bias may still remain, since: (a) any tariff structure, even if it is reasonably low, will tend to make investments for the domestic market more profitable than investments for exports; (b) exports normally involve greater business risks than the closer local markets; (c) production for the local market is intrinsically more profitable than for exports due to the incidence of international freight and port charges; and (d) marketing costs and efforts in export markets are considerably higher than marketing in the local market. There are good reasons, therefore, for India to single out "export" as a special area of support. Measures that could be considered include: (a) provision of tariff exemptions for exporters; (b) increased availability of export credit and insurance; (c) developing institutional support for export promotion, information, and facilitation; and

(d) extension of export benefits to indirect exporters. Further, the liberalization process should provide sufficient dynamism to enable exporters to adjust quickly to the evolution of market opportunities abroad and to focus on the more dynamic markets with growing potential. Intra-regional trade with other developing countries could also be encouraged to alleviate their dependency on markets in a few developed countries.

Policies for Encouraging Competition Locally

Policy reforms should not be limited to international trade policies, as has been done in many developing countries. The aim of industrial policy reform should be to improve the competitive environment, both internationally and locally, to bring market forces together. In fact, it can be argued that, in terms of sequencing of reforms, it may be essential to liberalize the domestic market even before international trade policy reforms are undertaken, in order to allow local firms to adjust their production, to improve efficiency, and to be able to respond better to international competition. In the local environment, there is a need to look at the adequacy of the regulatory framework for entry and exit of enterprises, local price controls, investment controls, corporate taxation, labor and other factor mobility, bankruptcy laws, etc.

The reform program should provide an adequate legal framework to facilitate the free formation and growth of a large number of firms and to check the formation of monopolies and cartels that could hinder domestic competition. Entry of enterprises would be facilitated by measures and legislation that (a) minimizes the need for cumbersome licenses and approval requirements for the formation of firms; (b) encourages the establishment of various legal forms of enterprises and associations with varying degrees of risks and return for entrepreneurs; (c) promotes the growth of "small-scale" industry; (d) discourages sector monopolies for production, distribution, and marketing activities; and (e) facilitates the establishment of foreign firms. Ease of exit is necessary to avoid resources becoming tied up indefinitely in uneconomic activities. The single most important measure to facilitate exit is to make bankruptcy laws more flexible and expeditious. In addition, liquidations can be facilitated by the banking system, which should be able to act energetically to bring financial discipline and induce the closure of unprofitable ventures. Similarly, while political and social questions must be addressed in a constructive manner, the government should abstain from bailing out enterprises in difficulty when they are no longer viable. Liquidation of nonviable firms can also be facilitated by the establishment of a national system of accounting and auditing that would allow more transparent operations. Industrial and financial restructuring programs should also be available for uneconomical firms that could become viable.

Even if an oligopolistic market structure were to remain, facilitating entry and exit of enterprises would render the market contestable. The constant threat of entry and of potential competition would force even the largest firms to produce efficiently, to weigh risk-return possibilities and to behave in a manner that most effectively promotes the public interest. Were they not to do so, they would be inviting new entrants who can provide the same output at lower cost and lower prices. Only firms operating over the long term at the lowest possible cost would survive.

Liberalization of domestic prices also encourages enterprise development and efficiency in resource allocation and use. In competitive industries, free market prices are essential to send the right signals to sellers and buyers and act as the equilibrating mechanism between demand and supply. In such competitive industries, controlled prices should be liberalized promptly. In monopolistic industries producing tradeable goods, domestic prices should be liberalized gradually (possibly under agreed upon semi-annual changes) in close consonance with trade liberalization, in order to ensure competition from abroad. With nontradeable products (such as bulky materials with very high transportation costs) or in industries operating under monopolistic conditions, administered prices should be set at their economic opportunity levels to reflect long-run marginal costs. The government could also let enterprises set their own prices following an agreed-upon system to reflect economic opportunity levels, using border prices or marginal costs as the criterion. The government could carry out periodic spot checks and apply substantial penalties in cases of noncompliance.

A third element to nurture local competitive policies is to neutralize corporate taxation and incentives. Many countries have used investment tax incentives to influence the pace and structure of industrial development. It is, however, unrealistic to believe that the overall investment level in an economy could substantially rise as a result of such incentives. A rise in the country's overall investment ratio can only come about with a rise in the savings ratio, if foreign investments are not considered. Taxation and investment incentives, on the other hand, can have partial equilibrium effects, as they can significantly affect the sectoral distribution of investments. It is doubtful, however, that in a general equilibrium sense, these effects will be positive. Within the industrial sector, these incentives have induced many regional and subsectoral investments which have been uneconomic and, thus, encouraged the misallocation of resources. Greater uniformity of tax treatment among subsectors and firms should be encouraged in order to allow the market forces of supply and demand to guide investment priorities. Departures from this uniformity, for example to assist infant industries or to encourage investment in backward areas, should be carefully assessed and temporary in nature.

Production Factor Market Policies

Policies and institutional rigidities affecting production factors, i.e., labor, capital, and technology, exert significant influence on industrial growth, competitiveness, and efficiency in many developing countries. Protective trade and other noncompetitive policies are often the original source of lack of competitiveness and flexibility in factor markets. However, these rigidities will not disappear automatically with the announcement of a liberalization program and may indeed jeopardize the success of trade and other liberalization efforts. Regarding labor factor markets, legislation may need to be changed to remove obstacles to labor mobility and facilitate the hiring and dismissal of workers, as required by economic conditions facing industrial firms. Other labor policies that may need to be reviewed include legislation of minimum wage levels in excess of opportunity costs and mandatory setting of salary structures unlinked to productivity. A worthwhile sectoral investment to facilitate labor mobility could be the establishment of retraining programs for displaced labor.

Regarding capital factor markets, an important additional matter is the need to eliminate controls on investments. Many developing countries maintain investment licensing systems to minimize excess capacity in some sectors, to prevent the emergence of monopolies, and to promote balanced regional development. These licensing systems, however, have normally failed to yield positive results and have increased economic cost for new investments, dampening competition. Investment licensing systems should be simplified or phased out, since entrepreneurs are better judges of opportunities and excesses of production capacity. There should be, however, appropriate legislation to encourage foreign investments. In particular, legislation should include protection against nationalization and protection for repatriation of capital and dividends.

Over the long term, in India, the development, adaptation, absorption, and efficient use of technology will be the key determinants of total factor productivity growth. Even in the short term, the ability to compete in export markets can be enhanced by technology upgrades, product quality improvements, innovations, and adjustments in product mix. Technological improvements will be stimulated by greater competitive pressures emanating from industrial and trade policy reform programs. But there are many market failures and externalities in the flow of information and technology markets that justify government intervention. Traditionally, India has directly intervened in the supply of technology through the establishment of public research laboratories and technical institutes to diffuse information on technology, university programs, and others. These supply efforts have had only a limited impact due to a lack of attention to the demand side. It is essential to improve the regulatory framework and incentives, as well as the financing facilities to encourage: (a) collaborations with technical foreign partners, (b) direct foreign investments, (c) procurement and adaptation of foreign technology, (d) development of applied research by local engineering firms and industrial enterprises, (e) greater interaction and more responsiveness of official research and development institutions to private industry requirements, (f) development of standards and technical specifications for the design and production of industrial goods, and (g) official certifications of the reliability and quality of components and products.

The industrial policies discussed so far are quite extensive and comprehensive, and of varying importance and relevance to different facets of Indian economy. Some generalizations, however, can be made about their individual priority, considering the main source of the economic distortion afflicting the industrial sector. In terms of impact on corporate revenues, the most significant potential distortions are foreign exchange rates, tariff protection levels, and prices. These major distortions allow for the establishment and operation of inefficient industries and inhibit new enterprise development. Furthermore, foreign exchange rates and prices are among the most volatile and fluctuating elements, creating substantial risks and uncertainties in the business environment. Therefore, the liberalization of exchange rate, tariff, and price policies should receive primary attention, not only because they are critical, but also because of the need to ensure their stability in real terms over time. Distortions in other industrial and trade policies, such as excessive wages, taxes, etc., are unlikely, on an individual basis, to affect corporate revenues to any great length. When taken together, however, they can be quite important in distorting the incentive framework.

Attracting Foreign Direct Investment

The world economy is increasingly being driven by foreign direct investment (FDI). Over 70 percent of world trade and the major part of technological innovations are now generated by multinational enterprises, which also carry out most international marketing and distribution.[18] If India is serious about globalizing her economy, it must attract more foreign investment. Toward this end, there is a need for clarity and transparency in national investment policy and for regulatory changes to facilitate long-term investment and day-to-day operations.

Foreign Equity Ownership

India's 40 percent limit on foreign ownership always came under strong criticism and was considered a major disincentive to foreign investors. Majority foreign ownership is often cited as an essential requirement, not only for retaining control over the operations of affiliates, but also for protection of proprietary know-how and commercial and trade secrets, in addition to enabling consolidation of the accounts of the affiliates with those of the parent company. This problem has now been taken care of. The new policy, adopted in 1991, allows direct equity participation up to 51 percent.[19] With majority ownership, MNCs can now seek full effective control and meet other essential requirements perceived by foreign investors as important.

It should be noted that the new policy on equity participation applies only to a group of 34 industries. India must revise its policy from time to time to attract specific industries, where current majority ownership is not permissible.

Further, although a large number of industries have been deregulated under the 1991 policy, licensing is still required for the following industries: coal and lignite; petroleum (other than crude) and its distillation products; distillation and brewing of alcoholic drinks; sugar; animal fats and oils, cigars and cigarettes of tobacco and manufactured tobacco substitutes; asbestos and asbestos-based products; plywood, decorative veneers, and other wood-based products; raw hides and skins, leather, chamois leather, and patent leather; tanned or dressed furskins; motor cars; paper and newsprint except bagasse-based units; electronic aerospace and defense equipment (all types); industrial explosives, including detonating fuse, safety fuse, gun powder, nitrocellulose, and matches; hazardous chemicals; drugs and pharmaceuticals (according to drug policy); entertainment electronics (VCRs, color TVs, tape recorders); and white goods (domestic refrigerators, domestic dishwashing machines, programmable domestic washing machines, microwave ovens, airconditioners).[20]

If major increases in FDI are sought, it may be necessary to deregulate some of these industries, especially those in which India has the potential to emerge as a global player. Besides, additional deregulation will strengthen foreign investors' confidence in India.

Foreign Exchange Regulations

In the interest of promoting investment and technology inflows, several changes and relaxations in the Foreign Exchange Regulations Act (FERA) are required, especially if changes with respect to majority ownership are to be implemented. At present, foreign companies, as defined in FERA, need to obtain the Reserve Bank's permission for a variety of transactions and face a large number of restrictions with respect to expansion, diversification of production, and foreign exchange transactions. Most of these requirements are still necessary despite the revision of the guidelines relating to foreign majority ownership. In other words, the provisions in FERA relating to companies with more than 40 percent foreign equity need to be revised. Apart from being able to expand or diversify, foreign majority-owned companies would also need to be exempted from obtaining the Reserve Bank's prior permission for various commercial transactions. In general, those commercial transactions involving foreign exchange should be permitted routinely. While it may be obligatory for foreign-controlled companies to furnish information required by the Reserve Bank for the purpose of exchange control, no undue restrictions should be placed on their business and commercial operations.

Local Content Requirement

An important policy in India has been the insistence on a high level of local content to be achieved in a short period of time. It is argued by foreign investors that local content requirements are not strictly imposed in most Asian economies and production of automobiles, consumer durables, and capital goods involves substantial imports of parts and components of higher quality than those produced locally.[21] Over the last two decades, several enterprises in Southeast Asia have developed considerable export capability in consumer durables and machinery products, such as transformers and motors, with relatively high imports of components. India could build similar strength if local content requirements are relaxed.

Phased indigenous manufacturing and increased local content have been an important feature of India's policy for over three decades. Apart from reducing foreign exchange requirements, increased local content has been a critical element in industrial and technological diversification in India and other developing countries, such as Brazil and Mexico. The extent to which the Southeast Asia experience of combining substantial maintenance imports with high export capability can be replicated under conditions in India is difficult to assess, particularly since most production is directed to the domestic market. What may be considered is a higher level of imports of intermediate products or components being linked to overall export performance of a particular foreign investment. The implementation of any guidelines on phased local manufacturing must also be flexible and subject to periodic adjustment in the light of actual experience.

Technology Transfer

While the increase in the number of technology agreements and collaborations during 1985-1988 has, undoubtedly, resulted in some technological upgrading in certain industries, it is doubtful whether it has achieved a level at which new manufactured products from India, particularly capital goods, consumer durables, and other engineering goods, can successfully compete in international markets.[22] Given the existing trends in Indian exports and the decline in exports of engineering goods, together with the major technological changes and breakthroughs in products and processes at the global level, a substantial increase in technology inflows would continue to be necessary. While certain manufactured products such as textiles, shoes, and some engineering goods have achieved global competitiveness, the number of such products has not increased significantly. This is largely due to increasing internal demand for these products and the growing technological lags in products and production processes in several manufacturing industries. India's lag in technology is revealed by the fact that, relative to others, India's payments have been very low. During the 1980s, for example, India spent only $280 million on technology, while Brazil spent $2 billion. If India wants sophisticated and up-to-date technologies, it must be willing to spend more on the import of technology.[23]

Technology agreements continue to face serious constraints. Apart from long delays, detailed guidelines or contractual provisions, particularly concerning technology payments, tend to be unduly restrictive. Royalty rates continue to be very low and are limited, apart from a few exceptions, to a maximum of 5 percent on net sales minus the value of imported items. Combined with a tax of 30 percent and a maximum duration of five to seven years, this tends to make the supply of technology and know-how far less remunerative than in other countries, including industrialized economies. Lump-sum payments, which are used to partly compensate for low royalties, tend to be determined rather arbitrarily and are not, in many cases, an appropriate substitute for suitable royalty rates. Minimum royalties are not permitted despite long gestation periods for particular projects. Foreign trademarks are generally not permitted on domestic sales, and intellectual property rights are inadequately protected in several fields. In view of these rigidly enforced guidelines, the supply of foreign technology tends to be greatly constrained.

Recent liberalizations in the guidelines on technology agreements are inadequate. The delegation of powers of approval to administrative ministries is of little significance to the foreign technology supplier or partner since the same guidelines have to be observed. The increase in royalty levels of up to 8 percent has been applied in very few cases and does not ensure substantial technology inflows, particularly after deducting imported materials and taxes. The increase in the period of duration has given some relief, but has also been applied only in relatively few cases. More importantly, delays in the processing and clearance of proposals persist.

The course adopted by the Republic of Korea should be of special interest in this context.[24] In 1980, a policy of automatic approval was adopted for technology contracts in several industries, ranging from heavy industries to electronics, for periods up to ten years or involving payments of up to 10 percent royalty and down payments of over $500,000 or, in the case of outright purchase of technologies, up to $1 million. Agreements with indefinite duration were also permitted in priority sectors where technological changes occurred rapidly. It was only following such liberalization that inflows of technology in the Republic of Korea increased very rapidly.

With soaring costs of research in most industrialized countries and high research intensity, new technologies have become far more expensive than established and mature techniques and processes in various fields. At the same time, the growing competition in new technologies has expanded their availability to new sources and has intensified the pace of technological obsolescence. To keep abreast of new technological developments in specific fields, a constant inflow of new technology, supported by intensive local sectorial research, is necessary. The adjustment of Indian industry to this rapidly changing technological situation may necessitate changes in policies and procedures with respect to foreign technology contracts.

Given the experience of the Republic of Korea and the changing technological environment, consideration should be given to the automatic approval of technology agreements under certain conditions and in selected industries, such as informatics comprising computers, telecommunications and systems, biotechnology and genetic engineering, capital goods production, including mechanical, electrical and transport equipment, and certain categories of petrochemicals. Levels of payment which may be considered for automatic approval could be 10 percent royalty for a period of ten years, subject to a total payment of $250,000 over the duration of a contract. All such agreements should be required to be registered with the Ministries of Industry and Finance, with copies to the Reserve Bank of India, for approval of remittances. In order to encourage inflows of foreign technology, it may also be considered whether the tax on payment of fees and royalties should be substantially reduced or abolished.

Monopolies and Restrictive Trade Practices Act (MRTP)

An important requirement for most projects in India involving substantial foreign investment is to obtain clearance under the Monopolies and Restrictive Trade Practices Act.[25] This is applicable both with respect to size, namely, fixed assets of over Rs. 1,500 million (approximately $60 million) or "dominance," defined as 25 percent of market share. The suggestions for revision include raising the level of fixed assets to Rs. 7,500 million (approximately $300 million) and modifying the definition of dominant undertakings to those with market share of over 50 percent for particular products or groups of products. A system of automatic approval for foreign investments up to a certain level and certain foreign technology agreements may still require MRTP clearance. Any changes in the legislation with respect to size or the proportion of market share which would constitute dominance would be welcomed by foreign investors. If no such changes take place, however, it would be desirable to provide specific guidelines and procedures for rapid processing of cases involving foreign capital participation from the MRTP angle.

Tax Policy

Taxation is considered as a major irritant in government investor relations in India. It has been pointed out that over 70 percent of all foreign investment in India was involved in tax litigation.[26] Moreover, tax policy is subject to sudden and frequent changes, which are often retroactive. A recent example was foreign oil drillers, who were invited to explore the area around Bombay by the award of tax-free status. A few months later, they suddenly became liable for a 50 percent levy as a result of a change in the tax law.

Foreign investors consider Indian taxes very reasonable by world standards. The problems lie in their implementation, and stem particularly from the setting of collection targets. To encourage investment, tax policy must be made more consistent, with liabilities remaining stable for at least five to ten years. In that way, investors would be able to make reliable cost estimates in planning operations. The government should also appoint a high-level tax official responsible for giving investors a clear and reliable assessment of their tax liabilities for the next few years.

Single-Window Clearance

An important criticism by foreign investors relating to India concerns the long delays in processing of applications for foreign investment and technology. A system of automatic approval and registration of foreign investment and technology agreements within certain parameters would largely meet the problem. It would still be necessary, however, to obtain approval for capital goods imports for meeting environmental requirements. In this respect, the concept of a "single-window" approach would become relevant. The "fast-track" approach, recently introduced by the Ministry of Finance, is an appropriate step in this direction, which could be extended to cover effective follow-up of all permissions and clearances that proposals involving foreign investment require. Since the number of such proposals may rapidly become very large, the "single-window" would need to be adequately manned. A useful approach with respect to certain requirements, such as public capital issue or environmental clearance, would be to determine specific regulations and guidelines and leave those to be implemented by the enterprise concerned. The responsibility would then shift to the enterprise, with the authorities exercising only checking functions to ensure that the regulations are complied with, as is the practice in most industrialized countries.

Summary

The role of FDI in India has been minimal, though foreign technology inflows are of vital significance for the manufacturing sector in India. It is, nevertheless, recognized by foreign investors that the country represents a major market as well as a critical base for production operations in various industries. The large pool of scientific and technical personnel also provides considerable potential for joint research and development programs between MNCs and Indian enterprises. At the same time, conditions for foreign participation may necessitate review of some existing policies and procedures. The liberalization during 1985-1988 with respect to industrial and technology licensing and capital goods imports have been welcomed by foreign investors. It has, however, been emphasized that if major inflows of foreign investment and technology, especially advanced technology, are to take place, it would be necessary to bring about further significant changes, in addition to those initiated in 1991 by the Rao government, in policies and procedures and, in general, to change the image of India to that of a country which welcomes foreign investment and technology, at least in selected sectors.

Enhancing Public Sector Enterprises Performance

Most public enterprises in India operate in an environment that effectively shields them from competitive forces, thereby potentially reducing the impact of reforms in encouraging entrepreneurship. Reform of public enterprises should, therefore, be an important element in a program to foster globalization.[27] Such a reform program should address some of the broader issues that are common to all revenue-earning public enterprises in the country, such as: (a) the degree of competition in the subsector, (b) the degree of financial autonomy and accountability, and (c) the degree of managerial autonomy and accountability.

Competition

Along with industrial, trade, and financial sector reform, public enterprises operating in competitive sectors should be subjected to competitive forces, including competition among themselves, with private firms and with imports. If necessary, large companies should be broken down into smaller competing firms, when economies of scale are unimportant.

In the case of monopolies or oligopolies, there may be a need to develop a pseudo-competitive system that could provide similar, though less intensive, pressures to induce state enterprises to undertake long-lasting and sustained searches for efficiency. In order to provide the equivalent to market "motivators" and "regulators," the system should: (a) require state enterprises to strictly adhere to well-defined objectives and targets, for example, through annual "contract plans" which may include export targets; (b) measure performance against these targets in a transparent and systematic way; and (c) provide large rewards for achievement (in lieu of market motivators) or substantial penalties (in lieu of market regulators) to induce managers to take the targets seriously. Without appropriate rewards and penalties, the system would be ineffective. Many countries, such as Korea, have found it useful to widely publish the results of performance evaluations, to exert public pressure for performance. Such a system may require the setting of ministerial secretariats and other processes.

In addition to the performance signaling system mentioned above, the government should make it clear that it will follow a "hard" budget posture vis-à-vis state enterprises; that is, if an enterprise does not perform, the government will not bail it out through subsidies and transfers. In addition, commercial banks should act independently and enforce financial discipline. Finally, state enterprises should be fully subjected to bankruptcy laws to ensure that nonviable or inefficient enterprises are liquidated. All these measures will put pressure on state enterprises to operate efficiently and profitably.

Financial Autonomy and Accountability

State enterprises should: (a) be able to set their own prices to reflect market forces in competitive industries, or opportunity costs in other industries; (b) have direct access to money and capital markets for their working capital and investments needs; (c) be able to set and be accountable for their financial liquidity, solvency, and profitability; (d) have no resort to government transfers or subsidies; and (e) should not be used by governments to finance their own deficits, such as by increasing arrears in government obligations. These measures will institutionalize financial discipline, encourage efficiency, and avoid preferences vis-à-vis private enterprises. The banking system and the capital markets are important to evaluate the performance of state enterprises. Government funds should only be made available to state enterprises for equity capital and for large expansion projects under reasonable debt/equity ratios. An additional important measure to make financial performance transparent is ensuring that if the enterprise is providing special social services at the government's insistence—such as employment in depressed areas—the enterprise is properly compensated to offset these additional costs. Ideally, these types of subsidies to a segment of the population should be given outside the state enterprise system.

Managerial Autonomy and Accountability

A third measure to encourage a greater market orientation for state enterprises is to give them greater managerial autonomy and accountability by rationalizing the relationship between the government and the enterprises. To realize that the state enterprise should be incorporated under commercial laws. Further, the role and responsibilities of the government, the Board of Directors, and the management should be clearly demarcated. The Board sets the policy and formulates the strategy, while the management is responsible for implementing them. The government exercises its ownership role. Decision-making authority should be delegated to managers. To facilitate decision making, the firm's management, accounting, and auditing information systems should be developed. In addition, to ensure professional and experienced management, the selection, appointment, promotion, compensation, and tenure of enterprise management should not be ad hoc, but should be based on a well-structured and transparent scheme. This is an important matter, since a common problem with many state enterprises is that managers are mostly political appointees, with little training and experience in management and finance.

A critical choice in providing market orientation to state enterprises is the choice of organizational form that would limit the role of government to exercise its ownership and control roles only. In order to coordinate, as well as to insulate, the influence of various governmental agencies, a focal point in the government should be established. Although the form of this focal point will have to be worked out, some suggestions can be made, since the degree of centralized control depends to some extent on the market orientation of the product. In competitive industries, the government apparatus can be quite simple, due to the facts that financial results can be used to measure performance, and that banks, suppliers, competitors, and other market participants will help in exercising discipline. In the case of noncompetitive industries, there may be a need for a large control mechanism, such as setting contract plans, price and output levels, and developing more detailed measures of performance. Some developing countries have established holding companies for this purpose, principally when there was a large number of small- or medium-sized state enterprises and a need for coordination on matters such as procurement and exports. The creation of sectoral holding companies, however, will tend to hamper competition. A better option would be to establish special units—either at the line ministry or under interministerial committees when several ministries need to be coordinated—to provide the government's ownership and control role. It is always critically important that the government acts only as a shareholder and refrains from intervening in the day-to-day affairs of the enterprise, which should be totally delegated to its management.

Privatization Policy

After achieving independence, India opted for a mixed economy with the public sector as the principal instrument of faster planned growth with social justice. In recent times, suggestions have been made for privatization of public enterprises. In India, dissatisfaction with the performance of public sector companies stems primarily from three aspects. First, they are monolithic and, for the most part, uncompetitive institutions. Second, they are inefficient. Third, they are a repository of excessive trade union power leading to irresponsible behavior. Briefly, there is an urgent need and desirability for considering privatizing state enterprises in India.

The circumstances that motivated the original formation of public sector enterprises in India, such as the lack of private sector interest and the lack of large pools of financing, have diminished over time.[28] Furthermore, India has been facing fiscal budget difficulties that could be alleviated by privatization.

While the above arguments comprise sound reasons to privatize public sector enterprises, political realities in India may not permit large-scale privatization, at least initially. If, in principle the government is interested in privatizations, however, it should quickly privatize two or three enterprises to provide a demonstrative effect and maintain inertia while a more comprehensive program is developed. Further outright sale of public sector enterprises may not be easy. The government may, therefore, embark on a program of privatization that includes such elements as: (a) economic and industrial liberalization; (b) a bigger role for the private sector in meeting investment targets; (c) growing importance of private capital as a source of funds; (d) improving management efficiency; and (e) joint-sector projects. The shift toward privatization will move slowly because of entrenched political opposition.

PUTTING STRATEGY TO WORK

The pragmatic implementation of policy is equally important in globalizing the economy. A variety of measures must be taken to launch the economy on a sustained course. India has gained considerable industrial experience in the last four decades which can be used as a foundation for future economic strategies. Right policies coupled with their adequate implementation would put India's various strengths into gear for sustained economic growth.

Political Commitment

India's political leadership must believe that in the emerging environment, and considering India's past achievements, outward-looking policies for trade and industry are essential for the country's development. The government, no matter to which party it belongs, must continually affirm its firm commitment to globalization of the Indian economy as the engine of economic growth. As a result, the policies for promotion of domestic rivalry, foreign investment, import liberalization, and export promotion would have a permanence that reassures firms that the rules of the game would not suddenly be reversed. Further, with globalization as the national objective, no other policy should be allowed to conflict with outward-looking economic policies. With so much attention given to the success of global economic policies, it should be possible to retreat from policies that prove ineffective.

Institutional Setup

More and more, the institutional setup for economic decision making looms large in explaining why some economies have been successful in their outward-looking economic policies. Take Japan and Korea, for example. What appears as common to their success in implementing outward-looking development strategies are: (a) an active private sector; (b) weak labor organizations; (c) an efficient bureaucracy; and (d) a set of strong institutional mechanisms that support the alliance of business and government. These factors together create a climate conducive to the conduct of business.

Initiating Companies to Export

The success of India's globalization strategy hinges upon Indian firms competing overseas. Overseas business evolves through several stages: (a) exporting through distributors; (b) distribution overseas through own-sales companies; (c) overseas production completely controlled by headquarters; (d) autonomous overseas operations; and (e) global integration of all overseas operations.

Most Indian companies are contented with the domestic market. Some companies have taken the first step, but have not gone beyond that. Exporting involves selecting the product, packaging it, shipping it, and in the foreign market receiving it, storing it, advertising it, and selling it to retailers, perhaps with arrangements for financing and for after-sales service. The time, risk, money, effort, and know-how required for these tasks explain why many would-be exporters simply resign themselves to producing for the domestic market, particularly since the Indian market is large and protected.

To initially encourage firms to export, however, buyers from abroad may be depended upon. If the conditions are right, they will come in and perform as many of these tasks as are needed to start and maintain a line for export production—for a price, of course. To make this happen, the government has to encourage Indian companies to export, on the one hand, and to create conditions to attract foreign buyers, on the other hand. The right conditions include: low production cost, good product quality, reliable delivery, high probability of ongoing supply, and an overall business environment that fosters rather than impedes export business.

This means that in the early stages of export promotion, marketing does not have to have the highest priority for many products. Foreign buyers will perform many, if not all, of the marketing tasks if prices and quality are acceptable and if deliveries are reliable.[29]

Based on the Japanese experience (and also the Korean), the trading companies have played a crucial role in developing their foreign markets. Should India pursue policies to develop general trading companies along the lines of Japan's *sogo shosha* is a question that requires probing. The incentives for general trading companies include preferential loans for stockpiling export products and higher ceilings on the foreign exchange holdings of their overseas operations.

As a matter of fact, some Indian manufacturers may like to rely on Japanese (or Korean) trading companies to initially enter export markets. The government should look into this possibility.

Going Beyond Exporting

The government of India has taken a variety of steps that have encouraged many firms to enter export markets. India's Export Trade Promotion Agency maintains offices in important centers around the world. Further, trade associations, such as the Confederation of Engineering Industry, have been formed to act as collective pressure groups on behalf of exporters. A variety of financial and trade incentives have also been enacted to push exports.

However, most firms have used these lures with a short-term outlook to make quick money. They have failed to establish a permanent foothold in the export markets and from there to launch a program of further international involvement, such as selling directly, starting overseas production, etc. The failure of Indian firms to move along the overseas business evolution cycle is a matter of concern that needs to be examined. Three questions are pertinent here: First, how effective have the initial measures of the government been (e.g., the performance of the Indian Trade Promotion Agency)? Second, what additional steps might be taken (e.g., provision of timely information)? Third, what may businessmen do to enhance their international involvement (e.g., establish a privately funded facilitating office in such important centers as New York and London, working in association with government agencies such as the Indian Investment Center)?

Organization Arrangements

India is a large economy to manage and the globalization program will increase the complexities further. In such an environment, proper and timely implementation of policy requires making structural changes at various levels in the government. For example, the Planning Commission may need to be reconstituted. Perhaps a new department should be added to the Prime Minister's office to look after matters relative to multinational corporations' technology purchases, export promotion, etc. Similarly, the role and effectiveness of such units as the Indian Investment Center should be evaluated and necessary changes made in light of overall organizational thrust.

The shape of exact organizational arrangements requires a thorough study on the subject, which is beyond the scope of the present work. However, it is important to remember that effective implementation requires one office to have the primary responsibility for the globalization program. This office would coordinate activities with different ministries as well as state government offices. The office should be the final arbiter in resolving conflicts, and the place to which firms, both foreign and domestic, may look for help and guidance.

Cadre of Professionals

The task of channeling the economy on a new path is by no means easy. Change is difficult for everyone, especially the vested interests who would find the new order unbearable. In addition, the benefits of global economy would become apparent only after a painful gestating period. To successfully steer the economy toward globalization, therefore, the country requires a cadre of professionals. India has an abundance of smart people. The Indian Administrative Service, as well as the Indian Foreign Service, produces highly capable people. To an extent, they can be credited for maintaining a democratic government even under extreme political crisis. But these people lack professional background, culture, and outlook to manage a business-oriented global economy. Efforts must be made, therefore, to develop new forms of training for the bureaucrats to equip them for the challenges they will face as they implement the new policy initiatives. Indian institutes of management can play an important role in this endeavor.

Program Coordination

There are several important ways in which policy reforms need to be coordinated. It is vital that implementation of domestic regulatory reform and the globalization policies take place over the same period of time, so that firms have new incentives to grow and to become more efficient, while the constraints on their doing so are removed. If domestic controls were relaxed without introducing greater competition from imported goods, there would be a risk that distortions in the pattern of investment would arise. Producers might overinvest in highly protected areas that offered opportunities for high returns, even if the economic cost of production were excessive. If external controls were relaxed without reducing domestic controls, then the industry would find it difficult to respond appropriately to foreign competition by changing investment patterns, product mix, technology, or inputs. Instead of efficient economic growth, such an opening to external competition could have adverse effects on some segments of the domestic manufacturing sector. This would quickly create pressure for reversing the policy reforms.

The easing of barriers to entry and growth needs to be accompanied by the relaxation of limitations on adaptation and exit. Unless this is done, producers will not have the flexibility needed to respond to changing market conditions by, for example, shedding old product lines, restructuring, or consolidating operations, and will be reluctant to enter new lines of business. Freer entry without increased flexibility to adapt or exit could lead to an even greater degree of capacity fragmentation, a major cause of present inefficiencies. Moreover, managerial or efficiency gains from increases in competition will remain limited while survival is assured.

Sequencing and Timing

The experiences of other countries forcefully demonstrates that the success of a globalization program, from direct controls on investment, production, and trade to indirect policies relying more heavily on market incentives and discipline, will be much greater if the initial policy actions are bold. An initial major shift in policy is required to ensure that the commitment to new policy is persuasive and, thus, yields the desired structural changes in investment and production. Moreover, without a relatively rapid expansion of efficient industries, the needed support for ongoing reform is unlikely to be forthcoming and resistance may increase. In particular, if exports do not expand quickly, then there is likely to be growing resistance to any general reduction in import protection.

In view of such concerns, the first stage of reform should ideally include export promotion, further relaxation of domestic regulations, and the establishment of guidelines for general import policy reform. The export promotion measures and generalized incentives would improve foreign exchange earnings and ease the transition away from quantitative restrictions on imports. They would also encourage firms to meet international quality and price standards and foster the more aggressive management required to respond to market shifts. These benefits would come at relatively low cost, as they would not imply any loss of domestic output or employment.

Concurrent further relaxation of domestic regulations on investment and employment would provide industry with increased flexibility to respond to export opportunities, increase domestic competition and, hence, incentives for productivity improvements, and help reduce the current disparity in profitability between the domestic and export markets. It would permit firms to move rapidly into new market niches created by shifting demand, technology, and resource patterns.

The pace of transition is a critical and sensitive element in any globalization program. Time is needed to build new factories and modernize existing ones, find and learn new technologies, redeploy workers and assets from activities that will no longer be competitive, develop new markets (including exports markets), and find new sources of financing. Too fast a pace would raise the costs of adjustment to the point where the government might be forced to reverse the process, while too slow a pace would delay the benefits of the program and give rise to resistance to further changes.

CONCLUSION

A country is a desirable global platform in an industry if it provides an environment yielding an advantage in competing globally to firms that are located there. The three key determinants of a good global platform are: (a) *comparative advantage* stemming from low labor cost, national resources, skilled scientific and technical personnel, and advanced infrastructure; (b) *characteristics of a country's demand* comprised of size and timing, sophistication and power of buyers and channels, and particular product features demanded; and (c) *local operating environment* referring to customs and conditions for doing business. India is well positioned as far as the first two determinants are concerned. If the government continues to forge ahead with its liberalization program to make the operating environment attractive, India would be an ideal global platform from which MNCs could launch business.

Indian leadership faces the twin demands of development and democracy in order to support a huge middle class that has the clout of ever-increasing buying power. Today, India is at the crossroads of change. It must take an in-depth look at how India can mobilize to compete and forge ahead in an age of increasing globalization of capital, markets, and production.

The process of change has already begun. India is trying to market itself to the international community by consolidating its preeminent position in the Asian region. It has begun to offer attractive incentives for international companies, including significant tax advantages, a cheap but skilled labor force, and affordable production facilities. At the same time, India has opened its doors to foreign investment in areas where modern technology is needed.

Yet more, much more, needs to be done. International success is a dynamic process, and the government must provide right and timely incentives, and create a congenial environment for innovation and training, the powerful sources of competitive advantage.

APPENDIX:
How Indian Firms Compete with MNCs

Nirma and the Detergent Market

Lever (Lever Bros.' subsidiary in India) started with a bar of soap and a cake (Sunlight). They followed it with a soap powder (Rinso) and, finally, with a synthetic detergent powder (Surf). Others in the market followed Lever. Tata (a large Indian company) had 501 bar followed by 501 cake, 501 soap powder, and then a detergent powder. Swastiks (another Indian company) were the first–even before Surf–to come out with a detergent powder but were soon overtaken by Surf.

Logically, a bar soap cake should have been followed by a detergent cake, not a powder. This was especially so when soap powders never really took off in the Indian market. India has always been primarily a bar/cake market. Further, thanks to Surf, all other detergent powders were "sophisticated" in the sense that they were in heavy cardboard packing, very well printed, and with powders which had a variety of ingredients to allow for optical whitening, high detergency, kindness to hands, etc. Lever started with large pack sizes and others followed suit. Some ten years after the launch, Lever introduced polyethylene sachet bags to provide a low-unit-price small pack which was aimed as a penetration pack.

Over the years many small-scale manufacturers had started selling detergent powder in regional markets, taking advantage of the government concessions available to them. The products were poorly presented, of low quality, and generally unbranded. In fact, synthetic detergents in the Indian market, despite very high rates of growth, accounted for only a fraction of the total washing market. This was primarily because of price. As vegetable oil prices increased, the price difference narrowed but, traditionally, vegetable soaps were still much cheaper.

Nirma (a small company) saw this gap and seized it with a product that was harsh on hands and clothes and had cheaper packing. Nirma also used the advantage of saving on the high excise duty by making it in a "cottage" industry, without the use of power and, thus, heavily labor-oriented. Their unique features in relation to other similar manufacturers were: a distinctive brand name and identity created and supported by highly professional advertising and a memorable jingle. They also did not set up their own sales force but built a loyal network of distributors around the country who earned higher margins than on Surf and other brands. In this way Nirma appealed to a whole new population for whom Surf was too expensive and to many current users of detergent brands for whom Surf and other brands were "too good" for use by domestic servants. Nirma, therefore, had an explosive growth and generally explosive effect also on the total market. Nirma had 59.5 percent of the powder market in 1988, versus 7.1 percent for Surf. Nirma followed on this success with a Nirma detergent cake which now has 34.2 percent of the market against the earlier very successful Rinso (which now has 21.6 percent).

Thus, Nirma's innovation was in taking full advantage of the tax concessions and equally, if not more so, in its approach of going after an existing mass market which had been ignored, with a product which satisfied the customer but did not give the customer attributes which added more to the price than to the utility that the customer got from them.

Balsara and the Toothpaste Market

Balsara is a company started as a manufacturer of products used to control odor and then branched to hygiene products and products used to keep toilet bowls clean. These were small markets and Balsara remained a small company though it was the dominant one among the many other small manufacturers.

It was the introduction of the toothpaste Promise that marked Balsara's entry into the big league. The toothpaste market in India has been dominated by multinationals, particularly Colgate, the others being Ciba, Lever, Geoffrey Manners, and Beecham. Interestingly, none of the others has been able over many years to make a dent into the very large market shares consistently held by Colgate. Both Lever and Ciba tried very hard. In the last 25 years Lever has had in this market brands such as S. R. Gibbs, Pepsodent, Signal, and Close-Up. Of these, the first two have been withdrawn, and the latter two lead a tenuous existence. It could be questioned whether Lever even makes money on their entries in the toothpaste market. Ciba, which had a few years of success when Chlorophyll was in fashion and pioneered the use of jingles on the radio, has not been able to repeat that success subsequently.

Geoffrey Manners has had Forhans as a specially positioned toothpaste (for gums) in the market for many years and has consistently held on to its modest share. It is not an ambitious brand and has not made any waves in the market. Another multinational which is also in the market is Beecham with Macleans toothpaste, again a very modest member of this large market. Hence, Colgate has been an enormously profitable and successful company, thanks to its continuing dominance in the toothpaste market. Its vast resources enable heavy advertising and it has a superlative distribution network supported by a good sales force. The product sets the taste and flavor preferences among customers. All attempts by other multinationals have failed in making a serious dent in their position.

It was this market that Balsara entered with Promise. They have been very successful, being now No. 2 in the market after Colgate, with a 22 percent market share (versus the 45 percent of Colgate).

What is it that enabled Balsara to succeed when so many larger and more experienced companies could not do so? Balsara went "ethnic." They recognized that cloves were the accepted remedy all over the sub-continent for problems with the gums, teeth, and mouth odor. They, therefore, launched a toothpaste whose major claim was that it contained clove oil. They also made sure that the base used for the product was satisfactory, as was the foam characteristic. They had the courage to invest in advertising, despite their small size as a company. While others tried to copy Colgate or to introduce product concepts picked up from their home markets in the U.S. or elsewhere in the west, Balsara instead went "native." This success has been sustained over the years.

Source: S. L. Rao, "Innovative Marketing Strategies: Small Enterprises Fight Large Established Companies," *Economic and Political Weekly*, August 26, 1989, pp. M-127-M-128.

Reference Notes

CHAPTER 1
MARKETS IN DEVELOPING COUNTRIES

1. "What is the Third World?" in *Third World Guide 89/90* (New York: Neal-Schuman Publishers, Inc., 1989), p. 12.
2. *The Global Century: A Source Book on U.S. Business and the Third World* (Washington, DC: National Cooperative Business Association, 1989), p. 17.
3. George Thomas Kurian, ed., *Encyclopedia of the Third World* (New York: Facts on File, Inc., 1981).
4. *World Development Report 1988* (Washington, DC: The World Bank, 1988), pp. 222-223.
5. Ibid., pp. 226-227.
6. Ibid., pp. 284-285.
7. "Indicators of Market Size for 117 Countries," *Business International*, July 30, 1990, pp. 252-255.
8. *Forbes*, August 22, 1988, p. 69.
9. *World Development Report 1987* (Washington, DC: The World Bank, 1987), p. 38.
10. *President's Task Force on International Private Enterprise* (Washington, DC: U.S. Government Printing Office, 1984), p. 70.
11. C. Fred Bergsten, *America in the World Economy: A Strategy for the 1990s* (Washington, DC: Institute for International Economics, 1988), p. 61.
12. Nikhilesh Dholakia, "Marketing in the LDCs: Its Nature and Prospects," in G. S. Kindra, ed., *Marketing in Developing Countries* (London: Croom Helm, 1984), pp. 10-28.
13. Ibid.
14. "Making the Most of Brand-Name Sales in the Indian Market," *Business International*, May 22, 1989, p. 155.

CHAPTER 2
U.S. BUSINESS WITH DEVELOPING COUNTRIES

1. "Leap Forward or Sink Back," *Development Forum*, March 1982, p. 3.

2. *World Development Report 1987* (Washington, DC: The World Bank, 1987), p. 42.

3. Ibid., p. 47.

4. *1987 U.S. Foreign Trade Highlights* (Washington, DC: U.S. Department of Commerce, 1988).

5. Ray Marshall, "Jobs: The Shifting Structure of Global Employment," in *Growth, Exports, and Jobs in a Changing World Economy* (Washington, DC: Overseas Development Council, 1988), p. 185.

6. *1987 U.S. Foreign Trade Highlights* (Washington, DC: U.S. Department of Commerce, 1988).

7. Herbert E. Meyer, "How We're Fixed for Strategic Minerals," *Fortune*, February 9, 1981, pp. 68-71. Also see: Peter Nulty, "How to Pay a Lot for Cobalt," *Fortune*, April 4, 1983, pp. 150-155.

8. Constantinos C. Markides and Norman Berg, "Manufacturing Offshore is Bad Business," *Harvard Business Review*, September-October 1988, p. 115. Also see: "AT&T to Build Plant in Thailand," *The New York Times*, June 24, 1988, p. D4.

9. "U.S. Trade Outlook," *Business America*, April 22, 1991. Additional information was obtained from the U.S. Department of Commerce.

10. Based on an interview with an official of the U.N. Center for Transnational Corporations.

11. *International Investment and Multinational Enterprises: Recent Trends in International Direct Investment* (Paris: OECD, 1987), pp. 186-210.

12. Bernard Wysocki, Jr., "Returning to the Third World," *The Wall Street Journal*, September 20, 1991, p. R1.

13. *New Forms of International Investment in Developing Countries: The National Perspective* (Paris: OECD, 1984), p. 106.

14. See: Raymond Vernon, "International Investment and International Trade in the Product Cycle," *Quarterly Journal of Economics*,

May 1986, pp. 190-207; and Louis T. Wells, Jr., "A Product Life Cycle for International Trade," *Journal of Marketing*, July 1968, pp. 1-6.

15. Subhash C. Jain, *International Marketing Management* (Boston, MA: PWS-Kent Publishing Company, 1990), p. 30.

16. Peter Drucker, "From World Trade to World Investment," *The Wall Street Journal*, May 26, 1987, p. 32.

17. Theodore H. Moran, *The U.S. Economy and Developing Countries* (Washington, DC: Overseas Development Council, 1988).

18. Thomas L. Brewer, Kenneth David, and Linda Y. C. Lim, *Investing in Developing Countries: A Guide for Executives* (Lexington, MA: Lexington Books, 1986), p. 8.

19. *Indo-U.S. Business Review* (Bombay, India: Indo-American Chamber of Commerce, February 1990), p. 5.

20. Ray Marshall, *op. cit.*, p. 188.

21. See Heidi Vernon-Wortzel and Lawrence H. Wortzel, "Globalizing Strategies for Multinationals from Developing Countries," *Columbia Journal of World Business*, Spring 1988, pp. 27-36.

22. See Anthony J. F. O'Reilly, "Establishing Successful Joint Ventures in Developing Nations: A CEO's Perspective," *Columbia Journal of World Business*, Spring 1985, p. 309. Also see: Gregory Stricharchuk, "Heintz Splits Upstar-Kist in Move to Raise World Canned-Fish Sales," *The Wall Street Journal*, November 2, 1988, p. B6.

23. *President's Task Force on International Private Enterprise, Report to the President* (Washington, DC: U.S. Government Printing Office, 1984), p. 90.

24. *World Development Report 1988* (Washington, DC: The World Bank, 1988), pp. 23-34.

25. *Agricultural Trade Highlights* (Washington, DC: U.S. Department of Agriculture, December 1988).

26. Richard Hemming and Ali M. Mansoor, "Privatization and Public Enterprises," *Occasional Paper, No. 56*, International Monetary Fund, 1988, p. 9.

27. *The GATT Negotiations and U.S. Trade Policy* (Washington, DC: Congressional Budget Office, 1987), p. 1.

CHAPTER 3
MARKET EVOLUTION PROCESS

1. Heidi Vernon-Wortzel and Lawrence H. Wortzel, "Globalizing Strategies for Multinationals from Developing Countries," *Columbia Journal of World Business*, Spring 1988, pp. 27-35.

2. See: Philip R. Cateora, *International Marketing* (Homewood, IL: Richard D. Irwin, Inc., 1990), pp. 303-306.

3. Lester R. Brown, *By Bread Alone* (New York: Praeger Publishers, 1974).

4. Erdener Kaynak, *Marketing in the Third World* (New York: Praeger Publishers, 1982), Chapter 1.

5. Hernando de Soto, *The Other Path: The Invisible Revolution* (New York: Harper & Row, 1988).

6. Marcus Franda, *Small Is Politics* (New Delhi: Wiley Eastern Limited, 1979).

7. Ford S. Worthy, "Why There's Still Promise in China," *Fortune*, February 22, 1987, pp. 95-100.

8. *World Development Report 1988* (Washington, DC: The World Bank, 1988), pp. 33-35.

9. Jeremy Main, "How to Make Poor Countries Rich," *Fortune*, January 16, 1989, pp. 101-106.

10. Leslie M. Dawson, "Multinational Strategic Planning for Third World Markets," *Journal of Global Marketing*, Spring 1988, pp. 28-49.

11. Walt W. Rowtow, *The Stages of Economic Growth* (London: Cambridge University Press, 1960).

12. William A. Stoever, "The Stages of Developing Country Policy Toward Foreign Investment," *Columbia Journal of World Business*, Fall 1985, pp. 3-11.

13. Y. A. Verma, "Marketing in Rural India," *Management International Review*, Vol. 10, No. 3, 1980, pp. 45-50.

14. F. Lisk, "Conventional Development Strategies and Basic Need Fulfillment," *International Labor Review*, March 1977, pp. 175-191.

15. Brian Tew, *International Monetary Cooperation, 1945-70*, 10th ed. (London: Hutchinson & Co. Publishers Ltd., 1970).

16. V. H. Singh, *Technology Transfer and Economic Develop-

ment: Models and Practices for Developing Countries (Jersey City, NJ: Unz & Co., 1983).

17. Thomas E. Hill, W. Warren Haynes, and Howard Baumgartel, *Institution Building in India* (Boston: Graduate School of Business Administration, Harvard University, 1973).

18. Theodore Levitt, "The Globalization of Markets," *Harvard Business Review*, May-June 1983, pp. 92-102.

19. Art Pine, "Africa's Poorest: Sub-Saharan Countries Take First Steps to End Economic Nightmare," *The Wall Street Journal*, September 16, 1982, p. 1.

20. J.M. Parkinson, "Marketing in Lesser Developed Countries," *Quarterly Review of Marketing* (UK), Autumn, 1985, pp. 1-14.

21. A. Kumar, "Sizing Up the Black Economy: Some Issues," *Economic and Political Weekly of India*, August 1985, pp. 1485-1488.

22. Robert Bartels, ed., *Comparative Marketing: Wholesaling in Fifteen Countries* (Homewood, IL: Richard D. Irwin, Inc., 1983).

23. Frank Meissner, "Capital-Intensive Supermarket Technology Can't Serve Needs of Poor in Third World," *Marketing News*, November 27, 1981, p. 15.

24. Y. A. Verma, *op. cit.*

25. "Asia: A New Front in the War on Smoking," *Business Week*, February 25, 1991, p. 66.

26. Jean Boddewyn, "The One and Many Worlds of Advertising: Regulatory Obstacles and Opportunities," *International Journal of Advertising*, Vol. 7, No 1, 1988.

27. Ford S. Worthy, "A Mass Market Emerges," *Fortune* (Pacific Rim Issue), 1990, p. 51.

28. Edward T. Hall, "The Silent Language in Overseas Business," *Harvard Business Review*, May-June 1960, pp. 88-96.

29. Herbert E. Meyer, "How We're Fixed for Strategic Minerals," *Fortune*, February 9, 1981, pp. 68-71.

30. James E. Austin, *Managing in Developing Countries* (New York: The Free Press, 1990), p. 42.

31. James Brian Quinn, "Scientific or Technical Strategy at the National and Major Firm Level," in *UNESCO's Role of Science and Technology in Economic Development* (Paris: UNESCO, 1970), pp. 85-86.

32. "The Cut Flower Industry in Columbia," a case copyrighted by the President and Fellows of Harvard College, 1978.

33. Anil Kumar Jain, *Economic Planning in India* (New Delhi: Ashish Publishing House, 1986), pp. 24-26.

34. James E. Austin, *op. cit.*, pp. 47-48.

35. Tagi Sagafi-Nejad, "Egypt," *World Development*, Vol. 12, Nos. 5/6, 1984, pp. 567-573.

36. Vern Terpstra and Kenneth David, *The Cultural Environment of International Business*, Third Edition (Cincinnati, OH: South-Western Publishing Co., 1991), Chapter 4.

37. Michael E. Porter, *The Competitive Advantage of Nations* (New York: The Free Press, 1990), Chapter 3.

38. Ibid., p. 118.

39. Jeremy Main, "How to Go Global–And Why," *Fortune*, August 28, 1989, p.70.

40. Yung Whee Rhee, Bruce Ross-Larson, and Gary Pursell, *Korea's Competitive Edge: Managing the Entry into World Markets* (Washington, DC: The World Bank, 1984), Chapter 5.

41. N. C. Nwaogwugwu, "Marketing Planning and Organization in Nigerian Enterprises," in Julius O. Onah, ed., *Marketing in Nigeria* (London: Cassell, 1979), p. 86.

CHAPTER 4
INDIA'S BUSINESS SCENE

1. *India–An Annual Survey* (New Delhi: Publications Division, 1991), p. 5.

2. David B. Barrett, *World Christian Encyclopedia* (Oxford: Oxford University Press, 1983).

3. *India–An Annual Survey, op. cit.*, pp. 55-56.

4. Ashakant Nimbark, "Indian Elections as Mythological Opera," *India*, February 1990, pp. 27-30.

5. "Into the Washing-Machine Age," *The Economist*, October 7, 1989, p. 91.

6. Tarun Gupta, "Managing Bureaucracy: Key Task of Revitalizing an Old, Slow System," *The Economic Times*, April 13, 1985, p. 10.

7. Jagdish N. Bhagwati and Padma Desai, *India: Planning for Industrialization* (New York: Oxford University Press, 1980).

8. *India: Poverty, Employment, and Social Services* (Washington, DC: The World Bank, 1989), Chapter 5.

9. T. N. Ninan, "Business and Economy: Reaching Out and Upward," in Marshall M. Bouton and Philip Oldenburg, eds., *India Briefing 1989* (Boulder, CO: Westview Press, 1989), pp. 40-48.

10. "Puppies and Consumer Boomers," *Time*, November 13, 1989, p. 53.

11. K. C. Khanna, "Strategy for Seventh Plan," *The Times of India*, January 27, 1985, p. 8.

12. *India: An Industrializing Economy in Transition* (Washington, DC: The World Bank, 1989), pp. 1-5.

13. V. M. Dandekar, "Indian Economy Since Independence," *Economic and Political Weekly*, January 2-9, 1988, pp. 46-50.

14. *India: An Industrializing Economy in Transition*, pp. 6-25.

15. Ibid.

16. *India: Poverty, Employment, and Social Services*, Chapter 2.

17. Ibid.

18. Ibid.

19. Ibid., Chapter 3.

20. *India: Recent Developments and Medium-Term Issues* (Washington, DC: The World Bank, 1989), Chapter 1.

21. M. L. Dantawala, "Growth and Equity in Agriculture," *Indian Journal of Agricultural Economics*, April-June 1987, pp. 154-158.

22. Ibid.

23. *India: Poverty, Employment and Social Services*, Chapter 3.

24. "Ballooning Growth," *India Today*, May 15, 1990, p. 45.

25. "Gandhi Starts to Use His New Broom," *New York Times*, February 21, 1985.

26. "Rajiv Gandhi Takes Charge," *Newsweek*, January 14, 1985, pp. 6-11.

27. *Economic Survey, 1988-89* (New Delhi: Publications Division, Government of India, 1990), pp. S76-S77.

28. Anand P. Gupta, "Financing Public Enterprises Investments in India," *Economic and Political Weekly*, December 17, 1988, pp. 2697-2702.

29. Raj Krishna, "The Economic Outlook for India," in James R. Roach, ed., *India 2000: The Next Fifteen Years* (Riverdale, MD: Riverdale, 1986).

30. William A. Stoever, "India: The Long, Slow Road to Liberalization," *Business Horizons*, January-February 1988, pp. 42-46.

31. Tarun Gupta, "Managing Bureaucracy: Key Tasks of Revitalizing an Old, Slow System," *op. cit.*, p. 10.

32. *Investing in India: A Guide to Entrepreneurs* (New Delhi: Indian Investment Center, 1990).

33. Louis T. Wells, Jr., *Third World Multinationals: The Rise of Foreign Investment from Developing Countries* (Cambridge: MIT Press, 1983).

34. See D. G. Gupta, "Companies Poised to Expand," *The Times of India*, January 24, 1985, p. 1. Also from interviews with India's Planning Commission officials.

35. "Ballooning Growth," *India Today*, May 15, 1990, p. 45.

36. *Perspectives and Issues and Implications of Alternative Growth Rates for the Eighth Five-Year Plan* (New Delhi: Planning Commission, 1988).

37. Mayank Chhaya and Milind Palnitkar, "The Great Lifestyle Revolution," *India Abroad*, September 13, 1991, p. 21.

38. Steven R. Weisman, "India's Tentative Turnaround," *New York Times*, May 29, 1988, p. 8.

39. Palakunnathu G. Mathai, "Stock Markets: Changing Times," *India Today*, October 15, 1989, p. 26.

40. "India is Becoming the New Asian Magnet for U.S. Business," *Business Week*, May 1, 1989, p. 132D.

41. "The Great Lifestyle Revolution," p. 21.

42. "Into the Washing-Machine Age," p. 91.

43. Ibid.

44. "India Busts Out of a Long Boom-Bust Cycle," *Business Week*, July 18, 1988, p. 86.

45. Anthony Spaeth, "A Thriving Middle Class is Changing the Face of India," *The Wall Street Journal*, May 19, 1988, p. 30.

46. "Puppies and Consumer Boomers," p. 55.

47. "Export of Maruti Cars to France," *India News*, September 5, 1991, p. 16.

48. "Indian Company to Make Telephones for Export to U.S.," *India News*, January 1991, p. 16.

49. "Ballooning Growth," *India Today*, May 15, 1990, p. 45.

50. "India Waits for a Lotus to Blossom," *Business Week*, Innovation Issue, 1990, p. 155.

51. Aprajita Sikri, "Tata Consultancy Sets the Pace," *India Abroad*, July 6, 1990, p. 12.

CHAPTER 5
MARKET EVOLUTION IN INDIA

1. Anil Kumar Jain, *Economic Planning in India* (New Delhi: Ashish Publishing House, 1986), Chapter 1.

2. M. L. Dantawala, "Growth and Equity in Agriculture," *Indian Journal of Agricultural Economics*, April-June 1987, pp. 154-158.

3. Jagdish N. Bhagwati and Padma Desai, *India: Planning for Industrialization* (New York: Oxford University Press, 1970).

4. A. S. Ganguly, "The Growing Rural Market in India," *Chairman's Speech* (Bombay: Hindustan Lever Ltd., 1984).

5. Manjula Narayan, "Rural Development in India," *India News*, December 1990, p. 3.

6. Navin Chandra Joshi, "India's Consultancy and Projects Exports," *India News*, December 1990, p. 3.

7. Khokan Mookerji, "Toward New Marketing Horizons," *Executive Speech* (Calcutta: ITC Limited, 1990).

8. Jay Dubashi, "Who Says India is a Poor Country?" *Times of India*, April 10, 1989, p. 10.

9. "India Becoming the New Asian Magnet for U.S. Business," *Business Week*, May 1, 1989, p. 132D.

10. "Of Color TVs and Washing Machines," *Business India*, December 11-24, 1989, p. 90.

11. "Ballooning Growth," *India Today*, May 15, 1990, p. 45.

12. William A. Stoever, "India: The Long, Slow Road to Liberalization," *Business Horizons*, January-February 1988, pp. 42-46.

13. "Of Color TVs and Washing Machines," *Business India*, December 11-24, 1989, p. 90.

14. Anthony Spaeth, "A Thriving Middle Class is Changing the Face of India," *The Wall Street Journal*, May 19, 1988, p. 30.

15. Viewed from India's living standard and cost of living, Rs. 10,000 is a lot of money. Scholars consider families with annual income of Rs. 25,000 or more as middle class. Thus, for many middle-class families, a television costs a big proportion of their annual income.

16. "Of Color TVs and Washing Machines," *Business India*, December 11-24, 1989, p. 90.

17. A total of forty-seven interviews were conducted consisting of eight marketing academics, eleven advertising/marketing research professionals, eight bureaucrats, and twenty marketing managers. Most of the interviews were conducted in the summer of 1991, mostly in Bombay and Delhi, with a few in Calcutta and Ahmedabad.

18. The roads in Bombay and Calcutta are too crowded and, hence, unsafe for a two-wheel vehicle (scooter/motorcycle), the mode of transportation within the reach of the middle class.

19. Most information on behavior changes is based on the author's interpretation of ideas advanced by different people interviewed in India.

20. Ashok Rudra, "Luxury-Led Growth Strategy and Its Beneficiaries," *Economic and Political Weekly*, July 2, 1988, pp. 1370-1372.

21. Khokan Mookerji, "Toward New Marketing Horizons," *Executive Speech* (Calcutta: ITC Limited, 1990).

22. "Into the Washing-Machine Age," *The Economist*, October 7, 1989, p. 91.

23. "Puppies and Consumer Boomers," *Time*, November 13, 1989, p. 53.

24. This section draws heavily on *A Psychographic Profile of the Indian Housewife* (Bombay: Pathfinders: India, 1987).

25. An outer garment worn by Indian women, consisting of lightweight cloth, about six yards in length. One end of the cloth is wrapped around the waist to form a skirt and the other draped over the shoulder.

26. Outerwear commonly worn by young girls and younger women in India, consisting of a long dress and a matching pajama.

27. Gathering to offer prayers either in a temple, at home, or in a community hall.

28. Adapted from: *A Psychographic Profile of the Indian Housewife.*

29. Alfred D. Chandler, Jr., "The Evolution of Modern Global Competition," in Michael E. Porter, ed., *Competition in Global Industries* (Boston: Harvard Business School Press, 1986), pp. 405-448.

30. Exhibits 5-5, 5-6, and 5-7 are based on a study that involved a random sample of 10,303 personal interviews of approximately one hour, 45 minutes each with women aged 18 to 45 years, all married. The interviews were conducted in 1987 in large metropolitan areas and a mix of large and small cities in different parts of India.

31. "Export Hopes," *India Today*, February 15, 1991, p. 64.

32. "Rajiv Gandhi Takes Charge," *Newsweek*, January 14, 1985, pp. 6-11.

33. "India Becoming the New Asian Magnet for U.S. Business," *Business Week*, May 1, 1989, p. 132D.

34. Nupur Basu, "Little Buyers Make Big Business," *India Abroad*, September 13, 1991, p. 24.

35. "The Art of Sell," *India Today*, December 31, 1990, p. 48.

36. Ibid.

37. Remarks made during a personal interview.

CHAPTER 6
U. S. BUSINESS IN INDIA

1. Cheryl McQueen, "Liberal Economic Policies and Steady Growth are Luring More American Companies to India," *Business America*, October 10, 1988, pp. 14-18. Information updated from the U.S. Department of Commerce.

2. Batuk Vora and Vidya Nayak Root, "U.S. Business Favors India vs. China," *India Abroad*, June 16, 1989, p. 17.

3. "Crafts for Export," *Commercial Bulletin of the Embassy of India*, July 15, 1989, p. 1.

4. Richard D. Harding, "India: New Policies, New Opportunities," *Business America*, May 9, 1988, p. 32.

5. Center for Monitoring Indian Economy, New Delhi.

6. This section draws heavily from: *Indo-U.S. Joint Ventures*

Partners in Progress (Bombay: Indo-American Chamber of Commerce, no date).

7. *Foreign Economic Trends and Their Implications for the United States: India* (Washington, DC: U.S. Department of Commerce, 1989).

8. R. Michael Gadbaw and Leigh A. Kenny, "India," in R. Michael Gadbaw and Timothy J. Richards, eds., *Intellectual Property Rights: Global Consensus, Global Conflict?* (Boulder, CO: Westview Press, 1988), p. 200.

9. "Indian Drug Makers: Brand X is Better," *The Economist*, July 1, 1989, p. 58; and S. N. Vasuki, "Pharmaceuticals: Exports Surge," *India Today*, April 30, 1989, pp. 64-65.

10. "Indian Scientific Strengths: Selected Opportunities for Indo-U.S. Collaboration," *Proceedings of a National Science Foundation Workshop* (Washington, DC: Spring 1987).

CHAPTER 7
PROBLEMS OF DOING BUSINESS IN INDIA

1. David J. Encarnation and Sushil Vachani, "Foreign Ownership: When Hosts Change the Rules," *Harvard Business Review*, September-October 1985, p. 152.

2. *Business International*, June 18, 1990, p. 200.

3. *Indo-U.S. Joint Ventures Partners in Progress* (Bombay: Indo-American Chamber of Commerce, no date).

4. *Indo-U.S. Business Review* (Bombay: Indo-American Chamber of Commerce, 1990).

5. T. N. Ninan, "Business and Economy: Reaching Out and Upward," in Marshall M. Bouton and Philip Oldenberg, eds., *India Briefing 1989* (Boulder, CO: Westview Press, 1989).

6. Ashok V. Desai, ed., *Technology Absorption in Indian Industry* (New Delhi: Wiley Eastern, Ltd., 1988).

7. *The Seventh Five-Year Plan, 1985-90* (New Delhi: Planning Commission, Government of India, 1985).

8. *Tax Incentives for Investment in India* (New Delhi: Indian Investment Center, 1988).

9. Stanley A. Kochanek, "Briefcase Politics in India: The Con-

gress Party and the Business Elite," *Asian Survey*, December 1987, pp. 1278-1301.

10. Rajiv Khanna, "Licensing and Joint Ventures in India," a paper presented at a U.S. Department of Commerce Seminar on India, March 1987.

11. Ashok Pratap, *Protection of Intellectual Property in India* (Bombay: Indo-American Chamber of Commerce, 1986).

12. "Indian Drug Makers: Brand X is Better," *The Economist*, July 1, 1989, p. 58; and S. N. Vasuki, "Pharmaceuticals: Exports Surge," *India Today*, April 30, 1989, pp. 64-65.

13. Pratap, *Protection of Intellectual Property in India*.

14. R. Michael Gadbaw and Leigh A. Kenney, "India," in R. Michael Gadbaw and Timothy J. Richards, eds., *Intellectual Property Rights: Global Census, Global Conflict?* (Boulder, CO: Westview Press, 1988).

15. "Investment Climate Statement–India," a paper prepared by Indian Investment Center, New Delhi, May 1990.

16. *Foreign Investment in India–Opportunities and Incentives* (New Delhi: Indian Investment Center, 1989).

17. See Robert Black, Stephen Blank and Elizabeth C. Hanson, *Multinationals in Contention* (New York: The Conference Board, 1978).

18. R. Jagannathan and Paranjoy Thakurta, "Indian Economy: Thank You, Sadam," *India Today*, February 15, 1991, p. 28.

19. See "Indian Industry: Way Below Par," *India Today*, January 11, 1991, p. 51.

20. See Prakash Tandon, "Maturing of Business in India," *California Management Review*, Spring 1972, p. 80.

21. Atul Kohli, "Politics of Economic Liberalization in India," *World Development*, March 1989, pp. 305-328; and Yoginder K. Alagh, "Policy, Growth and Structural Change in Indian Industry," *Economic and Political Weekly*, May 1987, pp. AN57-AN60.

22. Walter C. Neale, "India: The Secret Success Story," *Survey of Business*, Fall 1989, pp. 56-59.

23. Karen Elliott House, "Domestic Burdens Limit Global Role of Beijing, Moscow," *The Asian Wall Street Journal*, February 13, 1989, p. 1.

24. Bahbani Sen Gupta, *The Gorbachev Factor in World Affairs:*

An Indian Interpretation (New Delhi: B. R. Publishing Corporation, 1989).

25. See Gerald K. Helleiner, "Balance-of-Payments Experience and Growth Prospects of Developing Countries: A Synthesis," in *International Monetary and Financial Issues for the Developing Countries* (New York: UNCTAD, 1987).

CHAPTER 8
STRATEGIES FOR MARKET SUCCESS IN INDIA

1. *Investing in India* (New Delhi: Federation of Indian Chambers of Commerce and Industry, 1988); and interview with a researcher at the Indian Council of Applied Economic Research, New Delhi.

2. Nambi Marthandam, "Toy Tanks for Soviet Children," *India Abroad*, December 2, 1988, p. 6.

3. M. R. Mayya, "Coping with Growth," *India Today*, December 15, 1990, p. 3.

4. Ashok Pratap, *Protection of Intellectual Property in India* (Bombay: Indo-American Chamber of Commerce, 1986).

5. "India: It Has a Long List of Problems–But the High-Tech Quest Goes On," *Business Week*, August 10, 1987, p. 34.

6. Ibid., p. 36.

7. "India is Becoming the New Asian Magnet for U.S. Business," *Business Week*, May 1, 1989, p. 132D.

8. Cheryl McQueen, "Liberal Economic Policies and Steady Growth are Luring More American Companies in India," *Business America*, October 10, 1988, p. 14.

9. "Tie-Up for Lotus Computers," *India Abroad*, June 15, 1989, p. 17.

10. "Investment Climate Statement–India," a paper prepared by Indian Investment Center, New Delhi, May 1990.

11. "Foreign Controlled Enterprises in Indian Industry," *Occasional Paper No. 8* (Bombay: Export-Import Bank of India, April 1990), p. 17.

12. "Japanese Foreign Direct Investment: Hoping for the Best in India," *The Economist*, April 2, 1988, p. 60.

13. Khokan Mookerji, "Toward New Marketing Horizons," a

lecture delivered at the Marketing Man of the Year Award in Jamshedpur, India, January 27, 1990.

14. "Maruti: Export Hopes," *India Today*, February 15, 1991, p. 64.

15. Rajiv Khanna, "Licensing and Joint Ventures in India," *Indo-American Business Times*, May 27, 1987.

16. William A. Stoever, "India: The Long, Slow Road to Liberalization," *Business Horizons*, January-February 1985, pp. 42-46.

17. "India is Becoming the New Asian Magnet for U.S. Business," *Business Week*, May 1, 1989 p. 132D.

18. "Making the Most of Brand-Name Sales in the Indian Market" *Business International*, May 22, 1989, p. 1155.

19. "Building Sales in LDCs: Unilever's Tailor-Made Approach to Marketing," *Business International*, April 26, 1985, pp. 129-130.

20. *India: New Dimensions of Industrial Growth* (Cambridge, MA: Basil Blackwell, Inc., 1990), p. 41.

21. D. J. Encarnation and Sushil Vachani, "Foreign Ownership: When Hosts Change the Rules," *Harvard Business Review*, September-October 1985, pp. 152-160.

22. Yves L. Doz and C. K. Prahalad, "How MNCs Cope with Host Government Intervention," *Harvard Business Review*, March-April 1980, pp. 149-157.

23. "Betting on a Small Market: Uniroyal's Plan for India," *Business International*, July 17, 1989, p. 216.

24. Based on an interview with a Herdillia Unimers executive in India.

25. Rajiv Khanna, "Licensing and Joint Ventures in India," 1987.

26. "Making the Most of Brand-Name Sales in the Indian Market," 1989.

27. "Of Color TVs and Washing Machines," *Business India*, December 11-24, 1989, p. 90.

28. This section, as well as the following one on negotiations, is based on the author's insights into India. Interested readers, however, will find the following sources useful: Kasum Nair, *Blossoms in the Dust: The Human Factor in Indian Development* (New York: Praeger, 1962); V. M. Dandekar, "Indian Economy Since Independence," *Economic and Political Weekly*, January 2-9, 1988, p. 49; J. L. Nehru, *Discovery of India* (New Delhi: Jarwaharlal Nehru Memorial Fund, 1982).

CHAPTER 9
INDIA'S POLICY INITIATIVES:
NEED FOR NEW OUTLOOK

1. John K. Ryans, Jr., Lori Mitchell, James Baker, and William Shanklin, "Economic Development Programs Compared," *Business*, January-March 1987, pp. 47-51.

2. Rana K. D. N. Singh, "Perspectives on Foreign Investment in India," *The CTC Reporter*, Autumn 1990, p. 17.

3. Premila Nazareth, "New Delhi Round Table on FDI and Technology Transfer," *The CTC Reporter*, Autumn 1990, pp. 23-24.

4. Based on information provided by the U.N. Center for Transnational Corporations.

5. George S. Yip and George A. Coundouriotis, "Diagnosing Global Strategy Potential: The World Chocolate Confectionary Industry," *Planning Review*, January/February 1991, pp. 4-15.

6. Subhash C. Jain, "How India Can Compete Globally," *Business India*, June 15-28, 1987, p. 50.

7. "India's Economic Strategy for the 90s," Background paper prepared by the Confederation of Engineering Industry, New Delhi, 1990, p. 8.

8. Yip and Coundouriotis, "Diagnosing Global Strategy Potential," p. 6.

9. Alan Rego, "Tapping Export Markets Worldwide," *India News*, February 1991, p. 7.

10. Kenichi Ohmae, *Triad Power* (New York: The Free Press, 1985), pp. 149-164.

11. Ibid.

12. *India: An Industrializing Economy in Transition* (Washington, DC: The World Bank, 1989), pp. 6-25.

13. Richard E. Feinberg, John Echeverri-Gent, and Friedemann Muller, *Economic Reform in Three Giants* (New Brunswick, NJ: Transaction Books, 1990), pp. 103-134.

14. Dale R. Weigel, "Investment in LDCs: The Debate Continues," *Columbia Journal of World Business*, Spring 1988, pp. 5-10.

15. Edilberto Segura, "Industrial Trade and Financial Sector Poli-

cies to Foster Private Enterprises in Developing Countries," *Columbia Journal of World Business*, Spring 1988, pp. 23-24.

16. *India: An Industrializing Economy in Transition*, pp. 51-57.

17. Susan Lee Tatiana, "The Rising Stars," *Forbes*, May 5, 1986, pp. 106-112. Also see Alexander Nowicki, *Grass Roots of Indian Industry: Enterprises–Their Problems and Prospects* (Washington, DC: The World Bank, 1987).

18. Singh, "Perspectives on Foreign Investment," p. 19.

19. "Dramatic Budget Proposal for Deregulated Economy," *India Abroad*, August 2, 1991, p. 1.

20. *The India Times*, October 15, 1991, p. 7.

21. Abraham Joseph, "Japan's FDI in India's Industrial Development: A Case Study of Maruti Udyog Ltd.," *The CTC Reporter*, Autumn 1990, p. 26.

22. Tarun Roy, "Direct Foreign Investments: Don't Miss the Bus," *Asian Finance*, April 15, 1988, pp. 38-47.

23. This section is primarily based on information (including factual details) supplied by the Indian Investment Center, New York.

24. Yung Whee Rhee, Bruce Ross-Larson, and Garry Pursell, *Korea's Competitive Edge* (Baltimore, MD: The John Hopkins University Press, 1984), pp. 39-49.

25. *India: An Industrializing Economy in Transition*, pp. 96-109.

26. Nazareth, "New Delhi Round Table," p. 24.

27. Jagdish Prasad, "Privatization of Public Enterprises–Some Basic Issues," *India News*, September 1990, p. 7.

28. Krishna Monie, "Privatization, Indian Style, Boosts Government Coffers," *Far Eastern Economic Review*, April 28, 1988, pp. 74-75.

29. Yung Whee Rhee et al., *Korea's Competitive Edge*, pp. 64-65.

Index